Confessions of an Unashamed Asperger

I0099814

Ron Hedgcock

chipmunkapublishing
the mental health publisher

Ron Hedgcock

Published by
Chipmunkapublishing
PO Box 6872
Brentwood
Essex CM13 1ZT
United Kingdom

http://www.chipmunkapublishing.com

Copyright © Ron Hedgcock 2011

Edited by Aleks Lech

Chipmunkapublishing gratefully acknowledge the support of Arts Council England.

Ron Hedgcock

FOREWORD by Professor Tony Attwood

I have learned a great deal from Ron Hedgcock. Those who have attended my seminars will have heard several of his quotations describing his experiences and insights into Asperger's Syndrome.   He is now in his 70s, having lived with three wives; and has had a successful career as an actor.   He also adores cats, who are now his family and friends. His autobiography is unusual in that it covers seven decades and is one of the first to describe the ageing process and Asperger's Syndrome.   He has a wicked sense of humour; and in describing his thoughts, emotions and experiences, Ron is forthright and at times confrontational. His descriptions are authentic and will be endorsed by other adults who have the Syndrome.   His self-analysis is extremely interesting for clinicians, but his explanations will also be particularly valuable for the partners of those who have similar characteristics, and for family members who are trying to understand a father or grandfather.   Ron is a wise elder in the 'tribe' of people with AS; and his eloquent autobiography will be a source of explanation and insight for those who are discovering and exploring the world as perceived and experienced by someone who has Asperger's Syndrome.

Professor Anthony Attwood, - Brisbane Qld, Australia.
Author of the best selling – 'Asperger's Syndrome, A guide
for Parents and Professionals'   1998
& 'The Complete Guide to Asperger's
Syndrome'   2009
(Both published by Jessica Kingsley, London.)

FOREWORD by Dr Isabelle Henault

Ron's book brings a personal perspective to Asperger's Syndrome and its impact on intimacy, love and relationships.

Ron is an actor. As such, he compares relationships and marriage (where one partner has Asperger's syndrome and the other is neurotypical) to a play, where the lead role has to learn a script in order to relate to his co-star.   Ron acknowledges that for the partner of someone with Asperger's syndrome, every day can be a challenge.   By nature, individuals with Asperger's syndrome tend to be self-centred, which can create some confusion when it comes to intimacy. The couple may experience difficulties with trust, bonding and honesty.

In such a relationship, there will need to be adjustment to and acceptance of the several characteristics and personality traits of Asperger's syndrome.   This unusual type of relationship needs to be understood in terms of fidelity, sexuality and bonding, as well as the chemistry between the partners.

The information in Ron's book is invaluable for anyone who lives with an adult with Asperger's syndrome.   Both they and the professionals who are involved in counselling such couple will benefit considerably from Ron's personal experience.

Dr Isabelle Henault, Clinical Psychologist, Montreal, Canada.
Author of the book 'Asperger's Syndrome and Sexuality. 2005 (Published by Jessica Kingsley,London.).

INTRODUCTION

This collection of Essays is the result of a lifetime living with Asperger's Syndrome, or AS as it can be termed for short, and of some 12 years of knowing about it. I was not actually diagnosed until nine years ago, when I took the step of consulting with a Melbourne professional. Oh sure, I'd wondered, I'd puzzled and I'd speculated on the anomalies of my personality, but with very mixed results. It so happened that my then wife Brenda showed me a Library book that described persons that appeared to be very much like me. This was 'Autism and Asperger's Syndrome", edited by Uta Frith. Though I was impressed with the concept, I didn't really take it on board for several years; and I must stress that I felt no insult or rejection in potentially applying the label to myself.

Over the next three years two separate psychologists made the serious suggestion that I was AS; and one loaned me Professor Attwood's 'Asperger's Syndrome'. As soon as I took it up, I knew that this was IT. I had come home at last. I joined the State Autism Society, and linked up with several discussion lists on the Internet and excitedly contributed to the same.

After purchasing two or three current books on the subject, I proceeded to contact the authors of those I found to be most relevant to me. I had by then made extensive notes about my life and the meaning of AS in it; and feeling that I had something special to tell the world on the subject, impulsively took the step of offering a lecture to the State AS Support Network. This was not a particularly irksome thing to do, since I am a professional speaker. In my first presentation I made a point of varying and lightening the talk with brief performance items and comedy sketches. I must confess that these probably bore no specific significance to the subject of my AS; but I offered them to illustrate some of the skills and interests that are an integral part of my life.

The writings in this book are based on the speculations and conclusions that have absorbed me ever since my diagnosis. They include some auto-biographical material, of the kind that hopefully will give an in-depth understanding; while a brief personal history will be found as one of the Appendices to this book. Some persons with Asperger Syndrome seem to resent the suggestion that a 'mild' form of the condition can exist. One either 'has' it, or one doesn't. Nevertheless I feel, and am supported in my assumption by the Professionals in my life, that I indeed do show AS in a mild form. It is for that reason that I was inspired to title my basic public presentation with the heading Confessions of a Borderline Aspie. Much as I wanted to apply that name to the present volume, I considered that it may lead some to conclude that I have 'Borderline Personality Disorder' as well. This certainly (or hopefully) is not the case. So I reluctantly and discretely chose the present wording.

I am using conventional bits of jargon, as well as abbreviations in the form of certain familiar sets of initials throughout the book. For example, I early discovered that the majority of AS persons are happy to refer to themselves as Aspies - which happens to have become something of an in-house term - a pet label they apply to themselves. By contrast, those who are not Aspies are conventionally described as NTs. This stands for Neuro-Typicals, or in other words the 'normal' majority of the population, whose brains are 'wired up' as we phrase it, in the more familiar and recognizable form. The letters HFA stand for High Functioning Autism. I place Asperger people into that hypothetical grouping of the population, which is described as 'The Spectrum', a scale of developmental disorders, which includes the various forms of Autism.

In regard to my writing or lecturing about Aspergers, it might be said that I am blessed with a couple of advantages. I have a fluency in speaking, that I can apply with reasonable effectiveness to the job of explanation. As well, since my condition is relatively mild (and indeed as many have said, nigh invisible) it appears to me that I live very close to the norm of the population. Thus I am to some extent, able to look with some familiarity into each camp... that of the AS persons and that of the NTS. So perhaps I am enabled to explain to that outside world of the NTs, a bit more clearly than most, just what they really need to know about the world of the AS. Others have written about the How and the What. I am making an attempt to explain something of the Why. So herein I'm setting out to describe something of the mind of one Aspie as he deals with the world of people, and especially when he is endeavouring to communicate with a wife or partner.

But these descriptions of the Aspie mind represent possibilities only. Aspergers folk are just as different from each other as are the majority 'typicals' of our population. Already, many can see that there are things that they don't know, or can't understand about persons with AS; but I am attempting to describe or inform about significant things in the AS psyche, that NTs are not aware that they don't know. (I have a faint suspicion that a prominent American Secretary of Defence once made use of a similar phraseology.)

I make no scientific claims for what I have written here. I am not a professional in Medicine or Psychology, so my notes must be recognized as those of a lay- person's perspective, based on his years of reading and observation. Happily, this does give me a certain perverse sense of freedom from any professional constraint in my speculation. Let me make it plain again that the present volume is in no way to be considered as a scientific work. My intention is purely to explain my thinking, and the conclusions that make sense to me. I can say too, that in the long run, I will be happy to rethink any of my present' theories when new ones make more sense.

I guess I must advise the reader of one proviso here. Purists and Professionals will probably consider certain of my ideas and statements as being over-generalised and simplistic; and strictly speaking I don't hesitate to plead guilty. Keep in mind that the term 'Aspie' is an Aspergers creation, designed within the Autistic community, and hit upon to identify the AS individual from the inside, as it were. Similarly the term NT is an identification applied by us to those who are non-AS. Neither term can be described as scientific. They represent the way that AS folk often think about themselves and their opposite numbers. And so if I appear to quote in a dogmatic way about certain 'absolutes', all I am actually doing is describing common perceptions that an Aspie like myself might have about humanity. I am not offering 'text-book' information about facts which are and must be far better tackled by the professionals.

As well, I should warn the reader that I have a wide ranging sense of humour which can raise its ugly head, and give the impression of irreverence. I beg to be granted an appropriate indulgence. I'd like to add, 'After all, I am only one of these poor benighted Aspergers persons!" (But that might sound like a special pleading.)

Another thing which I must confess to the reader is that mine is not a tale of any sort of rescue or resurrection from disaster, or from wrongful diagnosis early in life. No-one could describe my personal life story as appearing in any way inspirational. I have not suffered from diabolical mistreatments, and I have never been incarcerated in a hospital for the mentally ill. Sure, I have in the last 35 years, consulted with some 6 Psychiatrists, and perhaps 7 Psychologists, along with another 7 Counsellors of various sorts and standards; - but the reason has usually been that I needed to talk over my marriage difficulties.

At times too, and most likely when not preoccupied with harrowing relationship situations, I was simply dead keen to explore my own psychology. This latter motivation gave rise to well-meant suggestions that I just had to be of the Narcissistic personality type. So, unlike many wonderful writers who have told so eloquently and movingly about their lives with various degrees of Autism, I can't proclaim or describe such a spectacular sort of story. Mine is simply not that sort of tale.

This book reflects the confessional style of discussion that characterises my public lectures. I want it to reflect something of the real me, with autobiographical material that may perhaps be of use to Psychologists or Analysts in understanding what might make a particular Aspie to tick. I have been forced to omit some significant material and anecdotes that would have explained some things in greater depth, for the usual reason that individuals involved are still alive, and it could be hurtful or problematical for them.

Many books have now been written by persons with varying degrees of Autism; and some are on my shelves at this moment, with innumerable underlinings and highlights where I recognized familiar ground. Primarily I was uncertain about the format I should use for this Opus of mine. Biographies and accounts of married relationships and other partnerships now abound, along with lots of excellent studies about Aspergers and how to deal with it. (and indeed, some on how to 'beat' it!) I am not qualified, as I stated before, to write with any scientific or psychological authority; so I determined that the only form of book that didn't appear to be in existence was a volume of essays on all sorts of relevant topics, from the viewpoint and pen of an Aspie. So here it is!

One other thing I'd say, and I want to remind the reader about this since it is crucially important. There is barely any characteristic that you will find in an Aspie that is not to be recognized to some degree in persons of the great NT majority of the world. You could say that we Aspies just tend to have a greater number of these features, and as well can be more significantly inconvenienced by them. I remind the reader again of that hypothetical and eccentric 'wiring of our brains' as the major cause.

In the sections relating to marital relations, a number of the problems I outline could appear little different from any number of non-Spectrum male/female issues. So I would point out to the reader that those same upsets and hiccups, that may hopefully merely interrupt or irritate NT couples who are otherwise pretty secure with their bonding and interpersonal chemistry, have the capability of completely disrupting and fracturing the fragile relationships that we people on the Spectrum attempt. Consider it this way, if you are AS and don't understand or recognize Love and Intimacy, then you will have little to fall back on, when things go wrong.

Ron Hedgcock

ACKNOWLEDGEMENTS

I must offer thanks to a lot of kind, patient and insightful persons and friends, for their help, suggestions and vital information.   Appreciation to certain ladies in particular, including my three wives, Barbara, Jane (now deceased) and Brenda, whose interactions with me over some fifty odd years, however difficult or painful, have taught me so very much. Thanks to friends of long ago, like David, Greg, and Ray.   Then in more recent times, those more AS-savvy colleagues like Jenny, John, Brett and Walter.   The patience and tolerance exhibited by these, and by many others, as they've endeavoured to cope with my eccentricities and gaps, has not gone unappreciated.

And I proclaim a very big tribute to certain professionals who have been directly concerned in my Asperger journey, whether as personal friends or official consultants, and have contributed so very much to my knowledge and confidence. These include (in the order of their historical influence) - Ruth, Zish, Sonya, Jan, Richard, Isabelle and Dom.

I acknowledge too, the contributions of my colleague, (also an Aspergian and a wise one to boot) William D Loughman, Geneticist and retired Laboratory Director, whose encouragement, good advice and sundry tit-bits of relevant information have proven invaluable to me. Thanks Bill.

I'm eternally grateful as well to those writers of AS books whose inspirational input has led me to wonderful discoveries. I think with admiration of Liane, Ed, Jasmine, Chris & Gisela, Maxine, Ashley, and Tony, all of whose writings are cited in my Bibliography.   Then to the many friends and colleagues on the Internet lines who have been so supportive and encouraging.   I can never pay sufficient tribute to Linda, and the many contributors to ASPIRES, as well as my associates in the AS Support Network of Victoria. These are folks who have become like family, and have been of profoundest assistance and moral support.

To you the reader - I thank you most sincerely for picking up this book, and I hope that it may contribute a few bits of understanding to this important matter in our modern world. Perhaps some of my suggestions and ideas may prove to be of use and interest in these still early but exciting days of AS research and discovery.

Ron Hedgcock. 2010.

Chapter 1   THE ALIEN CONNECTION

On Being an Alien

How does the benighted Aspie handle everyday life when he is faced with the vagaries of everyday people?   Does he simply have to put on a friendly smile or expression, and blandly avoid any real communication?   Does he pretend to understand everything that others say?   Or does he openly confess that he is confused and lost?   So often I guess, he discretely pretends that he is not offended by so many things that he sees and hears.

Yes, that's what we do.   We endeavour to gloss over the unpleasant sights and the distasteful ways in which people behave.   In order to avoid provoking the impatience and irritation of our fellows, we try desperately to fit in.   Even if we are bored in company, we try to look interested; and if sufficiently sophisticated, we endeavour to fabricate some of the gestures that we've read in the literature on Body Language.   What might this entail?   Well, we point the body and the feet toward the person we are with, making sure that we fix our gaze on him.   We avoid folding the arms, so as to remain looking interested and awake.   We frequently nod and murmur the appropriate 'yeah', 'uh huh' etc, and keep desperately alert in order to grasp at any point that we can pick up, and fabricate questions that look relevant.   We don't have the slightest bit of interest in the subject being discussed.   We possibly don't even understand just what is being told, or for that matter even pick up the some of the minor details.

And this is an important issue, I believe.   Aspies, in order to appear normal, will fabricate interest constantly in the conversations around them, when they are just anxious to escape and run as far away as possible.   Because we are so keen or even fanatical to be accepted, and to cause as little disruption to the status quo, we endure hours, sometimes every day, just listening in a weary fashion to the things that we are being told by our companion NTs.

We may feel no empathy with the other person; so I suspect

that we don't go through all this ultimately for their sake. I guess that we do it so that we will not be to blame for the other person being insulted or hurt, and also that we may retain friendships or associations that are important to us. We do it so that the wheels will keep turning, and the conversation will not be converted into a clinical and critical examination of our hearing or indeed of our very character. A huge amount of our family or social time is taken up with involvement in interactions and conversations or tasks that are actually foreign and incomprehensible to us.

The famous autistic Temple Grandin is described as an Anthropologist on Mars, and the account about her offered by Neurologist Oliver Sacks, was something of a revelation to me, just as it has been for many other Aspies. (1) Fundamentally, the thesis or fantasy there has become something of an in-joke among our community. Normally, it is we who are supposed to be the odd people out. But some of us get to imagine things back to front. We fantasize that you NTs are actually the alien and foreign ones, and perhaps fit to be little else but objects for OUR analysis.

So, listen, my NT reading public! Like other Aspies, I've studied your world for ages - in my personal case for some 70 odd years - and I feel I know it pretty well, although I can't say that I ultimately seem to belong to it. I feel close, and yet so very far too. At times, it is almost as though I exist on top of a wall in between the two camps...one for the Aspies of the world, and that on the other side inhabited by the NTs. This is why I describe myself in my lectures as a Borderline Aspie.

Many of my personal characteristics are of the Aspie. These include my motivations, my dreams, my fixed interests and my theories about NT people. However, my habits, my mores, my methods and processes of self-protection or sustaining, belong to that foreign world of the NT. In my efforts to succeed or get on in that same world of the NT, I've learnt many processes, and even tricks and gimmicks. I pride myself on the skills that I've learnt in which I've succeeded in giving signs that I'm the same as everyone else. This effort and process has been vindicated I think by the fact that so many of my long term associates who have classified me as a normal individual (albeit with mild eccentricities), have disputed the diagnosis of AS, and therefore have duly debated it, at least for a time.

My therapists have made it plain to me that the high intelligence has been a boon, in fitting me for most NT situations without too many disasters. No-one knows or suspects just how much anxiety or uncertainty I have gone through in social situations. **But** what may seem more unbelievable will be the degree of discomfort or at times, almost agitation that I may be going through, when engaging in the everyday, and the most normal social intercourse.

On Home and the Exile

It was only in recent years that I realized how a lot of my manoeuvres in company were pointed towards the tactic I describe now as 'looking for a home'. It was brought to my attention when I was at a celebration party for a film premiere, and I was feeling typically lost among the several hundred guests. I was carrying a security blanket (in the form of my favourite briefcase) and I just moved uneasily through the assembly, uncertain of what to do with myself.

While everyone else stood about with glasses of wine and chatted to their companions, appearing very much at ease, I felt lost. So after every two or three minutes, I would shift to some other group. Just what was I looking for? Well really, I don't know. As a non-drinker, I had no incentive to drug myself into a general 'lowest common denominator' state amid the human mass. The noisy chattering communion with other people, regardless of how much I might happen to share with them in activity or interests, quickly became for me little more than an obnoxiously loud noise, and therefore most unpleasant. Sure, a number of those present on that occasion actually happened to be friends and fellow actors, - but the difficulty I faced was largely to do with the Aspie inability to swap small talk, when that was the expected thing to do.

But to come back to my story; apparently for some hour or so, I was observed to be moving rapidly every few minutes from one group to another in the convention room -and presumably I had to be the only Aspie in the place. I had this action pointed out to me afterwards by a close friend, who found it not a little amusing. Now, I take this sort of behaviour as perfectly natural, and it hadn't occurred to me how funny it must have looked, until he described it. Then I had to analyse it all just to determine what was going on.

Without the advantage of having a private 'audience' of my own in front of me at such a mindless function, and lacking the opportunity to swap real thoughts and research with someone of like mind, I couldn't find any peace or comfort when remaining in one spot. Again and again at parties and meetings, I've gone through this same scenario, and only now have found the words that can enable me to understand and describe it.

However, this desperate process of searching about occurs only when I'm in the midst of a group that I am familiar with. Then my thinking goes something like this; - logically, if I know them, then I will have things in common. If I have things in common with them,, then surely I must be able to locate someone there who I can talk to. If on the other hand it is a group of strangers, then I don't meander about looking for a friendly face. I tend to stop in the one place and make do with my immediate neighbours or hosts.

In recent years I've become aware of carrying in my head an archetypal image or a sort of memory of myself as a Person in Exile. And thus, I am like a lost soul who just hovers helplessly about, studying the multitudes and longing to locate the presence of some fellow alien from the homeland that he's come from. I was and still am absorbed by stories, films, and pictures that deal with a person who having been lost, separated, or exiled for an extended period, is eventually reunited with his people and family, or perhaps even just restored to some earlier or more profound state of mind.

And it means that whenever I see a scene or read a passage that depicts the return of some such lost or rejected individual, I feel very deeply moved. It might be the tale of a man reunited with his daughter - just as I experienced for myself in my later years. It might be even more powerfully the tale of some sort of alien person who is temporarily situated amidst the culture of a foster family or civilization, and then joyously finds his way back to locate his original people.

Now in order to anticipate a rather obvious sort of Psycho-analytical explanation to the puzzle of this fantasy, it must be understood that I was never in any way a reject from my own birth family; and I duly maintained perfect relations with my father and mother up until their deaths. As long as either of my parents was alive, I always had a welcome among them; but in the process, it must be stated that I was actually never aware of being homesick.

I tried vaguely to make myself reasonably happy living in lodgings and with sundry landladies in my early days. But the happiness did rely to some extent on my detaching or divorcing myself from the awareness of those other obtrusive folk in the house. I think that this business of periodically wiping out other people's presence or influence has ever been a strong priority.

I sometimes wonder if this 'exile' fantasy is an unconscious awareness of the metaphorical exile that is the natural burden (or birthright) of an Aspie? Am I missing some imaginary or ideal home, on that planet and within that ideal society which Aspergers people typically never seem to find?   Another possibility is that the religious milieu in which I was raised, engendered an idea of the Christian longing for the archetypal destination of Heaven. The fantasy seems to hover there in the background of my mind, that somewhere out 'there' is some sort of extra-special spiritual home that awaits me. Maybe the members or inhabitants of that home would be of similar structure to me - and familiarly self-centred, perhaps?

On the Lack of Central Coherence (2)

It is hard to apply the lessons learned from one area of life, to the issues of another area, when you're an Aspie.   Each friend or associate that I cultivate, seems to reside in a different compartment from every other one.   When in company, I find it difficult to share the current scene and those other persons, at the same time as my partner. This is not through any sort of jealousy, but because this compartmentalisation meant that I was consciously exerting a real effort to switch my attention and interest, back and forth from my companion to the other. A partner represents for me a very specific and demanding sort of company; and takes a different kind of concentration and attention, than I can readily apply to other folk at the same time.

I find that my living is compartmentalised too. Each room of my house is like a different experience. Then the business of concentrating on any particular job or idea is a compartment too. And so to have someone call me out of my intense concentration is painful, and it was one reason for my lack of achievement in my working days. I didn't have that alertness and necessary ability to switch attention from one thing or person to another. It was always hard. I've occasionally had to repeat the last words spoken by a person who interrupts my train of thought, a few times, in order to realize just what the heck they are talking about. For an NT partner, to have a beloved who seems to lose track of day to day matters, not to mention the important things she is saying or involved with, must be unbelievable. I have always tried to persuade my partners to capture my attention first before delivering a message to me. I have written elsewhere about this matter. (3)

I can speculate a little on the question of just why we compartmentalise in this fashion that is so disturbing to NT persons. I think it stems from early days, when as children we were constantly battered by input, by words and demands and visions or information from the outside. It was profoundly confusing; but somehow we had to make sense out of the world and out of the various persons around us in particular. We tried to please them, and that was and still is a painful and difficult process. If we were conscientious and careful, we tried to invent some way to survive through it all. So the way I think that most of us find, is to concentrate our attention on the individual thing that is coming towards us; and that MEANS only one thing at a time. If we divide our attention and listen to all around, to try to watch and take in all the details or people, we will not be able to combine them. We cannot deal with them, or to process them. So we learn to cut out anything at that moment which appears to be irrelevant to the main thing that we are facing. I don't believe this is a conscious and voluntary process. We do this automatically, as one of our defensive mechanisms.

Just now, I believe, certain of those clever devils of researchers are trying to work out just whether the peculiarities of our neurological structures are the cause, or purely the result, of our behaviour and habits. Is it brain-wiring based? Or is it environment-based? There are advantages and disadvantages either way, of course. But regardless of the cause, this process leaves many Aspies with an extraordinary ability to focus the concentration. There is a single-mindedness at work, and consequently an over-serious determination, perhaps to the extent even of having the ability to be unaware of our own boredom.

On the other hand, we will exhibit a lack of that flexibility which the NTs expect of us and value so much. This unique concentrating ability is probably one of the reasons for the occasional and remarkable autistic talents described as 'savant'. As for me? - No! I've shown no savant abilities. Attractive and spectacular as certain of these may appear on the surface, I can't say I'd ever want to be saddled or restricted with those processes.

I might be slow at switching attention, of putting my concentration on to new or different things as they are thrown at me by the world outside, but I can do it after a relatively modest delay. Heaven knows, during my working days I've given myself the unenviable reputation of being an idiot on more than one occasion, when I looked completely bewildered at a sudden request that I wasn't expecting, to produce a particular file or paper that was quite familiar to me, since it was part of my everyday work. The more one's associates can understand what is going on here, the better; and the greater the success of one's interactions and relationships.

On Self-centredness

There is a clear difference between being selfish and being self-centred. The selfish person deliberately seeks out advantages for himself, and literally cares little for the feelings or losses inflicted on people. He cultivates methods and procedures that will enable him to do this; and in the process, will develop arguments and manipulations by which he sets out to convince the others that he is entitled to the advantage. He will probably have clever ways by which he can justify his actions to other people, as well as to himself; and will seek to give the impression of entitlement and of being in the right.

There would have to be a little of the con-man about him; and he would readily learn to read other people to his advantage. Above all, he is quite aware of the mental workings of other people, along with their processes and their weaknesses. It may be that all these skills and practices become an automatic matter, so that he doesn't need to even think about them. Thus he is likely to convince himself of his rightness and entitlement. Ironically, it is likely that our selfish person will have some striking short term and immediate appeal to others; and will exercise, and exploit a considerable sexual attraction. Presumably he will give every appearance of attention to and great interest in his fellows.

In contrast to the selfish person, the self-centred individual, like many Aspies, can be oblivious to the inner states of other folk. He may appear uninterested in them. He may seem detached; and others will feel that he does not appear to contact them, even in the most intimate situation. He lacks normal empathy, and usually will not be at all desirous of exploiting others. He would probably hate to feel that he has hurt or disadvantaged them. But the point is that his first and prime point of reference is himself. He may well feel terribly upset or remorseful when his actions or words prove to be detrimental. But regrettably, with his relative blindness towards others, he is likely to do very hurtful things. He might in fact, be most unselfish, and even most generous; but only of course when he actually becomes aware of the deficiencies or hurts of another.

He doesn't make for a very responsive or sharing partner, unlike the selfish person, who is capable of deliberately going out to make a good impression on a spouse, albeit for the worst motives, perhaps. He will frequently be in a state of confusion when he observes the eventual results of his actions which have not been easy for him to comprehend. He is not given to great courage, and may tend to take refuge in what might be described as political or pragmatic dealings with his partner. (4) The Aspie can often be described as self-centred in these ways. He frequently needs his partner to remind him of his duties, as well as the routine obligations to family or friends. He can't easily predict or foresee just what may be urgent or necessary from day to day. If the issue doesn't concern his own immediate needs and perceptions, then he is not likely to be aware of it. And further, he won't really feel confident or effective about many of the things that do come up. He will tend to shrug his shoulders and concede defeat, with the feeling that he can't stand against the strength exerted by those about him who are aware of what is going on.

If the partner offers strong opinions or promotes specific desires, then he will look for ways and words that will satisfy or placate her. He will tell her just what he thinks that she wants to hear. But he won't be truly with her, in any genuine fashion. As I indicate elsewhere in these essays, if the NT wants to know just what the truth is in the mind and heart of the AS person, she should listen to exactly what the AS person says, in the unguarded, unpressured and primary truthful moment. Under normal conditions, the actions and eventual decisions of the self-centred one within the family or social situation, are most likely to be chosen for purely practical reasons, and for the major purpose of avoiding conflict or argument. Of course some Aspies are profoundly argumentative and tough minded. But for the others as I indicate here, the last thing that they want in their relationship is to have to defend a case, or to justify a preference, in the heavy-going face of NT logic and argument.

On Grief and Bereavement

It was the specific fact that I had never felt genuine grief at the loss of any person in my life that convinced me there was something not standard about my psyche. About the age of

10 or 11, I recall observing to a mate that I felt I would not be devastated in any major way if I lost either of my parents. And I shocked my mother more than once with my cavalier attitude towards funerals and the deaths of people we knew.

This perception was convincingly demonstrated, or proven with the death of my mother in 1956, when sure, I did feel 'moved' to some extent, but certainly not in any way stricken with anything like grief. All the more striking perhaps, since while still living at home, I had probably been the closest of all the family to her. I spent more intimate time with her, in talking. Then on the occasion of the loss of my second child and daughter in 1963, (at the age of 9 weeks) the bereavement never appeared to me as a devastatingly tragic event. I certainly shocked people at the time with my rather matter of fact attitude.

It was not till years later, and especially with the onset of my discoveries about AS, that I realized it was essentially based on this curious Aspie brain wiring. To my shock, and with not a little humiliation, I realized my acceptance of these 'tragedies' was not based on some extraordinary and advanced spiritual or philosophical level of being at all Somehow the experience of super-painful grief over others appears to be tucked away in some remote corner of the brain that I have been unable to reach. But I must explain just the same, that death to me was and is very moving - even a beautiful, awe inspiring thing - but I seem to be incapable of going through any deep pain of grief. It was an anecdote told by Oliver Sacks that brought it home to me that this mental stance is not uncommon among persons with Asperger's. (5) I was fascinated to see that Edgar Schneider discussed the same characteristic in one of his books. (6)

My next experience was the death of my father in 1987. Again this was not a grieving time, though Dad had been a tremendous influence in my life, and in many ways something of a hero. I had a few tears in my eyes, but I can honestly say that these did not appear to be symptomatic of a shattering experience.

I have to admit that the biggest grief I've experience over

death has been at the loss of certain of my beloved cats. Somehow my Moggies seem to have some sort of status of being like integral parts of my own psyche. Actually I can't envisage these creatures as sharing in that 'Alien' classification that all humans, including family and intimates, seem to have for me. All the same, the grieving and the tears over the loss of my cats lasted no more than a few days; and I had no hesitation in replacing them, to become totally absorbed in the furry little replacements almost immediately.

Curiously, I think I can describe as a powerful grief one particular experience, when I had to give up and eventually sell a housing unit that I had loved greatly. It had been the very first home dwelling that I had ever actually owned and lived in by myself; and somehow like my cats it was representative of some deep and integral part of myself.

One Psychiatrist friend suggested quite seriously that my lack of grief over death was based on some sort of denial of my mortality. But I am sure that she was wrong. I'm convinced that I would most be aware of this if this were the case. It would rise to haunt me, and I'd most likely be afraid to ponder the issue. However, this has never been the case. I can think about death, talk of my own mortality and quite cheerfully write wills, or prepare for my eventual demise and my funeral, as I would like it to be. As a deliberate exercise, I have from time to time tried to force myself to confront the many negative or diabolical faces of death and dying. Still no effect. I'm not sure if it is because of the Aspie compartmentalised brain system, but I found it very difficult, if not impossible to do.

Whenever I pictured the traditional horrors or loss of death, the concept would simply not stay securely in my mind. It would rapidly retreat, and leave the very barest of discomfort, and certainly no sense of fear. The business of preparing my Will, or of planning ideas for my eventual funeral, has appeared to be quite a fun exercise. With my abominable theatrical sense, I have seriously toyed with the idea of preparing a video tape of myself offering a farewell message (embroidered with some typical favourite joke) to be played at the funeral. I would dearly love to think that my friends would get together, chat about me, have a chuckle over some of my worst jokes and puns, and metaphorically wish me luck as they wave me goodbye.

I am reminded here of one of the earliest jokes I ever heard. It came from one of the radio sketches of the wartime comedians – Flanagan and Allen. (7) It still tickles my funny bone as a great classic. It ran like this.

"Don't you think our times are bad?"
"Our times are terrible!'
"I'm glad I belong to a Suicide Club."
"Suicide club?   Then why don't you go and kill yourself?"
"I can't."
"Why not?"
"I'm behind with my subscription!"

As far as the death of a partner is concerned, it would not represent any huge shock or horror for me. Indeed, I suspect that a violent argument or fight with her would represent a worse occasion and experience for me than even her death would be.   Strictly speaking I can't recall any time in my life when I've been able to picture any person, real or imaginary, whose presence in my life could be so crucial that their death would be devastating for me. It is the relationship I enjoy with them while they are alive that is the emotionally significant thing. Then when they have to go, they just have to go.

Looking back on what I have observed in other people, or (as has been highly influential or instructive to me) in films or stories, about death and grieving, it has tended to be puzzling. In the early days of my life, I often passed it all off as being just one more example of what I call the 'language of love'. The reader might refer to my essay in the present volume with that title. It seemed to me that it was little more than the way that people communicate over the things that are of importance; and thus the expressions of sorrow and grief that I observed or read about were the conventional ways of communication for the sake of society.   Even at times, I wondered if the individual who I observed in such grief was strangely deficient or pathologically inadequate.

Confessions of an Unashamed Asperger

It was only with many years up my sleeve, and indeed within these last 12/15 years, that I came to understand to my shock, that the discrepancy was actually within me and not with those other grieving ones. It was with sheer incomprehension that I heard on radio interviews, descriptions of the moaning cries of pain being wrenched out of the bereaved persons, and the sorrow that lasts for years and never goes away. I read the In Memoriam notices in the papers, and looked with disbelief at memories of relatives who died decades before. Eventually I had to come to grips with the truth of the matter, and it represented the factor that made me so sure there was something peculiar about me. And thus I was led to Asperger's Syndrome.

Now this newfound understanding of other folk's experience makes no difference to my inner experience or perception. Watching 'tragic' scenes or grieving people in movies or on TV can sway me emotionally, in a way that real life simply fails to. I sometimes suspect that it is some kind of sentimentality that gets to me under those circumstances; and Edgar Schneider tells of having the same experience. (8) I would postulate that whereas a 'tragic' or grievous situation in real and daily life, commands my attention and perhaps some kind of remedial action, - the parallel but abstract situation in book, film or music leaves me totally free to contemplate it, and literally swim or wallow in the sea of appropriate emotions. There is then no demand, no urgency or requirement to keep a level head. This is crucial to the conscientious Asperger.

I have had to be terribly careful when speaking about my feelings, when confronted by others who are dealing personally with death and the dying. I can of course only call on my native sympathy in such cases, which I have the greatest difficulty in backing up with clichés and other inadequate verbiage. One thing I have found very hard, is to write or offer appropriately chosen words and sentiments of sympathy for folk in bereavement. I have had to fight back a strong urge to be facetious or even comic at those times. It strikes me more and more clearly just how inadequate some of us Aspies can be, when confronted by authentic and down to earth human issues.

References.

(1) Sacks, Oliver.   An Anthropologist on Mars,   Page 233.
(2) Jacobs Barbara   Loving Mr Spock.   Page 70.
(3) See Essay   On Talking to Me
(4) See Essay   On Politics in Relationships.
(5) Sacks, Oliver.   An Anthropologist on Mars.   Page 197.
(6) Schneider Edgar   Discovering my Autism.   Page 51
(7) Flanagan and Allen. Comedy Sketch.   'Oi'   1940s?
(8) Schneider Edgar. Discovering My Autism.   Page 52.

Chapter 2   LOST AMONG KIDS

On The Mystery of the other Kids.

At school, just somehow or other, the other kids knew things that you didn't know. They knew the rules of getting on, of being understood and appreciated. They knew how to handle the teachers, and how to play off one parent or teacher against another. They knew how and when to laugh. They had the right balance of spontaneity and calculation. They were sophisticated. By contrast, your own naivety was painful. The things that appeared natural and real to you were ludicrous and ineffective among your fellows. Sure, you made a real effort to create friendships. You tried to join in games, but you were out of alignment with the others in timing, and in appropriateness.

And just so - as a school student, I was something of a mixed blessing. For the greater part of my time I was liked and appreciated by the teachers for my quietness and good behaviour. I tried hard to get through the studies in the various grades, and eventually just managed to pass at the High School Leaving level. This was in strict contrast to my brother's record of high achievement, as he was undoubtedly of a very gifted standard. Because he took a great interest in sport, concentrating on cricket and tennis, he retained some reasonable degree of acceptance by other boys. He also had the advantage of being tall, which must have given him some sort of increase in moral stature. I rarely excelled in classes, and certainly I was never popular with my peers. I inevitably set myself up for teasing, and minor degrees of bullying, and there is no doubt that my lesser stature made for an increase in vulnerability.

My attempts at making friends tended to be like futile gestures for the most part. I saw all the others about me in coteries of mates and companions. And it inevitably gets to be one of these alien others – an individual of a totally different sort from myself - who becomes the Prefect or Class Captain. Naturally such a privileged individual will be found in the thick of activities. He will have an extroverted nature, will probably be pretty good at sport, as well as being reasonably prominent in the academic sphere.

But the criteria for this popular choice totally escaped me in those days. We Aspies don't register or recognize these factors in any appreciative way, at least not at the critical period of our lives. How well I remember being left out in this situation – sensing the classical rejection that was so familiar. A greater amount of my envy and incredulity was based on the fact that I was just so certain of my innate respectability; and this state of respectability was in my eyes the major qualification for just about any position of authority and recognition in the world. Of course it didn't occur to me until many years later that I was actually not in the least bit suitable – just not in any way appropriate to hold an authoritative position among my peers at that time.

Of course when you think of it, I was not among my peers at all. Those others spoke a different language. They lived through each day in a different rhythm, being interested in totally alien things; and indulging in horseplay and crude teenage misbehaviour that was foreign to me. No, they were not my peers. They might just as well have belonged to a different age group and an alien society. It might be said that anything real about them was outside of my scope of vision, because I observed them distantly almost as though through a window.

The only thing I could see in the selection of Prefect or Captain was a title and a recognition that I craved. But in envisaging myself in the position, I couldn't comprehend the fact that in the job, I'd have been required to show that unspoken state of human understanding which the NTs of the world displayed or appeared to possess without even trying. I could not grasp the fact that in that desirable position, I would be required to accept responsibility, and to show leadership, along with that extraordinary quality of Empathy (or bonding) with the others!

On My School Results.

My marks were never particularly spectacular. I just scraped through at Mathematics, and the accompanying Geometry, etc. I actually enjoyed the early stages of Algebra, but got left behind in later stages. At my father's suggestion, I dropped the Science and Chemistry subjects and took on the 'Commercial Course' of Shorthand, Typing and Bookkeeping. The latter I only just managed to pass, while the former two were very mixed in their results. I tended to learn their fundamentals very well, but when the other students were starting to speed up, I dropped behind very badly. In them, as in all other activities requiring rhythm, I simply failed to exhibit the necessary physical coordination.

To this day, I can still type, but irregularly and with many mistakes. Thank heaven for the word processing facilities on the computer, permitting me to do away with those dreadful correction ribbons, which on the older typewriters turned out to be my biggest expense. Being able to touch type, however badly, has certainly been a blessing over the years. But despite the problems, I believe my father's advice was sensible in the long run.

French was the only language taught in my school, and for the most part, I quite enjoyed it. My standard though in French results tended to resemble my results in many other subjects, as I got worse as the years went on. English was probably my best and most consistent subject, though I did find the business of writing formal essays very hard work. The section of the English course that was most appealing to me was drama, though it was not treated at that time as being of the slightest importance in the curriculum. There was no separate subject made of it, of course, but I always tended to shine whenever the opportunity came up to act or read parts in classroom plays.

I undoubtedly came across to my fellow students as either a snob or a prude, which didn't help my reputation or my playground life. At no time did I speak the language that they seemed to speak. Usually I got on well with the teachers, but it never occurred to me that they were anything other than alien machines, who simply churned out school material. When the idea was suggested to me, many years later, that by studying and understanding the characters of the teachers, one could serve up to them in one's assignments precisely the stuff that would appeal to them, and thereby gain one better grades, I was astounded. Such a thought had never occurred to me. I suppose I rarely thought of teachers, any more than other persons, as having an inner life or consciousness. They were aliens, the same as all others. I got by with them by being polite and to some extent appearing keen or conscientious in class. I was characteristically naïve, but tried to be myself as much as I could.

The other classes I was saddled with were Sheet Metal and Wood work. I barely matched any standard, other than a vague Pass, as typically my manual skills were weak. Thinking back, I'm quite sure that my teachers and my parents expected or hoped for big things of me; but all that happened was that I barely got through those higher grades; and thank heaven that I did.

So it can be said that I was not a particularly successful scholar. It may be that the style of schooling in those times was inadequate for me to really learn the proper processes of study and application. I do listen with more than a hint of envy as young people blithely describe the optional extra studies at school these days, in Psychology, in Drama and even in Criminology. Near impossible for me to visualise, when I compare with the curriculum that was thrust upon us when I went to school. Any time we kids were given tests on Vocation and Intelligence, which was very seldom, my own results showed that I was well above average; and certain embarrassing predictions were made that suggested a great academic future.

The demands of a regulated and institutionalised study programme really didn't work for me. On the surface, it appeared likely that I would succeed; but in the long run, whether due to laziness, bad study habits, or some other more obscure deficiency in my character, I was only really happy when engaged in the business of choosing my own study material, and pursuing it at my own speed. The temptation for me is always to read specifically for sheer enjoyment. And when studying obligatory and formal stuff, I literally had to force myself to take in the contents for future regurgitation. I was especially out of my depth when attending University, and found myself attending classes and lectures in a vaguely obedient fashion, and as sheer routine.

It must be understood that I was not held back by the type of pain or discomfort that attended many Aspies in this strange environment. Liane Holliday Willey gives good descriptions of these difficulties in her own life. (1) But unlike her, I had no trouble coping with the mechanics of time, direction and travel.

Again, despite a very high IQ, my best application in study has been limited to a middle range of intellectual work, and certainly not in the upper brackets of academic learning, which tend to leave me cold, and even confused. As it happens, I'm not a particularly profound thinker. Reading really advanced books in higher learning, does not come easily to me. The texts I had to peruse when doing Psychology and Philosophy during my all too brief stint at University left me simply uncomprehending most of the time; and I found it near impossible to take down intelligible notes while listening to a lecturer.

On Leading and Following

From an early age, our poor benighted Aspie sees with the most pained bewilderment that he is not like the others. His attitude and expressions both in body and in speech will inevitably be different, and may be hard for others to understand. He will probably have laid the groundwork for his special interests and his fads from the time before he goes to school; and when other kids are keen to do the normal play, to share in the unspoken fashion or to get excited over the latest craze, our Aspie is preferring to live in his dreams, rattle on about his pet topic, or read books about his obsessions. He most likely won't be able to play team games, and consequently can't be part of any 'in' group. He won't pick up the latest talk, and may simply not understand what others are on about. He will have learnt early that others will never choose to do what he wants, neither will they pursue the topics of conversation that he initiates, or rather that he tries to initiate.

It is not uncommon as I indicated, for the high functioning AS child to be well appreciated by the teachers for his serious application to school work, and for that very same non-conformity to the instincts of the herd. The result is that among his peers, he may well have a further strike against him, because of his 'good' behaviour, and the fact that he may tend to obey the rules. So in order to find some sort of acceptance, he can only set out to become some sort of blind follower. He sees others fitting into a group, as they are led by some strong minded individual. He may not gain any particular kudos by such following, but at least he feels that he is not being left out. Unfortunately to his surprise, he can be extraordinarily inept even at this very job of 'following'.

Perhaps it is only with the attainment of adulthood, and then engaged in some sort of profession or job in which his individual skills and perception come into their own, that he will start to shine. But his skills can backfire on him if he is promoted to supervisory positions. From management's point of view, it is logical to offer him suitable promotion after years of successful performance of his work. But disaster can all too easily follow if he finds then that he has to engage too much in the way of interpersonal contact with his fellows. The business of understanding subordinates and dealing with their individual needs and quirks is not the best or most comfortable thing for him to be doing.

Often it will be that our Aspie performs at his optimum best if he has the opportunity to work by himself, utilizing his own initiative while he has the minimum of inter-action with the others. Then his skills may well show up to advantage. So it can be expected that in early years, I never took the lead. I didn't understand just how one went about the business of ordering people around. I tended to follow others dutifully, because these others seemed to have an instinctive confidence and self-assuredness in giving orders. As I grew older, I still hated to be 'boss'. I couldn't feel confident to tell or show others what to do. If authority was specifically given to me in the short term, as in a meeting or group, or most importantly at a later stage, in directing a play, then I could feel more comfortable. But it must be noticed that this confidence was essentially based on a non-personal relationship going on, in limited times and circumstances.

Now marriage gave me the experience of a new form of leadership. As a parent I found that I could cope with my children when they were very small. But the business of having any sort of authority over or with a partner, in the same way that she appeared to have over me, was inconceivable. I felt that – well, if she gives me 'orders', or asks me seriously or confidently to do something, then she must have some sort of god-given authority that I don't understand. So I must do it. As well, she sounds just so damned sure of herself, in a way that I could only manage in very rare circumstances.

As a follower, I don't mind being given 'orders' or instructions, so long as I can understand them. But I must admit that I can display a rare talent for mis-hearing or misunderstanding what I've been told. (2) I do frequently require rather more detailed explanations of how to fulfil a job in the work place than other folk seem to. In this regard, on the occasions when I had to instruct a new body in the routines and technicalities of my own job, I automatically went to elaborate lengths to prepare detailed instructions and form filling in the way I would have wanted or needed myself. I was then shocked and not a little embarrassed to find that the new recruit picked it all up with alacrity, and barely required any of the examples and hypotheticals I'd so carefully created.

There are definitely some things I can do to order, and other things I can not. Years ago, one of my friends had some sort of job with a Government department, which had him, among other things, patrolling side shows on a local Agricultural Show. He had to investigate issues of exploitation of minors, for one thing; and he was prepared to march into some particular tent show and tell them that they were offending, and had to close up forthwith. He was just so terribly sure of himself, and of course had to use and apply his own initiative with great forcefulness.

I can still see just how foreign such a job of work would be for me. To some extent it reminds me of the sorts of things that school teachers have to do in wielding their authority, and having to make up their own minds all too often. I could never feel comfortable taking a position of authority over the things that other people might get up to. You have no legal power; and the greatest sanction you can apply is perhaps to withdraw a privilege.

The whole idea of holding some sort of legal or serious contractual responsibility over other parties is something I find pretty horrible. I can't imagine, even with appropriate training, that I could ever take on such areas of duty. Perhaps it might be within the framework of a family situation that this fear and reluctance could show itself up in the most common sort of situation.

The business of having to keep growing children in order - of expressing myself as not only a concerned but also as an authoritative parent, who manages just the right balance between caring and discipline - would scare the life out of me. I was able to maintain such a stance during the earliest infancy of my daughter; but this process was interrupted by the breakdown of the marriage. I was thus protected, you might say, from the necessity of having to be the father of a teenager. Looking back it might well appear to me that not only was I shielded from such a situation, and from responsibilities that would have ill-befitted me; but as well, my poor children were rescued from having to deal with a father who had not the slightest idea of how to handle growing kids in an integrated way.

I imagine that it will be clear that if as an Aspie you have difficulty getting across to adults and in particular, intimate partners, you will undoubtedly have problems in dealing with your children at a later date. This sort of responsibility is terrifying and confusing to me. Again and again within the Aspie community, we observe and read about the difficulties that Aspie fathers have when they try to handle the complicated understanding of growing kids.

On Team Games

Team games of all sorts have always been a problem to me. They tend to fit for the most part into the area of physical balance again, as well as instinctive coordination with others, which is inherently problematic. I guess many sports have difficulty for those like me. It was really only the games that gave me the opportunity to perform the necessary actions on my own that made sense to me. Thus cricket was possible in a limited way, largely because it is not a body contact sport. Well I remember as a child how my brother, who is a fanatic for that game, did persuade me by bribery and blackmail to bowl balls to him; and so I developed a bit of a keen hand as a bowler, while regrettably not being able to bat for toffee-apples.

Tennis might have been a possibility, but about the age of 14, I took up Badminton, which was more to my liking than any physical activity I'd tried. I enjoyed the light weight of the racket, and the unique freedom to move according to one's instinct, and not according to any rules. I was restricted though, in not having any great power in my wrist. So I could not 'smash' the shuttlecock in the way that others seemed to be able to do. I hated playing doubles, for obvious reasons. That was a team effort that again just left me floundering. I must say that strictly speaking, playing partnerships in just about anything was and is hard or unpleasant. Even if it were in the more non-physical playing of card games like Euchre, I could not bear anything except a three handed cut-throat. Having to be responsible for or answerable to another participant in just about any activity is odious.

Billiard type table games appealed very greatly. I sometimes fancied learning to ice-skate, though my very few sorties onto the rink tended to end with disaster. I suspect it was once again a matter of coordination and balance as well. Horse-riding and Archery had appeal, though I never actually tried the latter. In my brief time doing National Service Army training during the 1950s, I found that I was a pretty reasonable shot with a .303 Rifle. I fear however that I would have been a menace to my own side if I'd had to keep trying with an Owen or a Bren Gun. My frantic attempts to control such automatic weapons, especially the former, were a source of much laughter, as the darn things jerked upwards in my hands out of all voluntary direction.

I admired Basketball, but my attempts to control a ball proved a sheer impossibility. In any case, being on a court with a coordinated group of team players was confusing to me - indeed, just as disconcerting as was my one and only attempt to join a group of boys on the Football field. (This is of course the Australian Rules game I refer to here. Probably few of us Australians in those days had even heard of Soccer or Rugby in its many forms.) That very idea of getting out on a field, and competing physically for a ball, was just impossible. This ball, like that in every single team game I know, just never seemed to anticipate just what I required it to do. It always appeared as though the rest of the team had some mystical affinity with that curious object. These guys seemed to know automatically just where to go, how to move and avoid the other players in the most amazing fashion. They consequently left me floundering about in confusion; - and most bewilderingly of all, miles from the play. Also, it must be added that physically, I was a natural coward, and that ever-present possibility of falling, of being hurt, bumped, scratched or of having a bone broken, honestly did not appeal to me in the least.

For similar reasons, I never engaged in fisticuffs, or physical combat of any kind, and as a consequence tended to be bullied and pushed around, sadly like all too many children with AS. Luckily, no really serious beatings of any consequence ever happened to me during those milder or safer school days of the 40s; and I did manage to talk my way round the looming possibility of it in a few cases. I was most fortunate, (or else protected by some divine intervention) when in the Army, that I was never directed into any form of hand to hand combat. I'm quite sure that I would have been absolutely hopeless in such activities.

On A Highly Strung Nature

It didn't help during my boyhood to be cursed with a rather delicate and highly strung temperament. It clearly made me further subject to bullying and the tormenting that some kids like to inflict on the sensitive. As I explained, while my peers were acting out all through their schooldays the normal physical adventuring and finding out about their masculine lives to be, I was on the other hand lounging about and reading books, thinking, fantasizing and dreaming. It didn't make for a very comfortable life among the others.

Luckily I was never one of those hyper-sensitive AS folk who has to put up with a physical battering from the material things about me. I wasn't disturbed by dazzling lights or electronic buzzes or hums. Strange environments or big crowds didn't phase me out. My worries were essentially connected to personal interaction with other folk; and as might be imagined, the worst environments for me turned out to be school, and then the Army when I did my National Service training.

As I have argued elsewhere, I think it is of considerable value to determine for every Aspie from earliest age, just whether he is of a tough minded disposition, or of the tender minded type. As one who largely supports the 'Nature rather than Nurture' origin of human nature and behaviour, I think there may be all sorts of influences that we inherit genetically that give us this tough or tender characteristic. But I don't think there are too many among our fraternity who truly find a middle path. With the extremes that are typical of the Aspie, we are typically either one or the other in predominance. And the Aspie who is tender will almost certainly be possessed of a highly strung nature.

I recognized from an early age that I was possessed of the latter; and I developed various means to protect myself, with every attempt to avoid too much in the way of pressure. In my schooldays, for some reason or other, with my romantic imagination, and an inadequately informed mind, I pictured myself as a Philosopher, and I developed a memory bank of quotes and proverbs about all sorts of things in every-day life. They were designed, I can see now, to offer glib answers and simple obvious ways of coping with all sorts of issues. Many, and probably those that I happily avoided quoting to other kids, were from my Biblical and Church background. I think I must have learned fairly early not to push religious quotes at others, though it would have been all too easy for my Aspie mind to take some sort of moral high ground as a foundation for snobbery. I didn't mix with the others, and I was clearly often seen or judged to be a snob. This would naturally promote the predictable sort of treatment from my peers, who would not understand just where I was coming from.

Inside, I felt quite sure that the only rule one had to follow for success and popularity was to be respectable, and polite. I could never comprehend or anticipate how there was as well (or rather) some extra, human quality of 'Being' that along with its accompanying 'Folk Psychology', actually got you on well with other people. I never learned about it in home or at school; and for that matter, I fear that much of it I still have never learned.

There was never any native toughness in me. It was a gentle family that I came from, and though my brother and I may have had our odd differences, it was essentially with the barest resources of fire and guts that we conflicted. There was never any cruelty, nothing I had to literally fight against, or protect myself from in the home life. I displayed a fundamental gentleness and sensitivity from the beginning. Like many Aspies and Auties I had not the slightest inkling of how to protect myself against bullying or ragging from other kids; and though I was lucky enough never to have been genuinely 'beaten up' by the others, I was certainly treated in harsh and distressing ways, when my naïve and silly perceptions of things influenced my behaviour or my words at school. This 'Good Boy' syndrome may have endeared me to certain of my teachers, but it was detrimental when I had to stand up among my peers.

It is to be expected that one of the areas of difficulty lies in the inability of persons like myself to cope with physical rough and tumble. Not having the impetus for physical activity, or for the slightest inclination to fisticuffs and body contact sports, I was at a big disadvantage when confronting other boys who took the business of roughness for granted. And under pressure from others if it was too physical and unremitting, it was possible for me to lapse into a state resembling hysteria. And as it could be imagined, it was all too easy to get the label of being a bit of a 'Girl', or a 'Pansy' as we referred to the effeminate and the Gay in those days. The demand that one must conform to the expected styles of masculinity were I guess much the same then as they are today. If you can't take and dish out the appropriate 'boy' treatment then you are headed for trouble as you react in shock and fear to the others.

Predictably, my early defensive stance as a Philosopher didn't help me very much. It was perhaps something like a process of building up a structure that made me think about issues and ethics from an early age, and to avoid the otherwise natural feelings of inferiority and shock. The Puritan attitudes of my family, or of my mother, were not conducive to living in this world. She herself had always been unsuited to dealing with the realities of life. Look at it this way; if you are in a constant state of shock and horror at the fact of the world having such evils as alcohol, tobacco, swearing, and gambling in it, you naturally tend to avoid all those in that world who indulge in such things. The newspapers and the radio gave me the picture of a pretty frightening and degenerate world which is not only evil and condemned in itself, but which is probably out to get you as well and to drag you down to its level.

As one might imagine, it was not a good training for dealing with the big wide world outside. It is probably impossible for anyone today to imagine and conceive of such an attitude. Films, television and the Internet must nowadays have the effect of ensuring that everyone is sophisticated and aware. To this day, I'm still an abstainer from alcohol, and I still don't indulge in a range of those 'evils' that I was taught to avoid as a child.

I still do have a rather highly strung disposition. But perhaps I've developed newer and more effective ways of dealing with issues in my life. A big influence in my early thinking and adaptation were Dale Carnegie's Self-Help books. (3) That sort of 'pop' Psychology with tips on how to deal efficiently with ethics and relationships has had much bad press; and Carnegie's work, though still in print, is regarded by many as being built on insincerity and political type manipulation. However, I can't really see all this. What I do know is that Carnegie taught me a great deal about how to deal with upsets and disappointments in daily life, as nothing else ever did. To this day, I give the impression most of the time of meeting difficulties with a calm approach. I make sure that I never fail to look carefully and systematically at things when they go wrong.

But I must admit that the biggest difficulties I still face are those situations when another person is putting pressure on me and perhaps bluffing me with intensity and sheer persistence. If things go on and on too unremittingly, I can lose much of my confidence, and feel that I can't deal with things in my own way. I seems then that I'm being dragged into that other's alien world and am getting lost.

One of the major processes of calmly dealing with problems is to stop what I'm doing, to cut my own automatic reactions to the issue that is hitting me, and to avoid jumping to conclusions. By not crying over spilt milk and accepting bad things as quickly as possible, if not immediately, I am avoiding one of my pet peeves, and that is to make sure that other people as well are not being dragged to get into a big stew over the issue. That way they will not have any motivation to put me under any pressure or to enforce their remedies. I don't want to add their upset or judgmentalism to the difficulty I'm already facing.

Clearly if you yourself don't jump up and down, complaining or expressing violently your worries about what to do, or of how to get out of a situation, then the other NT person will not be so likely to intrude, or pressurise you to accept their point of view. As well, they are not so likely to point the finger and read you a lecture on how you have happened to bring this problem on yourself. I guess, against all common wisdom, this fits into my contention that a problem shared is actually a problem doubled!

On my own Children

Curious isn't it that even after all these years, I find that being with children for more than a few moments, I'm floundering and feeling anxious and out of my depth. Because I move as you might say in the child's direction and try to put myself and my speech into their world, children seem to like and trust me. It is ironic that I find it all so bad and stressful. I've never felt particularly comfortable with any child that was not my own.

In fact, I even felt decidedly disquieted with them. Being with a child just wears me out terribly. Interesting to recall that despite my own obvious child self, I actually resented being a kid when I was young. I couldn't wait to be 'grown up'. It represented everything that I wanted.

I recall before my first marriage, my fiancée asked me to spend a half day with her as she looked after her little nephew. I reluctantly agreed after some discussion, and when at the end of the day I was told just how easy and successful it had been, and how happy the little guy had been, I had to break it to her that it had been a nightmare of stress for me, and that I was absolutely worn out. She couldn't believe it, as I had apparently put on a good display of being happy and friendly.

In regard to children of my own, I always took it for granted that I would be a father; and as it happened, I had three children with my first wife. As time has gone by, they have gone out of my life. It may well have been something to do with my AS, because though I always seemed to get on well with them, they came to regard me as irrelevant in their lives. Luckily I never had any essential desire or need to have children. It would never have troubled me if I'd actually been unable to father any. So though I certainly got a degree of joy or interest from the children in their early years when I was connected with them, and I do feel a minor degree of loss, it has not been a serious hurt or set-back in my life to be out of touch in this way.

From the start, I believed that I would get on well with any kids I might have, though I was burdened with fears during the first pregnancy in particular as to whether I was capable of actually liking them as babies. As it happened, I did get on well with my daughter through her infancy, and did a great deal of talking and communicating with her. I think I must have been living through a lot of my own child self in my dealings with her.

It has been of great fascination to me to observe a few of my male friends in recent months with their attitudes towards their children. There's Joe, a tough unsentimental guy who has four grown up children of his own. He described to me the profound sense of awe or wonder he felt at the birth of his kids. This was concerned with that incredible way in which the woman carries and then produces a real living human creature. He confessed to me that he really enjoys 'Bubs' as he calls them; and I have marvelled at just how he shows every sign of pleasure as he chats to the small offspring of his family and friends.

Then I think of Ben, a close colleague who has been married for just a few years, describing the sensational feelings he had when his own little girl was born. The 'most precious moment of my life' he put it. I've watched him as he displays his deep protective devotion to the little one; and I know he would sacrifice just about anything for her. He told me that he always looked forward to having children of his own, and that this experience with his first had been a key point in his life.

Doc, a professional who has seen the very best and worst of men during his working life, described to me how again and again, despite their status as criminals and murderers, some have shown their passionate devotion and possessiveness towards their babies. When talking of his own little lad Steve, with the greatest of sincerity and assurance he told that he would gladly 'take the proverbial bullet' for that boy. Having him, he said, was undoubtedly about the greatest experience of his life.

Now, am I just so profoundly self-centred in recognizing that all this is inconceivable to me? Surely, I can't be all that removed from human feeling? Oh, I can imagine the possibility of sacrificing my life in an emergency situation, to save or rescue a child or partner. But I can't see that it would be based on any such thing as a deep world-shaking love. I could only imagine it as a response to some special instant of exigency, rather than as an on-going dedicated prepared-ness.

Knowing what I do now, and with the understanding of all that can go wrong, with possible birth defects, or troubles that might afflict the new-born, I don't believe I would ever have any children if I were to do it all over again. For similar reasons, as well as being armed with my new-found knowledge of my Aspie brain wiring, I would never get married either, if I could make the same choices all over again.

References.

(1) Willey, Liane Holliday. Pretending to be Normal. Chap. 3.
(2) See Essay On Interpreting Words.
(3) Carnegie, Dale. How to Stop Worrying & other titles.

Chapter 3   EYE CONTACT AND OTHER ASPIE PROBLEMS

On Eye Contact

Like a great many Aspies, I have never been particularly keen on looking into other people's eyes. However, I guess I must have been trained or brain-washed from an early age to look at people in the eyes when I talked to them. My work in theatre further accustomed me to eye-gazing. But I don't seem to get any of the benefits and blessings that one is supposed to gain from the practice. For me it is a pragmatic action that will bring some sort of confidence to the NT mind and heart of the other party. Maybe as well, the practice does allow me some form of concentration and focus, when otherwise my attention can wander back into my own inner world.

But there are other dimensions in eye contact that are valued by the NTs. At least that is what I'm told; and it's what I've read in innumerable pieces of writing.   What on earth can it possibly mean for people to convey messages via the eyes? Now if by 'messages' one means that others may decipher psychological information from movements of the eyebrows, the narrowing, closing, or a wide opening of the eyelids, then perhaps I can concede it may be possible. But in that case, why describe the process as conveying the message by the eyes, specifically? Oh sure, we know that there is such a phenomenon as the widening or reducing of the pupils; but these are involuntary effects and merely indicate depth of interest or excitement. The process of staring or of looking away may suggest something to an astute observer; but just what precise conclusions can you come to when you see them? Logically speaking, it would seem to me that any of these variations could indicate a whole contradictory range of ideas or mental states.

Strictly speaking then, the greater part of expression that one observes in another is made up of muscular movements in the face as a whole. There is the smile, - in its many forms. We might think of the tilt of the head or the sounds coming from the mouth.   But the idea that lovers or any other intimates, can simply look at each other and have nothing but their eyes convey messages!!!   Well, words fail me.

I am reminded that the desirable steady gaze is actually part of the stock in trade of the confidence man, the shonky real estate salesman, or maybe the investigating detective.   For that matter, is there a lover, or for that matter any dedicated sex addict who does not use his eyes in the time honoured and utterly believable fashion of clear, open and steady gaze? But how can you get specific meanings out of these things, in any way that is reliable?

If, by any chance, lovers can and do read each other at the same time that they are sharing eye-gazing rituals, maybe it is other factors unconnected with the face at all,   that   are conveying the essential messages.   The exudation of those mysterious body scents known as Pheromones may be occurring at the same time for example, and this may be the active factor.   But these may be emitted simply as a sexual signal and attraction procedure. (1)   If there is some other sort of sensitivity that is being activated at the same time as the eye gazing, then we seem to approach some sort of a mystical or psychic awareness.

 Unfortunately, I don't think that there's any reliable evidence that people in the big wide world who claim to be able to read people so significantly, actually achieve better results during their mating procedures. I have to admit it does amuse me when people claim to be picking up messages from the eyes, when for the most part it is likely the cues come from the things the other person is saying, factored in with a whole lot of other features.   There might be the body posture, the consistent reliability in their utterances, and their track record in relating behaviour in the past.

It amazes me just how people can be influenced by all sorts of personal factors in their interactions with each other. Consider the desirable firm handshake, for example.   As an actor, I can quite readily choose just what sort of handshake I apply at any time.   Presumably, I could apply just about any routine or ritual of meeting people that I want.

For the most part, I don't take in these clues or suggestions from my fellows. Even though I might register the eye gaze I get from another or the style of handshake, I don't come to any conclusion. I don't try to read anything into it, as I talk to or think about the other. The action is for me something separate from the person, and doesn't influence what I think about the inner nature of them. Sure, I might well decide that the topics of conversation, the habits or cleanliness of the person, or his philosophy in life, are not my cup of tea. I may decide that I don't like him or her. But it is essentially based on my total perceptions of the other party, not on subtle 'messages' that I am supposed to read via some sort of intuition. I certainly know little about the thinking processes of the other, from what I observe, or about their honesty, or decency. I won't be able to picture their motivations, or develop any conception of how to predict their future actions. I would work solely on whether or not I like them, based on their actions or outer show.

Now I'm not out to claim that my conclusions are reliable or that my likes and dislikes in people have a superior validity as a tool of judgement. In fact I can recall many times in my life when I have been led by some completely superficial factor like the lines on their face, or an odd spoken phrase or word that they've emitted, to decide that I didn't like or trust them. On occasions, I fear that I was misled purely by a face or voice that, as the old saying goes, only a mother could love. Yes, I have frequently picked the wrong person to like, and the wrong person to mistrust. However, there are also many instances when I've known a self-proclaimed empathic NT to be diabolically wrong when they rejected or distrusted the nicest person, just because of some obscure and (to me) subliminal factor that put them off.

In regard to eye contact, well, we all just do it, and as we are used to doing it, somehow we can't do anything else. I know that the practice can keep my mind from wandering away from the conversation that is going on. Maybe it just happens to be one of those habits that should best be classified as politeness.

Of course, it might all be a culturally based matter. There are some Asian peoples, I understand, who might give the appearance of the Aspie in their communication habits. The women in particular have learnt not to stare another in the face when talking or in answering questions. This, we are told by school teachers and Immigration Officials, can give a bad impression to the uninformed.

So the same can apply to us Aspies. It must be understood though, that often we simply don't think particularly well or analyse efficiently, when we have to look another straight in the eye. And perhaps our memories won't readily come up with the required information if we are concentrating on this disconcerting gaze of the other. We may well find it detrimental to keep our eyes open at all while we set out to describe effectively just what we are thinking about. To be confronted by another's gaze is to be confused by input that we can well do without.

On Loneliness

I think it can be truthfully said that an inherent loneliness is the lot of every Aspie. We don't understand our fellows, and our fellows don't understand us. Rarely do we have any concept of the real nature of another person. The face, figure, voice and habits and history of the other person are all that we can know and observe. Any change in their personality or habits may cause him or her almost to become unknowable. So the presence and person of another is always something of a mystery.

Since it is seldom that any other person comes close to us in a way that is truly real or intimate, it seems that we are almost always isolated. I might suggest the analogy of a Westerner, who gets lost in some dense unknown jungle. Just consider what this has to be like. You don't know the language of the inhabitants. You never really know just what the rules of living there are. You tread carefully and delicately in order not to aggravate the inhabitants. You look for and value above, all any kindness and gentleness that might come to you from the 'natives'. You try to develop and manifest trust; and apart from the process of pure survival, your major mechanism is based on taking care that you don't rock the boat. You are desperate to make sure that the inhabitants get only the simplest of messages from you. You try to determine what is being signalled and displayed by them, and all you can do is base your decisions on the literal messages that are apparent to you. There is no-one, however, who is such satisfying company for you as yourself; and though you are aware of what you need, you don't know how to get it.

Just so in daily life, our Aspie will usually know just what he needs at any given moment; but he is somewhat at a loss as he tries to determine how to get it. This jungle of a world is strangely cruel, too fast, complex and indecipherable. Yet amazingly, those other NT inhabitants seem to manage to live together, in some sort of complex conspiracy that will leave the Aspie feeling out of alignment. Now the occasional and admittedly very welcome NT who actually succeeds in entering our world, or who remarkably manages to contact us in our own world, will have had to make a major shift in his thinking and understanding. But it breaks every convention he has established. Just about all the people dealing processes that he has spent a lifetime in cultivating may have to go by the board. Even if he has dealt with the more regular areas of what may be described as disablement - whether with the blind or deaf, the wheelchair bound, and even those endearing individuals with Downs Syndrome, he may well be totally flummoxed when confronted with his first Asperger.

I guess that a 'heavy' Autistic at least gives every indication and signal of being a difficult deal. But when it comes to his meeting with a high functioning Asperger, our NT is presented with all sorts of tricky and misleading indications. When he sees this person, who may look pretty normal, who manages to eat, travel, sleep and talk on the phone efficiently, and who may also be coping with a job or marriage, he will be taken aback when he finds that his familiar communication processes seem to be inadequate. This high functioning Aspie may be so accustomed to living 'as if', or as Liane Holliday Willey put it in the title of her book, 'Pretending to be normal', that he may only rarely in the day to day situation give clear signs of his inconveniences or detriments. So the NT may get to the point of even disputing for a time that this person has anything at all unusual about him. (2)

Confessions of an Unashamed Asperger

We Aspies search for and periodically find avenues whereby we can be efficiently alone, with the appearance of being engaged and suitably occupied. I expect that lots of us have made a point at times of pretending to be involved in something of our own, just so we wouldn't be interrupted, or drawn in by others against our will. And let's face it we do have our crucial avenues of activity and occupation. Look at our hobbies or our reading - our gardening, perhaps, or especially nowadays, our work at the computer. And here I cannot omit from the list our involvement in that most Aspie of all activities, our 'Stimming'! How could we possibly get on, if we weren't entitled to enjoy that privilege? And what a puzzle it represents to the eye of the NT!

I'm often asked if I get lonely. I have to answer that yes, I do feel mildly lonely at odd times. But let me make it plain that I've proven that the mere fact of having my loneliness just technically assuaged by the company of another bears little guarantee of giving me any satisfaction. The regular presence of another, however close or 'intimate', can all too easily bring a far worse set of disturbances. As it happens, the most painful loneliness I ever experienced was when I was with a partner in a 'dead' marriage. I felt I had sold my soul, as it were. I was floating round in a limbo, where the partner alone seemed real, and somehow I wasn't there. I craved to be myself once more, and to be able to think without interruption; and even to talk to myself, without having to be just a sounding board for the other party. It was very sad and very destructive for me.

So in answer to the question, I can say that generally I don't tend to get lonely in any serious degree. My cats give me the companionship and closeness that I crave. My books provide me with a special excitement as I communicate with myself. My friends give me the periodical communication that stimulates me. And when engaged in professional performance, my audiences give me the feedback that offers the desirable kick of affirmation and applause.

I must say too, that the relationships I've had with AS folks on the AS Internet lines have been emotionally fulfilling. And a great deal of my sexual need is satisfied by my day to day friendships with women, despite the absence of any literal sexual activity or purpose.

On Knowing another Person

A long time ago, I heard the saying 'What you are speaks so loudly, I can't hear a word you are saying'. Now that is a statement that I find totally incomprehensible. It is assuming that one can truly know the essence of another person.

In my early life, I took it for granted that I understood well enough just what it meant to know someone. But as I got older and saw just how the NT population interpreted the matter, and just how it was discussed in the literature, I realized that I'd never actually had a clue. With my Aspie brain, and despite my sophisticated reading and observation, what I still mean by the word, is just the fact that I can identify an individual. It probably means little other than that I have talked to them, and that they are equally familiar with me. You know the sort of verbal usage... "Have you met Joe Bloggs?" "Oh sure, I know Joe... I was introduced to him three hours ago."

For me all I can ever know of a person (and that includes a wife or a partner) is what I may observe of their face and figure, their voice and their habits, their history or just whatever I may happen to recall of what they've said. There is no coherent combination of all these factors to make up a particular person. I only know a collection of individual parts. (3) And if none of these is singularly disruptive or unpleasant to me, then I may determine that some sort of relationship is possible.

I can't really detect or define any consistent and reliable being even within a wife or partner. I would have to admit the fact that this clearly makes confidence and trust in the other, a very delicate and indeed difficult thing, as the partner may swing in and out of the desirable state of trustworthiness constantly. In my eyes, a partner remains one of the Aliens of this NT world, despite being the particular one whom I share most time with, along with accompanying life experiences. In particular as well, she is one who has offered herself into a physically mutual access with me. She has agreed on accommodation with me for mutual benefits.

I always entered marriage with the view that its essence was a mixture of cooperation, politeness and an agreed process of mutually 'giving in' to each other. The business of having conflicting wills and preferences was always a puzzle. The partner was and always would be for me a mystery, and ultimately unpredictable. In my married days I had to work very hard to cope with the interruptions to my life's flow that she represented, because they represented part of the price I had to pay in order to get from (or through her), those very few benefits that a relationship was expected to give me. I now live alone in my later years, because I have realized that sharing is not at all worthwhile for me.

My problem is thus the business of 'living with' and 'sharing'. In my married days, I was never concerned with questions or facts about a partner's inner nature. Since I don't really have pre-conceived ideas about the inner being of a partner, I am not so likely to be shocked or disturbed by any revelations about their real feelings or experiences and nature. In general, so long as any truths about the nature or history of the partner don't directly affect me or the relationship, and in particular are not likely to rebound or cause trouble later on in a practical or pragmatic sense, then I could imagine few of them that might worry me.

I fantasise that NTs merely talk themselves into believing that people have a knowable reality or personhood. And I think that I've seen plenty of evidence of this in my own marriages. On a number of occasions, my partners have reacted with shock when they had to conclude correctly that they didn't know me particularly well. They had come to all sorts of wrong, though perhaps logical, ideas of what constituted me, as well as my thoughts, preferences and feelings. But just maybe this is all based on the degrees of honesty and openness which are engaged in between the partners - and so, something else that I can't really comprehend. (4)

That outside world of 'People' is a big scary place to many of us AS folk. People are unpredictable and intrusive. However we may get to like some of our fellows, they still remain aliens to us. So for me it is with a definite jolt that I switch off my own inner contented or stable processes that I may make the effort to receive and register the input of the people out there.

What I have come to realize over these last 51 years, since I married for the first time, is that the longer I live with them, the less I actually know my partners. Now by contrast, it appears that the NT person in each case feels herself to be more familiar, more natural and more real as time goes on. By contrast, I become more restrained, nervous, and indeed more fearful of the partnership. I could perhaps speculate to explain it in this way. When a couple is first together, they are in many ways on their best behaviour. They relate in what is actually a very limited and careful fashion. And this limited style is obviously closer to the AS mind and habits. But then, in the mixed AS/NT marriage, the relationship will develop in a rather lop-sided way. The NT will, as I suggested, settle down, and become very much more herself. But the AS partner as in my case, is likely to remain virtually where he is - where he started. He is not likely to change. The careful guardedness, being part of his essential nature, just won't alter. That individual you see at the beginning is what you will have permanently. What you see is what you get!

So in my marriages and partnerships, I remained just as intimate and real for the rest of the relationship as I had been at the beginning. Well, at any rate, for as long as restraint and fearfulness didn't develop. Sadly, I would say intimacy, in any desirable sense, just didn't happen in any of my marriages. I never developed a real sense of confidence or trust in the other party; and she remained just as alien to me (albeit as a friendly or harmless alien) all the way through. After fifteen or twenty years, I had no sense of knowing this other person any better than I did at the beginning. Consequently the partner's contrasting growth of confidence, sureness and naturalness meant that she spoke thought and acted in some intimate 'relationship' way that I could never achieve or match. Her language, her expectations and her relaxed way of treating me or other family members became disturbing or frightening to me. Her confidence and certainty, indeed her very familiarity could be destabilising. And I'm not the only Aspie who has disconcerted his partner with the revelation that even in the most intimate moments he is probably still not being truly spontaneous. (5)

There is a curious formality or politeness that can come out of me even in the most intimate situations. This gives something of a detached and maybe distant appearance. I can sound unrelated at those times, and perhaps uninvolved in my attempts at intimate talk. It will represent something of a state that can appear cold and artificial. The other party may well feel that she is not contacting any sort of a real me. And that is probably a pretty accurate perception.

Now these AS traits are disconcerting enough for the NT; but let's face it, that contrasting and confusing naturalness of the NT partner can be even worse for the AS one. However puzzled or shocked the NT may be about her resident Aspie, she will most likely still come to conventional and logical conclusions about his psychology. They may feel right to her, but can be totally misguided. It is what she has trained herself to do with people all her life. Our Aspie on the other hand, is likely to have no workable theories at all about her, to work from. He is simply confused and lost.

We AS folk are persons of habit and of system. The unpredictability, the spontaneity of the NTs, and indeed, their very naturalness and intuition can become very scary. When you don't read another person, you have to depend only on what you observe and hear (or what you think that you observe and hear) in a literal fashion at the given moment. The messages, the suggestions, the natural exchanges and comments commonly taken for granted, and confidently interpreted among NT folk are simply bewildering to us.

Momentary emotional fluctuations are taken by us literally, as bearing permanent truth. The thing that is said in a moment of heat by the NT becomes too easily set in stone by the AS person. His fears will probably have trained and led him to be very defensive. He can well recall and still take literally the minutest things said or done to him many years before. I can find myself cringing at comments or reproaches made by my partners twenty years ago, or even by school teachers some 60 years ago. Heavens above, I still squirm at the memory of things that my parents said when I was small.

On Living 'as if'.

It was a lovely title that Liane Holiday Willey gave to her first book – 'Pretending to be Normal'. Years ago, I would never have dreamed that I had the gaps in my consciousness that have since been uncovered. Because of my obliviousness to other people's reality, I thought that the world looked perfectly normal. People looked 'real' and life seemed predictable. My own day to day experiences had consistency and everything seemed to tell me that my inner happenings and interpretations of the same just had to be identical with those of everyone else. But naturally, I was left with puzzles that virtually said "why do other people seem to have opinions and observations on life and truth that don't match my own?" or "Why do other people appear to live according to a rhythm that doesn't match mine?" It was like marching to the proverbial different drum.

Through study, and reading books on relationships and Psychology, and above all in dealing with my own marriages, and observing many hundreds of people throughout my lifetime, I realized that I had not misread these indicators. The majority of these other people, and the authorities that spoke for them, did have perceptions that were definitely not like mine. All along, it had seemed to me as if I was not missing anything. Anything I talked of to others seemed to have the same details, the same logic, the same premises. I had this illusory impression of pure normality. Unlike the person who is physically disabled, maybe deaf, blind or held back by illness or injury, I could find nothing that obviously stopped me in my day to day activities or pursuits from doing just what I wanted to do.

So it was a terribly shocking thing to recognize that there were many things that I had been unaware of not knowing! It's one thing to be aware of the fact that Person X over there handles Mathematics better than I do; or that compared with Person Y, I'm a complete dunce on computers. But when for years I thought, as a well read and verbally skilled individual, I was using words such as 'love', 'intimacy', 'sexual chemistry' in the same way as my peers, only to discover that I understood them in a totally different and seemingly deficient fashion, it came as a big shock to the system, and a hard learning experience.

Despite my good IQ, and with all my wide reading, all I could learn was that others used the words differently. It's just like finding that your fellows are speaking in a foreign language. I'm egotistical enough not to feel deficient or inferior because of this. But I must admit that just at times, especially within the delicately balanced conflicts and misunderstandings of relationships, I do feel unfairly disadvantaged. So I've had the temerity to try explaining in my public lectures some of the insights I've been lucky enough to develop about the different world which I inhabit. I try to tell the public about some of those thing, that regardless of their family experiences with AS, they still don't know that they don't know.

Like the majority of Aspies, I frequently take refuge in a stony silence during intimate confrontations. It appears useful if not necessary, in order to avoid falling into states of chaos or panic.   I am then better able to avoid having my emotions swayed all over the place, as I experience the partner's emotions and fluctuations. I can then safely observe and contemplate rationally, rather than being shaken off balance. The point is that when I am confronted by another person's momentary fluctuations, it is possible for me to be virtually taken over as it were, with the result that I cannot think very clearly.

I'm quite sure that it will be most disturbing for the other party too; but on all too many occasions when I actually expressed my emotions and reactions in an open and honest way, the other party just got more and more upset. I was also more likely to cave in and say 'Yes!' to just about anything suggested or asked, without meaning it, or for that matter, without understanding it and its implications. The blank face and distant observing consciousness enabled me to pause and clearly consider what was being said or thrown at me with minimum confusion. I would not then jump to conclusions. I could wait to see if further information were forthcoming. It must be appreciated that the stony face is not deliberately chosen at that moment. It certainly comes naturally, because for the reasons given above, I have to shut off, in order to study what is being said. And I simply can't concentrate on what is being said if I'm going through emotional states in response.

It appears hard for the Aspie to take a middle road in most things. He will tend to extremes, both in his likes and dislikes, as well as in his talents and understanding. He can usually be classified as either a visual thinker or an aural thinker. He has talent or interest in the Arts, or he is drawn towards the Mathematical and Engineering areas. He is decidedly quiet, or he is talkative. He is physically tidy, (and maybe obsessively so), or else he is haphazard and disorganized. He may be anxious and defensive, or aggressive and domineering. Sexually, he may be disfunctionally immature and even Asexual; or he may be thoughtlessly promiscuous. He may be specifically obsessive or casually detached. Those characteristics which come naturally to him, will likely be exaggerated throughout his life.

One of the common signs of AS is an awkwardness in expression and something of an uneasy style of speech. Maybe a curious formality may manifest. However, self-presentation and clarity of speaking have been professionally developed in me. So the casual acquaintance will feel sure that I for one am perfectly regular, since my speech and eye contact do appear to be normal and friendly. I can only assume that I'm efficient at pretending, and yet I cannot imagine how the observant or so-called intuitive person comes to miss those signs of discomfort or effort that distinguish both my intimate and my small talk, and of which I'm still so deeply conscious.

My urge or maybe my sheer compulsion to fill the gaps in communicating by speaking lightly or facetiously can be embarrassing. It happens so automatically that I feel carried along in my talking. Luckily my most aware colleagues have become capable of just quietly directing me back to the seriousness of things with a brief word. I'm usually alert enough to be able to swing back out of my lightness, to resume the thread of the discussion without disruption. Hopefully the outsiders are not aware of the shift that is happening, or the adjustment I'm making.

With the expectation that I join in a conversation, my instinct is simply to be quiet. The swapping of words pauses for a moment and the direction points to me. In order to fill the gap in the sequence I fall back on routines and standard lines. Automatic pleasantries like "How are you?" or "Nice Day" will be inappropriate; so I will use some of the many glib phrases and quotes in my repertoire that are intended to express interest and understanding. But as it happens, with all the sophisticated vocabulary in the world, I must eventually run out of 'lines', and will start to repeat myself, or indulge in my urge for facetiousness and comedy. As I become aware of what I'm doing, I just hope that either they don't remember, or else that they aren't the same folk that heard it all last time.

How embarrassing it is to hold the idea that others are thinking about you... 'Ah, he can't take anything seriously, this fellow.' Or perhaps something like 'Why the hell does he have to make a joke about everything?' I find it very tiresome and artificial when I have to speak routinely or repetitively about the everyday things that one conveys to people; and this is a major reason why I cover it all up by comedian style verbiage.

Just now, I heard an interview on the radio with a very mature and genial gentleman, who made a couple of relaxed comments about his wife of almost 50 years. It just struck me how totally easy the remarks were. I just couldn't identify with this sort of attitude. The business of being in a marriage, the routine being with another, the finding of comfort with, the being real throughout... none of these has ever happened for me. I've constantly had to fabricate them.
I've had to play-act them.

As with so many NT conditions and situations, it's not that I look on and crave to be able to experience it differently. Rather when I observe people behaving in their NT fashion, I look on in a state of wonder. I study them without comprehension. As I've stated elsewhere, I sometimes feel deep down that I actually resent the way NTs behave. It can have almost an embarrassing feel to it. I wouldn't be comfortable trying to say the things to or about a partner that come naturally to the NT person. And this means both good and bad things!

The only times that I came close to being natural in my relationships were when I was with a spouse who took on all the initiative in running the relationship. The naturalness of my second wife in that case, was the very thing that made it happen. And as long as there were no essential stresses or tensions, she would carry things along. I just fitted in unthinkingly, and for periods it worked. I couldn't do it by myself.

My sense of time is very potent. I have a powerful urge to be on time for all events. I endeavour to allow plenty of time to prepare myself. In fact when it comes to appointments and meetings, I usually get all things ready some day or more ahead, so there will be the minimum to do in the morning. But I was not ever thus. As a child I was tardy, and indeed famous, or for that matter a figure of fun, for being late to school in the mornings, due to a reluctance to rise from bed. Consequently in my early working days, and probably up till the time I did National Service training, I was often running late for work. Terribly embarrassing, I must admit. I did learn or train myself to be prompt. Not sure to this day whether it was due to sheer maturity. But perhaps the Army forced a worthwhile change; but I became almost obsessional in handling time.

But I do hate deadlines imposed by any other. I hate to have to produce whatever is required on demand. When I'm preparing lectures or other written things, I usually have them done a long time in advance. I guess that it is one of the many reasons that I could never have followed my brother and become a Journalist. There's simply no way on earth that I could churn out anything asked for at short notice.

Confessions of an Unashamed Asperger

On People Reading People

As Barbra Streisand (almost) sang... 'People who read people, are the luckiest people! ...." Well, as I said. Almost! Years ago, a young lady I worked with in an office, sat near by, and would commonly chat with me during the morning and afternoon tea breaks. We covered all sorts of pleasant matters in our conversation. One particular day, I was giving her an explanation of how I really felt about some subject, when I became aware for the first time, how her eyes were fixed on me, and it seemed so unyielding and pointed. I was characteristically blank about her gaze for a few moments while I mentally processed the observation, when it suddenly hit me like a ton of bricks. 'The wretched woman is READING me! How Dare She???' I felt a surge of indignation.

Oh, I didn't indulge in recriminations and our friendship was not spoiled. But I did venture to ask about her attention style. She explained how she always fixed her eyes on anyone she was conversing with, so she could pick up the unspoken messages and the meaning behind their words. Well, I must say I was terribly shocked. Nothing could be more foreign to me. Such a procedure seemed intrusive and inexcusable. When I talk to someone, I want them to register absolutely nothing other than what I am saying. I want to be taken completely literally. I am composing and delivering a specific message for that person at that time, and they are simply not to be privy to any other information. If it's good enough for me to take in from them purely the content in the form of those specific words that they are delivering - why isn't it good enough for anyone else in return????

Some 23 years later it still hits me in the same way. Is this because of my secretive tendency? Is it because of my native compartmentalising process? Maybe it is a bit of both. As I see it, each individual person sits in his own specific and unique compartment, and is entitled to a specific and appropriate selection of facts and thoughts. And no other party (as far as I'm concerned) bears an automatic entitlement to precisely the same inroads or intimacy. I suppose it is in this way that I can control my interaction with each person, and avoid, as it were, any cross contamination between their utterly different relationships with me. Every single one of my associates has a function or area of knowledge and experience of me that is not shared by any other at all.

I never think to inquire into people's motives. It always feels irrelevant to me. I am so literal that I often feel I wouldn't care about anything that has not been expressed. The outer form and expression of a person is the thing that seems of any importance, and is generally the only thing I want to be concerned with. I don't get the faintest idea of the genuineness of a person's attitude. For sure, it might mean that I can be manipulated, or used by the wrong person. Even if an individual didn't greatly care about me or my life, the fact of that one being kind or civil to me is the important thing. Despite the fact that I have been badly used by some few persons during my life, the whole thing has I think been balanced out for me in the long run. I don't believe that I've been let down any worse than have many of the NT persons I've known, who prided themselves on their protective insight and that much vaunted empathy. At the same time, because I seldom take offence, it is rare that anyone can upset me when they haven't meant to.

I recall being criticized by one of my wives for regarding casual acquaintances as close friends. I have no perception of depth in a person's nature. I can get the greatest joy from momentary encounters or associations. The only thing that distinguishes deeper friends and intimates from casuals for me is the way in which the deeper ones seem to last longer or make themselves more available; as well as the fact that these deeper ones may encourage the on-going sharing of interests that I rarely get the chance to enjoy. The same thing can be said to apply to my relations with the opposite sex. The big difference between the women in my life, lies in the degree of affectionate intimacies that may be initiated or encouraged by that other.

We Aspies can be seriously misread or misinterpreted by even the closest of our friends and intimates. We retreat behind that blank face I've talked about, when we hear or learn of things that we should by all NT standards react to with some degree of emotion or shock. Often we simply take in some information with care and open-mindedness; and regardless of how threatening or painful it may have been to hear it, we can recite the details back or comment on them with a distant air of problem solving or detached analysis. This peculiar form of Aspie demeanour can be most disconcerting to others, and as well as for the average Therapist who is not used to it.

I think there can be two or three reasons for this. One is that it will not be until we've recited the details over to ourselves, or until we've checked by repetition and had some sort of confirmation from the other, that we start to see exactly what is being considered. When one doesn't have an instant gut reaction to things, it may often be hours or even days before the thing that was said gets to be digested and measured up by our very systematic brains. We can't react quickly because we have not felt any inner response. However alarming or serious may they be, the things that we are told can appear to us just like data or fiction on a printed page, and don't seem to relate to ourselves. They appear to have originated somewhere out 'there' away from ourselves, and represent cold unemotional information first and foremost.

Another reason is that in our early childhood we were probably too inclined to be impulsive in our reactions to things. So, under the discipline of parental or school authority we learned to restrain ourselves, - as for example to hold back from jumping to conclusions. This became so habitual that after many years we will have avoided any recognizable reaction for a time. In fact, our intuitive and childlike automatic responses got us into so much trouble that we have developed a whole series of mechanisms for deflecting our impulses, so we get to the point of being unaware of what is happening in the psyche. We only let ourselves feel and analyse and duly confront the situation or stimulus well after the incident has passed. A big benefit in this is of course that we will not have acted dangerously or impulsively in a fashion that might have caused something particularly bad. It would be all too easy for anyone on the Autistic Spectrum to be over-hasty to self-protect. I guess it's a bit like the old suggestion that one should count up to forty before responding to any stimulus with anger.

Because of our propensity for observing the most alarming things with a cerebral detachment, many of us Aspies can be of immense value in emergencies. Our practical and disinterested involvement may give us big advantages in taking the most expedient remedial action.

On Literal thinking

The NT mind will find it very disconcerting to observe just how literal is the thinking of the AS person. It is well documented in the literature that we often have little facility in the way of detecting sub-text. We don't detect under-currents, or read the minds of our fellows. It can be very hurtful for others, especially for a partner who simply cannot conceive that one who has lived with them for any number of years still has no concept of their inner nature or needs. This AS person, this partner, after 20 years, can still regard the spouse as a stranger - as an alien. And each opinion or thought that is spoken about by the spouse, can sound like a brand new thing, something that is not familiar or anticipated, even when part of an on-going topic of concern. And so, I take the things told me by a partner as being literally true. I don't look for an underlying message or emotion. In return, I expect that my words will also be taken literally. When I converse with another person, I am intending him to register exactly what I am saying.

It is really quite funny to think back to occasions when an NT I've been talking to, ignored the naivety of my expression, and became quite sure that I'd been dropping hints, and suggesting things or asking favours that have been far from my mind. The sophisticated NT seems so incredibly proud of her ability to read sub-text. She is so used to detecting hidden meanings, and to probing into the mind of the other, in order to bring to light the things that are not being said. Often this process is an attempt to put into practice some sort of empathy. But honestly, I don't really think that these processes work too well with the Aspie.

Confessions of an Unashamed Asperger

When you don't feel empathy, or when you are not aware of the inner states of your fellow humans, you certainly don't have a realistic or educated idea of what goes to make them up. Other folk can give the appearance to us Aspies as walking and talking 'objects' only, and not as humans. As I've already said, no matter how long we may have known them, it tends to be that our long term partners, are still mysteries to us.

It is quite possible for the Aspie to take in the sight or image of anyone, even of our nearest and dearest, and just experience multiple bits of information. Now for me, I can clearly picture and determine a set of characteristics that identify a partner in my life. I know her face and figure well. I know her voice and her habits, and many of her expectations and dreams. But these are still like tables of details in a book or a technical file. They don't really represent any clear or reliable guide to what she may say or do at any particular time. Regardless of what sort of recent experience I may have had with her, I still find no guarantee or confidence in any knowledge or expectation. She is ultimately much the same unknown that I came across years before. As I described in another essay, it tends to be true that my earliest experiences of the partner will have actually been the most confidant or certain for me, (albeit however misguided). (6) At that stage, I'll have taken in essentially the simplest of details of her personality and emotional life, and those will be the greater part of what I am anticipating from then on. Any suggestion of a growth of understanding between us will be foreign to my nature.

Just thinking back to the most innocent and youthful loving period of my life, I recall plainly how I had no conception of anything that I might learn in the future about my partners. I never dreamed for a moment of trying to work out or calculate anything about any of my wives. My knowledge of them was simply an ever changing set of observations, based on the moment to moment things they did or said.

I tend, as an Aspie, to remain relatively static in my nature and in my emotional life. I guess that I pride myself on being consistent and predictable. At least that is the way I see myself; and it is precisely how I feel that I am presenting myself to the world and to the partner. But the partner at the same time is trying to detect and uncover more and more of the hypothetical inner, the secret and the real self of me. But the machinations of intimate relating don't come readily to the Aspie. It rarely occurs to him that there could be anything detectable behind the partner's façade.

An old piece of folk wisdom suggests that 'A man hopes that his woman will never change, while a woman is always hoping and seeking to see her man change'. I think that there is something of considerable importance in this statement, and it especially applies to the Aspie. Women, among whom AS seems to be less common than in the male of the species, do appear to have some sort of greater investment in the business of getting to know the inner self of the other. And particularly intelligent and aware ladies seem to envisage and long for that curious development in the psyche of the partner, known as 'growth'. Men perhaps look for something of the consistency and familiar stability that they knew in their mothers, and hope for the same to manifest in their chosen womenfolk. The complexities of developing interests and the growth of wisdom (or whatever) are not so attractive to the male lover.

The AS individual may be happy enough for his partner to learn, study and to tackle new things and skills, as long as he is not drawn into the business of involvement against his will. He is probably still content (or lost) within his own inner world; and would find it unpleasant at least, and maybe deeply painful to have to step out of his chosen fields. He can't comprehend why sharing or combining on things should be at all desirable. He is content with his own life and his own dreams. Why on earth should any other want to get into it, or persuade him to enter and participate in hers? In the life of the Aspie in particular, people and associates are often chosen specifically, because they have similar interests and passions. So unless there is an already present sharing of interests, why feel the need to divert to someone else's new passions? We Aspies tend to be predominantly 'Things' persons, not 'People' persons. Oh, we may be drawn to study or work on people issues, but it would then represent more of one of those Special Interests, or as a profession rather than just for the love of people in themselves.

I never inquire into, or even wonder about the sincerity or innermost thoughts of a partner. It rarely seems either relevant or interesting, or even, for that matter, respectful. I am interested only in how I'm being treated moment by moment, or in the specific message that they are currently transmitting.

My literal thinking causes me to occasionally speak naively and unthinkingly when talking to a partner about my own issues. What I say can appear just so simplistic, obvious or unsophisticated that the comments I make are actually not trusted by the other. I may be accused of lying or of implying something completely different. This result may also be triggered off by some degree of discrepancy between what I say, and what may show in my facial expression or body language. Since I am having to work hard in order to join in a conversation at all, it is possible too that the process of deliberate contrivance of my contributions, instead of just pouring out naturally, will seem suspicious to the partner.

References.

(1) See Essay on   Sexual Chemistry
(2) See Essay on   An Aspie you Ain't!
(3) See Essay on   Central Cohesion.
(4) See Essay on   Secrecy and Privacy
(5) Slater-Walker G. & C. An Asperger Marriage   Page 57
(6) See Essay on   Knowing Another Person

Chapter 4   ROUTINE, COLLECTING, AND OTHER ASPIE THINGS

On Routine and Ritual

For the normal child there is a comforting security in the way that all daily issues are tabulated and handled by the concerned parents. Naturally, a small child isn't required to keep track by himself of the momentary needs and the timetable of meal preparation and school schedules. It may well be a source of irritation to him that the parent so often interrupts the most fascinating and absorbing of activities in order to call him to eat or to get ready for bed or for school. But ultimately the constantly reinforced guarantee that the parent has the child's best interests at heart tends to get across; and the child will learn to bow to the parent's counsel and direction, albeit with varying degrees of reluctance.

However the learning process engaged in by the Aspie child is not so predictable or achievable. The actual relevance of that common sense timetable routinely imposed by the NT (and thereby Alien) individuals round about is not so obvious, perhaps possessed as he may be of unpredictable body timetables, and maybe certain bizarre feeding requirements as well.   In fact this whole business of getting his needs consistently catered for in accordance with the requirements of others is not obvious to him; and the resultant feeling of losing control can send him into panic and confusion. But things can change for him when occasionally he achieves a successful encounter with simple objects, or maybe when he dictates a sequence of actions for himself. He may well then seek to replicate the security and comfort on future occasions by handling the same objects, or maybe demanding some similar arrangement in future.

Perhaps an occasion of experiencing of an appropriate and comforting time of day for a meal will lead the Aspie to demand in future a similarly precise and unchangeable starting time for the meal every time. Some unique and specific arrangement of knives and forks in front of him at the table may come to represent security. It may offer a unique and familiar order that contrasts with the otherwise unpredictable or uncontrollable meal times that are fashioned normally within the chaotic arena of these NT adults.

It is an unsuspected inner world that the Autistic or Aspie child inhabits; and it is a world that cannot be conveyed in words or concepts to the NT adults about him. It is by no means a little or insignificant world; and it has different sensations, rules, distractions, pleasures and even, you might say, a different set of inhabitants. And naturally in a huge world-wide fraternity of AS folk, there will of necessity be a near infinite variety of such inner worlds. So often it is with discomfort and shock that we on the Spectrum are called from our inner native land back into the material NT world, most often by the demands of others; and somehow we endeavour to create ways and means that can make the transition more comfortable and to our liking.

I would not presume to say why any specific set of moves, sequences or timings might be chosen or preferred by a particular Aspie. Suffice it to say that each of us has his own process, and if encouraged, can often develop for himself the appropriate systems to make the transition a bit more reasonable and liveable. With our poor central coherence, we do tend to lack the ability to understand separate or disconnected instructions, procedures and preparations that are imposed from outside. Those big and disconcerting adults with whom we are enmeshed in our families seem to operate and to come to us with no rhyme or reason. They dictate timetables, and order actions and schedules that don't match our inner preferences.

I would postulate that in order for us to cope, a personally discovered (or deliberately chosen) pattern will help the transitions from that inner world of familiarity, through to the outer world of confusion. This pattern may be a particular sequence of how the day's clothing is to be put on; or perhaps just how a set of toys or collection of objects should be arranged on the mantelpiece. While when we have reached adulthood, in order to deal with many of the curious and unpredictable jobs that are laid to our fulfilment, it may be most useful if we have the freedom to arrange the desk or working space.

We do best if we can have everything sorted or positioned exclusively by ourselves in order to allow for an automatic grasping or reaching for the things. It may look bizarre or obsessive, especially when on occasion we can exhibit the greatest blindness to artefacts that have been removed and then duly replaced by others in positions that dont conform to those that we have chosen or defined for them. This characteristic can appear alarming and indeed pathological to the outsider. But those who observe us closely should be able to see just how it makes for expedient working and comfort. Thus it becomes clear just why, for example, the compulsion   to follow some unique routine of a walking direction or drive home or to work may well be comforting and even necessary.

Now in my case, I have to admit that I don't have too many issues that are based on such rigid sequences of procedure. But when I am enjoying my autonomy in solitary living, the night and morning procedures are among the most important things that give me peace and security. Though however valued these rituals are to me, they are not essential.

So I must make it plain that the big and most important thing to make my routine happy and totally comfortable at night will be a freedom from any distraction - the absence of any other person about the house - there would be no interruption from another voice or presence. So I don't have anything to distract me from the inner life, which is peaceful and quiet. And this quietness, this freedom from another person's presence, is what makes bedtime so very very special for me. My rhythm is not disrupted. I don't have to repeatedly switch my consciousness outwards and away from my inner world.

Oh yes, self-centred indeed! Any attempt to 'cure' this inward-living and navel gazing habit would need to be pretty powerful and penetrating to give me the conviction that it was worthwhile. In everyday life that very business of routinely paying attention to my fellows is essentially hard work. But I allow for it just the same, and daytime is the time that it is best done. It represents the environment in which dealing with other people, and the business of living with its exertion, its effort, and for that matter, with its tiresome unselfishness, is the order of the day. But evening and morning with their perfect solitude, represent the times when I don't have to set myself to these tasks and efforts.

I do engage in many simple (and, I believe or hope, relatively unobtrusive) rituals and routines during the day. My seemingly repetitive, indeed near scripted, talk to the cats looks just like this. However childish or inane, it fills my particular need for communication without the burden of intention, pressure or argument. The cat can't and won't criticize. I can enjoy the fun of pretending to myself that I understand just what she is saying. In some ways my cats are like extensions of myself perhaps.

What are the other key routines or activities which mean much to me? Well, acting, singing and theatrical performance all have represented some form of routine and predictable, progressive activity, that can be pleasant, fulfilling and creative.

On Clubs and Societies

Since he lacks comfort and self-assurance to a greater extent in the personal company of other people, the Aspie will often seek a 'home' in clubs and groups. It may be painful to deal with a purely social gathering, or a party/celebration type of setting; but a meeting of like-minded people is easier to cope with and indeed desirable.. From an early age, I joined in with groups and societies as they represented suitable means of access to information and activities that complemented things that I was doing. For make no mistake, I was always taking up or pursuing hobbies, studies and new skills.

In my mid childhood, I became a member of one of those children's radio clubs that tended to proliferate through the 40s and 50s, - but which largely evaporated with the coming of television. This particular club was based on mythological imagery, and centred round the Greek Myths and Heroes. It was called the Argonauts Club. Unlike my brother who duly contributed a number of entries to the various departments of the Club, I mainly just listened to the session each day, rejoicing in my personal membership designation of Heraclea

49, which, for heavens sake, I still remember after some 60 odd years.

It must be understood that in the outside world I found very few school friends, and just a few church mates. So I didn't really have much in the way of social life, and even tried on a number of occasions to create my own societies and groups. My efforts were rather weak in this respect, as I had not the slightest idea of how to organize or run them.

But probably the most exciting affiliation effort of my youth was achieved in my early teens, when I became fascinated with stage magic, and attempted to become an exponent of this unique theatrical art. At the age of 12, and well encouraged by a kindly and very patient family, I proceeded to inflict my developing (and at times painful) conjuring performances on an unsuspecting and innocent world. I was fortunate enough to make contact with a guy who had been a professional magician in his younger days, and together with four other interested parties we formed a local magical society, which duly affiliated with an Australia wide body. Just a couple of years later, on transferring to the big city for the start of my working life, I was able to join with the parent group of the Society.

The other associations that were important were the parties of fellow actors while I was studying theatre or rehearsing a play. This realm of theatre was another milieu in which I felt at home. In this for me no time schedule was too hard; and no sacrifice, money or effort could be considered as wasted. The other actors and the directors became something resembling spiritual kith and kin.

School represented just an odd activity and environment that gave me nothing much in the way of personal satisfaction or companionship; and I cheerfully attended Cinemas by myself. I was natural that through my early years, the Church was the major social structure outside the home. For that matter it tended to dominate everything within the home as well. From babyhood, it was quite normal for me to attend Church along with my parents, as often as three times on many weekends. Youth groups and Sunday School were important and reasonably enjoyable – as well as predictable; and I can't say that I ever rebelled against these in any fashion. It would simply never have occurred to me to do so.

Non-Conformist Church services in my childhood, within the Methodist Church, did provide a certain minor form of ritualistic Service, which was easy on the eye and pleasing to the heart.

In those days of the 1940s, within the Methodist Church in Australia was an organization for men and boys that offered a regular ceremonial meeting that was based, in its mythology and symbolism, on a romanticized (and Christian) image of the Court of King Arthur. It was called The Methodist Order of Knights, and my brother and father were well entrenched in the group, gaining a great deal of satisfaction from it. Our father was a highly respected lay preacher of the Church, as well as sometime organist, choirmaster and Sunday School Superintendent. But also with his inherent love of ritual, long promoted by his pleasure in Freemasonry, the Order of Knights was greatly suited to his temperament as well. I quickly discovered that ritual appealed to me in the same way.

It was with my introduction to high Church ritual within the Anglican Communion during my late twenties to thirties, that I found a Christian form of ceremonial that was most satisfying, I eventually proved to be a good student and practitioner of ceremony. A few years later, my entry into the organization known as Rostrum, offered an entry into a totally different form of ritual which has proven to be of great value. Rostrum is something of a British form of the 'After Dinner' public speaking society, in which one may learn the various skills of oratory, and for that matter a certain mastering of Chairmanship and Meeting Procedure. Heaven knows this latter especially is a very ritualistic system, that is applied to just about every club and society that one can ever belong to as well as the Government. Knowledge of the standard rules can assist one in almost any organization, to make sure that the business will work well and efficiently.

As I have said, I was deeply entrenched in the Methodist

Church during my youth. But there was a very significant period in my late 20s to 30s when I engaged in a close affiliation with another Church, and for several years actually belonged to the clergy. At the time it filled something of a void, you might say, after the break-up of my first marriage. It certainly did give me some much needed structure at that time, not to mention some interesting and stimulating experiences. Much of it was pleasing; however when it came to the requisite Pastoral work I was totally out of my depth, and duly passed jobs over to my fellow clerics, who were more suitably human (and more appropriately NT) in nature. At best my affiliation did represent a wonderful experience; but for any number of obvious reasons I could not fulfil the most important part of the work, and eventually had to resign from the Clergy.

I guess that the discomfort and inadequacy I exhibited and felt in personally interacting with the members of the congregation was one of those important experiences of my life that convinced me that something was a little bit askew about my style of being. I literally found myself getting afraid of facing the people after services, and simply couldn't in all honesty do what was required of any Pastor. Clearly one has to be possessed of an affinity with people and some degree of empathy in order to fulfil the job. It simply doesn't work if you live life in a state of detachment, and fail to truly contact those about you. I guess too, that when the only talk you can engage with them is in the form of routine and pat phrases, you rapidly run out of anything to say.

Oh sure, my sermons were greatly appreciated, as was my work in teaching. Clearly my skills in the public and platform areas were being honed and developed at that time. Also, I was an enthusiastic and devoted Ritualist, and loved leading the Ceremonial. But a Pastor or true Minister of any sort? No, I simply wasn't! As I mentioned earlier, my father was well entrenched in the business of ritual within his Lodges, and though as a child, I knew nothing of the inner working of this august body, somehow what I heard or learnt of it felt strangely familiar; and I bore a natural sympathy towards such activities.

It automatically seemed to me that the idea of a dedicated space or area, of duly appointed ritualistic officers and personnel, and of sacred or special artefacts and symbolic pictures, was just so right. Certainly it was appropriate that I should eventually link up with symbolic and ritual organizations. These fulfilled my natural inclination towards ceremonial to a considerable degree, and pleased me far more than membership within a more open and pedestrian 'Meeting' type of group would do. The member felt that he was a precise unit in something very special. There was initiation into the various degrees of the organization. One had the opportunity to wear special and simple forms of regalia which were designed, along with the ritual and the discourses, to intensify one's involvement with the ideals and purposes.

And so it was that my reading and fascination with religious and so-called esoteric subjects drew me at 21 to form the most significant affiliation of my life, when I joined the Fraternal Order known as the AMORC, with which I am still happily associated, some 50 odd years later. And herein I made some of my most long-term and understanding friends. It was with my entry into this fraternity that my love of and proficiency in ritual came into its own. It gave me a greater understanding of the processes and beauties that my father long before had come to locate and value within his Masonic Lodges. The engaging in ceremonial that multitudes of persons had participated in over long periods of time and maybe over many centuries, is a thrilling experience and one of the great joys of my life

Within groups like the ones I detail here, I was able to find something of the 'Home' that I always sought for. I was not left out on a limb when in such a crowd of these, my fellows. There was always someone to talk to, and no demand that I should engage in that appalling expectation of small talk. Perhaps the more rare gregarious side of my Aspie nature is at its most contented and fulfilled when engaged in such work, practised alongside those special persons who share the same ideals and aims.

However, I can make some horrible blunders in the simplest

of such appropriate company. There was one group I belonged to that practised meditation; and when we had a Christmas party, I offered to provide recorder and tapes of music as background. Naturally I chose my own personal selection of music, based on my regular association with the folk involved; and that was naturally serious meditation music. There was very quickly an agonized cry of protest from the others (rather to be expected, as I realized later), and some light Christmas songs and carols were substituted. Clever me was just not capable of anticipating or of reading that essential atmosphere of 'Party time'. Typically I went into automatic pilot mode, and associated these perfectly normal people with the agenda that we generally worked together on; and the last thing I would have though of would be light music. I must say to hear someone at an event suddenly shout with excitement, "Okay, now let's PARTY!!!" leaves me in a state of incomprehension. What can it possibly mean to a person like myself? Given a choice for me between serious and exciting discussion on one hand, and light fun on the other, the reader can readily figure out just which I would choose! A classical Party Pooper, I fear.

Social situations have always been a problem for me. From the earliest days I had the idea that one is supposed to join in and enjoy, even if it kills one. On the only couple of occasions that I had some sort of Birthday or Christmas party celebrations at my home for would-be school friends, I innocently and naively looked forward to them; but found in the event, that I had to work hard in order to find and drag the various bits of enjoyment out of them. Maybe the greatest benefit I eventually got was more in the way of the principle of it... in the bare fact that I actually had had a party at all. What an achievement, what an opportunity! (but opportunity for what?)

But probably my favourite funny story about the social situation concerned a party I was invited to when in my 40s. By myself, I landed in at this rather large house, and was duly ushered into the lounge, where some close cuddly dancing was going on. A fat lot of use to me of course, since I don't dance at all. So I moved on. There in the dining room a whole lot of alcoholic drinks were being swigged down, and I moved on again since I don't drink. In the kitchen there were some individuals puffing on marijuana, which was every bit as useful to me as the previous offerings.

Other activities of a private nature were going on in the bedrooms; and I came to the conclusion that there was not one thing that would interest or involve me in the whole place. But then with a bit of good fortune, I discovered the family cat in a corner of the hallway, accompanied by a new set of fluffy kittens. I settled down right there and played with them for some hour or more, and was left undisturbed; until I excused myself and left with a reasonable degree of satisfaction.

Thankfully, I've had very few celebratory dinners or parties in my whole life. One, and the last, was virtually forced on me by a group of my theatrical friends who arranged to land at my place on my 60th birthday. I had discouraged the idea when it was first mooted, and didn't really believe that they would turn up. But as it happened, they didn't take my word for rejection, presumably thinking that I had meant something in the realm of "Oh please, don't go to any trouble on my account". So they turned up, only to find on top of everything else, that I was in miseries with a bad attack of the flu. The very last thing I would have wanted at that time was to have to entertain anyone.

Occasionally I do accept dinner or celebration invitations. Strictly speaking I don't really mind all that much, if I can sort of disappear in a seat at a long table, where one just listens to a few speeches, and exchanges the most innocuous small talk with one's neighbours. It is not too bad for me either, if the company consists of no more than one or two close friends. I can cope with this, though I will probably murmur excuses to leave early, before I get caught up with the others in the real nitty gritty of sharing. Naturally, if I can share in a gathering at which there will be discussion of issues that are significant to me, then I will be pretty happy to be a part of it.

On rare occasions I have found myself at some sort of dance meeting, and have been confronted by a whole lot of people just spinning round about on the floor, and I've looked on with amazement. The whole scene appeared to me like a universe of atoms or electrons just whirling mindlessly and impersonally about in their orbits. It has appeared almost hypnotic to me, and certainly miles beyond my comprehension.

On Collecting Things

How typical it is for Aspies in the process of pursuing their special interests, to collect things. I'm reminded of the old story about the woman who went to her Psychiatrist with the complaint that she was having trouble with her husband. He got unduly upset over her love of pancakes, she complained. The Psych opened his eyes wide, and smiling said: "Well, there cant be much wrong with that. I like pancakes too!" The woman answered: "Oh goody, you must come and visit me. I've got boxes and boxes of them." I must say that she sounds just like an Aspie.

Collecting things is pretty common around Aspies; and very often the objects collected and sought after, are odd and unique. We hear about the boxes and files crammed with railway timetables or news cuttings on dinosaurs, etc. No wonder we get the reputation for eccentricity.

Of course there are plenty of regular Neuro-typical persons who collect and display special collections every bit as much. I have friends and relatives who have shelves of porcelain owls, or china dolls, or even of those ghastly old-fashioned souvenir teaspoons. I take delight in a collection of glass, china and plaster cats that stand on my crystal cabinet. But my collecting of these little figures is in no way to be considered as compulsive. It would not disturb me unduly if they were destroyed or lost. This assemblage of cats represents to me more of a bonus among the joys of life, rather than a necessity; and I rather suspect that the processes of collecting among adult Aspies represents a comfort to them, rather than being like the painful and pressurised activities of the Obsessive Compulsives.

Less in public view in my boxes and shelves are relics and reminders of just about every occupation, hobby or enthusiasm I've ever pursued. I do like to file away just about all books, pamphlets and news articles that relate to my areas of research. I find it hard to toss out or burn any printed material that has the slightest bit of information that might be of future use or curious interest to me. One very special kind of printed material that I compulsively file away is in the area of humour. Any good jokes or cartoons that tickle my funny bone do get kept. Much of the more serious stuff I retain is kept with a potential use as research for later reference. So consequently I've got dozens of cartons and plastic storage boxes filled with various bits and pieces in my cupboards and in my garage. It will be appreciated that the business of shifting house becomes a big and tiresome one.

Let me make it plain that I've had good value on many occasions from these same bits and pieces. I give a lot of talks and lectures; also, I write quite a few letters to colleagues and to various sites on the Internet, not the least of which in more recent times have been the discussion groups on Asperger Syndrome. The 'junk' in those cupboards have provided me with innumerable reminders and bits of information or illustrations for the expositions that I deliver.

But naturally the major things I collect are books, and there are shelves of books in a number of rooms about my home. In the office where I'm presently working at the computer, there are reference works, dictionaries (upwards of 50 varieties perhaps), sundry encyclopaedias as well as collections of special interest topics like cats, health and history. In the library next door are volumes of poetry, largely selected for public readings and performance, along with my pride and joy, a major collection of books on Art, which number some 800 or more. On the wall opposite these are the books on Theology, Christian History and Paganism, as well as the more important volumes on the various esoteric subjects that are among my passions.

In my bedroom are two big shelves of books on Theatre, Film and Acting, with a large selection of plays; and in the Retreat room upstairs are the books on Psychology, Literature as well as rare collections and special treasures. These collections do not sit idle. They represent a real resource, a working library.   My great delight on visiting a new town, and especially a big city, is to get stuck into the second hand book shops. And I really do have to keep a strict reign on myself to avoid overdoing the spending.

Why does the Aspie collect?   Well I guess there's little difference between the process of making collections of material objects on the one hand, and mentally assembling or memorising lists or details about things on the other. Somehow it is pleasing otherwise we just wouldn't do it. As I've previously said, I assume that this is one of the big differences between Aspies and Obsessive-Compulsives. We don't generally go about it anxiously or in fear. We fulfil our compulsions or urges through a love of the process, and for that matter with a joy at the eventual achievement.   There will possibly be some inner sense of being special, at having talents, faculties or arcane knowledge and collections that are superior to those of the folks about us. We become aware that the objects of our study or assembly are different from those of others, and we can duly and superciliously raise our eyebrows, and secretly retain some sense of being clever.

How many stories are related by the professionals about some Aspie or Autie, who on being first introduced, has instantly inquired if the Psych is well informed on dinosaurs, astronomy, railway engines of 1932, or whatever?   It is apparently quite common that on receiving a negative answer, the 'Savant' however young, will just shrug his shoulders and withdraw in order to   indicate that he has no interest in talking any further.

Chapter 5 PLEASURABLE PURSUITS

On Peak Experiences

It is not some sort of self-hypnosis, but as a rule, I can at any moment look at simple detached and isolated objects and have a happy sort of 'peak experience' – however mild it might be. The object might be the straight edge of a wardrobe, or the outline of a tree against the sky; or again as mundane a thing as the flat surface of a CD deck. I can focus on any of these and blot out all things round about. The object can then become literally 'beautiful' to me and quite absorbing. The key factor about any and all of these appears to be that the chosen objects are essentially 'parts' that have been virtually abstracted out of their natural context. And I presume that the process is based on the Autistic tendency to concentrate on or even to see just the part or segments, whether of things or of people – something of a classical 'not seeing the wood for the trees' syndrome.

It appears to be a source of great amusement (or at times frustration) to NT observers, when they observe the ecstatic delight with which AS folk regard small things like odd coincidences and special number sequences. I'll never forget that wonderful time a few short years back, when the Internet simply buzzed with Aspies all over the world comparing notes about the very remarkable dates that were showing up on the calendar. As an example, there was the 1st of February, in the year 2003. This of course, offered that wonderful dating sequence of 01.02.03. Or if the present reader happens to be American, we'd need to quote the 2nd January in that year.

An even better one was very special indeed. And I was among those who spotted it and drew attention to it when it showed up. This was that wonderful day designated as the 20th February, in the year 2002. But that was not all. If you looked at the time of day, you could discover that at two minutes past eight that evening, you could put the time down as 20.02pm. And thus the time and date together would read 20.02 on 20.02, in the year 2002. That sequence was of course unique. The only comparable date possible in times past or future would have been at one minute past ten, on the tenth of January, in the year 1001. It can simply never happen again. Observing and rejoicing in such wonderful sequences is a prime experience for Aspies the world over.

A minor moment of the same variety occurred several years back, when I noticed that the speedo on my motor scooter was registering 11110. On seeing that the number 11111 was coming up, I deliberately drove the machine into a quiet street, so that I could gently coax the throttle, in order to observe and enjoy that moment when it hit the anticipated registration. A similar interest in the speedo occurred in the television series Monk, when that hilarious Obsessive/Compulsive just had to watch the numbers spin in the same way, just when he was supposed to be paying attention to something else. Actually, Monk shows every sign of having Asperger Syndrome as well as O.C.D.

I must confess that I happen to be one of those fanatical individuals who took up the challenge that was centred round the correct date of the Millenium the other year. While common sense and opinion maintained that the specific peak and turn-over moment was at midnight on 31.12.1999, just as it hit the number 2000, I, like a lot of other picky individuals pointed out that the end was actually one year later. I was astonished to discover how many highly intelligent people had got it wrong. Of course, I am aware that strictly speaking, a Millenium based on a more accurately calculated Christian Calendar of Anno Domini, would have actually ended some few years previously. But that's another story (and every bit as picky!).

Sure, I know just what the reader is thinking. 'Small things amuse small minds!' All too true, and I'm not in the least bit ashamed or embarrassed about it, just as I would affirm that no Aspie alive should be, either. I might add that if nitpicking of this kind represents the worst depths of degradation that any of us Aspies ever sinks to, I can't say that I'll be too unhappy about it.

Just why are such 'silly' little things so desperately significant and world-shaking to the Aspie? Well, I think it's because they show up as serendipity, as a happy and exciting contrast against the common mass of things and facts that are otherwise confusing and illogical in the world about us. So often it appears that there is nothing in creation that seems to have any rationale about it; and the people who inhabit the world, however kind and well-meaning, appear to be unpredictable and awkward. And so when we locate some sort of special pattern in the things about us, no matter how obscure or coincidental, we take notice with a real delight. It seems that it will remind us, or perhaps more accurately suggest to us very comfortingly, that not everything in the world is chaotic or unpatterned.

Just on these odd occasions, it seems that we are able to observe something (and even as in this case nothing more than a series of numbers) popping up out of the blue, and what is more, actually unbidden, that will give us the longed for vision of order in all the mess. The Universe, we are reminded then, is not after all just a state of painful chaos. There can literally be joy and pattern as well. Life has a sense, for that moment at any rate, of being worthwhile and sensible after all.

On My Love of Art

Among the many fascinating books that I grew up with, was a huge family Bible, with beautiful embossing in gold on the leather covers. It was a Protestant edition published within 'Bible Belt' America during the 1880s. It particularly interested me as a child because of its 2000 engraved illustrations; and I would pore over these with a lot of satisfaction. The other big art influence on me was my father's set of three big volumes that contained 100 of the world's greatest paintings. And to this day, the interest has never faded.

Personally I can neither draw nor paint, but I developed an interest and gained a certain expertise in the knowledge and processes of what is called Iconography. This is the study of subject matter and symbolism in art works; and I have applied this knowledge to two major fields, - the great Western paintings of the Renaissance, and the history of Christian art. Now, one might ask just what sort of an idiot or fanatic would concern himself with a pursuit like this? Heaven knows, such a study sounds tailor-made for a picky AS person, and I guess I've proven just that.

Curiously, despite all the study and the possession of an extensive Art library, I am still not anything in the way of an art critic. I know nothing about techniques, quality, schools of art, and the strict history of painting. My encyclopaedic knowledge is confined almost entirely to this obscure topic of subject matter. The works of all the great Masters interest me, perhaps up till the end of the 19th century. And over the years, I've amassed a collection of thousands of slides with which I design and deliver lectures on various topics, both for Art lovers and for uninformed lay people.

For all my love of beauty, I can't claim to be particularly artistic in the way I furnish my home. My arrangements and choices of decoration definitely bespeak a bachelor's establishment. Perhaps I do manage to achieve a dignified sort of look to the public parts of the house, with the greatest number of items and furniture designed and chosen for sheer practical usage. I've often felt that my home resembles something of a combination of museum and library as well, since ultimately my books take pride of place in all rooms.

I really do get lost in wonder and admiration when I look at the home of other individuals, frequently recognizing the hand of a woman therein. I see the skill and the imagination involved, as they have arranged things, and for that matter, applied a real vision in the way that furniture and artefacts have been selected.

On my Favourite Music

I am grateful for the musical background that was with me from my earliest years; though naturally I didn't appreciate it until my adulthood, when I had a couple of years of singing lessons. I didn't retain my singing voice, nor did I develop any facility in reading music. Similarly the two years in my childhood learning piano achieved nothing either, though that failure might best be attributed to my problems with physical coordination.

It was due to my father who was highly skilled on the pipe organ, that I grew to love that instrument, as well as a great deal of sacred and choral music. It was also thanks to my father that I was provided with an absence excuse note for school, in order that I could attend a special matinee screening of Walt Disney's 'Fantasia'. This introduced me to Tchaikovsky, Beethoven and Dukas (the latter via the all important 'Sorcerer's Apprentice' starring Mickey Mouse.)

My trips to the ballet encouraged my appreciation of instrumental music, and led eventually to a delight in opera. In this latter genre, I can admire Verdi and Puccini, while my favourite works just have to include The Mozart cycle, and above all his Magic Flute. I love the great Rossini works, and Beethoven's heart-wrenching Fidelio. I've also got a great liking for the operas of Offenbach, especially his Tales of Hoffmann. I must confess that I've never been grabbed by Wagner. He just comes across to me as pretentious, and I simply can't take him seriously. In Hoffman I am deeply affected by that overwhelming inner battle of Antonia, when she is being spiritually seduced by Dr Miracle. And something of great beauty is the duet 'In the Depths of the Temple' from Bizet's Pearl Fishers.

The voices of some opera singers can readily move me to tears with their beauty, and I could quote a few of those that mean most to me. Among the female singers, I think of Australia's Yvonne Kenny, and in America - Frederika Von Stade, Teresa Stratas and that incomparable soprano Rene Fleming. Her rendition of the much aired 'The Last Rose of Summer' has to be one of the most exquisite performances I've ever heard. 'To the Silver Moon', from Rusalka by Dvorak is another piece that leaves me breathless. Male voices that I love include the Swedish Tenor Jussi Bjoerling, Paul Robeson and Lawrence Tibbett. Some of the Viennese artists like Erich Kunz, Richard Tauber and Fritz Wunderlich are very special to me as well. In orchestral works, I love Beethoven, Mozart and Tchaikovsky, with a few special favourites by Paganini, Vivaldi and Schubert.

It is curious that I lost almost complete awareness of Pop music around the mid 50s; and thus I got familiar with only the barest minimum of the early Rock stars like Elvis, and I missed out completely on the Beatles and Rolling Stones etc. (Can you believe that? It's true!) My total ignorance of Rock and Roll material since then is alarming to say the least. My ears are now literally offended by the diabolical noise and the heavy beat behind the greater part of this output, and I do my level best to avoid being attacked by it. I still love the great stage musicals and operettas. I grew up with a deep appreciation of Rogers and Hammerstein, Cole Porter, Jerome Kern, Irving Berlin, and the remarkable Noel Coward. Kern's Showboat stands for me at the top, along with the greatest works by Johann Strauss and Franz Lehar.

I can enjoy a lot of the very earliest productions in the Jazz idiom; and as well, curiously enough, a certain number of the more melodious and sentimental of Country and Western songs. Though any trained singing voice I had all those years ago has long since dissipated, I can still belt out a few old-fashioned comic songs without too much trouble. British Music Hall numbers are still within my range and fit well into the areas of entertainment that are part of my repertoire.

On a Humour so Perverse

It will not be too surprising I guess to find that with his profound inner life, the Aspie will have his own very unique sense of humour. It may be that it depends on whether he is a visual thinker or a verbal/hearing thinker, as to just what sort of humour will appeal to him.

Amusing incidents and dialogue that he witnesses on TV or film may well pass him by, if they are based on subtleties of relationships, or unspoken and tension-filled interactions. Humour based on sarcasm or lies may be totally misunderstood. Indeed it is not unusual for Aspies to mistake the specific point of a joke entirely, and dream up their own reason for the humour. I did this constantly, with some of the most bizarre conclusions.

In the accounts of the life of the famous 'Elephant Man' Joseph Merrick, it is told how he entranced he was when taken to one of those spectacular London Pantomimes of Victorian times. But with his literal and serious nature, he tended to take it as real, and to believe that to some extent the events in the burlesque story were really happening. For example, he mused afterwards as to whether 'that poor fellow is still inside the gaol'. Anyway his experience of the comedy was interesting. Certain of the subtle humour was simply lost on him, while the slapstick and blatant hilarity of banana skin type jokes just delighted him. Any tricks or jokes played upon the policemen in the story were particularly pleasing, as he no doubt recalled the harsh treatment that the constabulary and other officials had dealt out to him, when he was still regarded as nothing but a freakish outcast from humanity. (1)

Now I'm not suggesting that the sadly mistreated Merrick was any kind of an Autistic. Indeed the records, I think, seem to indicate that he was well and truly NT, despite being subject to depression and other burdens. But I think that his childlike reaction to the fun on stage may well resemble certain of the types of humour that AS folk respond to so often. The obvious the clearly spelt out and the theme of pride or high position leading to the fall will probably represent a powerful stimulus for laughter in the Spectrum community.

We are told, and it is pretty well demonstrated, that all too often the greatest comedians are persons who have had the greatest of burdens, and who have suffered from 'humours' of the deepest cast. And so they can depict and expound on things that the sadder persons of our world will identify with. Aspies are so often used to being figures of fun and derision; and so will feel a profound sympathy with individuals in films and TV who go through problems with their peers. And just so, too, will they get the greatest of enjoyment from seeing characters who resemble their own tormenters and superiors, being dragged down to earth, and getting their come-uppance.

Personally, I have never been particularly fond of satirical humour. Political and social comment in humour tends to leave me cold. I like the pun, the shock unexpected final catch-line, along with the custard tart, the unintended double meaning and the witty retort. For me, please, no comic shots at public figures that are supposed to exploit their foibles and mistakes - at any rate, certainly not as routine. It may be different in the case of very serious issues, when some major reform may be triggered off or brought about by a humorous expose. But satirical commentary just for the sake of cutting down tall poppies in a disrespectful fashion I find distasteful.

Another factor that will frequently come up in Aspie sense of humour is a delight in specific sequences of events within a story. Then there might be the repetition of particular gag lines, and funny sayings associated with a particular character. The Aspie child will frequently get the greatest kick out of watching a favourite episode in a TV series, over and over, despite eventually getting to learn every single line in the dialogue. His memory for some of these sequences can be astonishing, and lots of us have had this sort of experience. It seems that we never seem to get tired of these repetitions, to the raised eyebrows and despair of our parents and confreres. In the process of grasping at our glimpses and visions of the funny, we Aspies at all ages do behave just like small children, with hysterical roars of laughter at virtually nothing, as far as our families can see. Those things that are delighting us so very much can rarely be shared with others.

One of my happy memories of childhood is the profound enjoyment of humour that existed in the family. I must add that with the puritan tendency in that 1940s church- centred world, many themes and forms of talk were regarded as improper. It would no doubt seem ridiculous today, but forbidden words in our home, included devil, hell, chuck (out), backside, rotten. The way that 'bloody' has moved into the common vocabulary would have been unthinkable then. These days, even Ministers of Religion (in Australia at any rate) will say 'We need bums on seats!' One could receive a very severe punishment at my school for using such a term.

For my mother's sake, everyone in the family was terribly careful never to say anything that could be construed as suggestive or crude. That kind and loving lady, it must be said however, did have a good sense of humour. She enjoyed a laugh, though she showed no personal signs of creativity in wit; and as far as I can recall, never told a joke, or attempted to write a verse or limerick. As for the rest of us, though - my father, my brother and I - we were all addicted to jokes, funny lines, and for that matter, to the production of comic verse. And I was delighted to discover that my daughter has continued the trend.

One of my disappointments in childhood was the fact that I was never credited with being able to be witty, or to compose funny stories. I still regret that I am not consistently witty. Everyone else was good at being funny. When I tried to, I all too often put my foot in it and found myself in hot water for saying something inappropriate or even obscene without knowing it. I just longed to be funny. My journalist brother on the other hand, was a wordsmith from an early age, with a versatile wit. His productions were always careful and inoffensive. But in these later years, I can be humorous at times, and I will make good use of standard or much repeated funny lines and anecdotes in order to please my audience and lighten the presentations.

It was fundamentally not until my early adulthood that I discovered something of the facility I can now exercise for writing comic verse. I can still get the pleasure out of writing pieces that I confess might best be described as schoolboy humour. I compose limericks; and have churned out many verses in a genre known as 'Ruthless Rhymes'. For the benefit of the uninitiated, I must explain that the Ruthless Rhyme is usually a gory or bloodcurdling piece in four lines. Many of the examples that came out in the old days were also known as 'Little Willys', since they told of the simply dreadful things that were engaged in by a precocious lad called Willy. The gimmick was that there would be some ironic or laconic comment offered by a family onlooker in the last line, with a fond sense of 'Oh the little pet. Isn't he a clever kid?' Or it might take the form of a completely shocking or irrelevant observation.

One of the classics in the genre ran something like this;

> Little Willy, full of life
> Slew his brother with a knife.
> Mother, smiling at the noise,
> Murmured "Ah boys will be boys!"

The gory exploits of Little Willy get progressively worse and worse; and my own productions were quite appalling at times. But before the reader recoils in horror, I would remind him that it is not uncommon for Aspies to be somewhat immune to many of the conventional taboos that plague our society. We share this characteristic with small children who instinctively delight in spouting outrageous words and jokes. Way back in the 50s/60s, there was an amusing little piece composed by the British team of Flanders and Swann, (originators of the famous Hippopotamus Song - "Mud, Mud, Glorious Mud" etc). It was a cute commentary on this proclivity for playing with naughty words that small children enjoy, to their parents' discomfort. It opened, if I recall correctly, with the lines...

"Ma's out, Pa's out; let's talk rude. Pee! Po! Belly! Bum! Drawers!"

The reader is to be advised that the latter ejaculatory words are to be delivered rapidly and in distinctive rhythm. Not very alarming by today's standards, but in early/mid last century, often quite enough to give Mum a heart attack!

When it comes to us Aspies, maybe as part of our compartmentalised way of experiencing things, we separate words away from their meaning, with a delight in play and repetitious cleverness. We can say things in words that we don't associate with anything wrong or with political incorrectness. We are oblivious to just what we are saying. Comments about death, and other taboo issues, can flow out, without any intention to be disrespectful or crude. Words to us can often be just that... words! And we can play with them in a childlike sort of fashion that is most disturbing to the NT onlookers. This characteristic is of course, not to be confused with the verbal eruptions of those persons with Tourette's Syndrome, which are compulsive and often painfully involuntary.

Confessions of an Unashamed Asperger

As examples of my less offensive versifying, I might offer the following limericks;

> I was bet by my friend in the college, he
> Could devour any work on Philology.
>   Then this gutsy young brute
>   Ate a whole Latin root,
> And his hungry young wife Etymology.

> I inquired of the birds on the knoll
> If my parrot's new plumage looked droll.
>   But with laughter unkind
>   Those birds all declined
> To reply to my new pinion poll.

I must confess that these latter contain some rather bizarre puns, but they give me great pleasure. My comic verse can be at times quite reasonable (albeit with no claim to literary excellence). But the more serious verse that has issued from my pen tends to be either naively sentimental, or else suggestive of antique ballads.

With the Puritan upbringing at home, I was taught from an early age to despise rude words and stories. But by necessity, this Victorian restriction came to be modified at last, when I was sent off for my National Service Army training, at the age of 18. Surrounded as I was then by dozens of un-brainwashed and less inhibited young men, I had to learn painfully to cope with them at that point. Strictly speaking, I have grown to appreciate certain risqué jokes, just so long as they are not particularly crude, or based merely on unpleasant language. Any clever plays on words will appeal to me to this day, and within my repertoire for recital I have a few doubtful pieces that I discretely save with the utmost discretion for the right audience.

I taught myself to tell jokes well; though I regret bitterly that I am still not consistently good at being creatively funny. In speeches and lectures I can be humorous at times, and I will make use of standard or much repeated funny lines and anecdotes in order to please the audience or to lighten my presentations. I tend to have a wide range of likes in humour.

I can laugh at custard tarts, banana skins, slapstick of most kinds, as well as crafted word play or cheap puns. Some of the best laughs I've enjoyed have been on watching some of the great British comedians, such as the Two Ronnies, Benny Hill and Marty Feldman.

I get joy and excitement out of acting and directing comedy and farce on stage. The latter is very demanding, as any practitioner will tell you. The timing is vitally important, and the process of combining or coordinating with your fellow performers is fine cut and demanding. I may not be able to dance or perform fancy choreographed movements and sequences, but this farcical sort of coordinating has been no problem to me. The blending with another on stage cannot of course be impromptu or spontaneous. It is dictated by the script and by the demands of the director and requires a great amount of rehearsal. Therefore it has proven to be straightforward for me to perform. Among favourite comedy recitals that I've engaged in, are performances of sketches, monologues, and comic poetry readings.

One of my worst habits, I guess, is to try to be 'funny' at all sorts of times and in all sorts of places. For example, when you don't have the normal sense of relationship towards one's fellows, you don't really sense the appropriateness or necessity of consistently greeting other people properly. You can even be affected by a certain embarrassment in routinely doing the appropriate thing. Sure, on a first meeting, I will approach the other with respect and shake hands or whatever. But on subsequent occasions, I feel rather impelled to come out automatically with facetious or bizarre expressions. But I can't really be certain whether all this is through boredom or a sense of inadequacy about the situation or contact. Or is it on the other hand a feeling that the dull routine contacts with others, however fleeting, can be made just that little bit more exciting? Maybe this is it. The human communication, the quick contact that is for NTs something of a real and natural experience, will seem for me like an opportunity for a laugh, for something to be different as well as creative. So I will feel impelled to approach others, even those I don't know very well, with the urge to be 'funny'.

Confessions of an Unashamed Asperger

A degree of this, I think, goes back to my childhood and that desperate wish I so often felt to be clever and witty. Perhaps I was fed too much on the clever and anarchistic wit of comedians on stage and screen, or on radio. I think back to those people I admired so much, for the way they developed and used catch phrases that made people laugh. Look for example, at Groucho Marx. (And I must confess that those wonderful Marx Brothers have been among my heroes since childhood.) There is a story told of Groucho - how at some deadly serious Board or Policy meeting, he would be just as likely to rise and announce with deliberation. "Gentlemen, I have the grave duty of informing you that Napoleon has just escaped from Elba'.

It came as the greatest disappointment and hurt for that matter, that whenever I tried to use such a 'funny' line myself, whether in personal conversation, or less frequently, in inappropriately serious situations, it would go down like a lead balloon. Perhaps it is the fact that Aspies are inherently lost or misplaced in company, and thus some of us attempt to hide our discomfort, our alienation, by being bizarrely funny. We will blithely pick the wrong moment or occasion to try the stunt. My Aspie logic told me that if some famous comedian or important individual was able to get laughs by tossing in a comic line, then so should I. It took me a long long time to learn to judge something about the right time and place; and I still frequently get it wrong.

In virtually any company or situation, I still find myself automatically playing with the words that are being spoken in the group. I wouldn't be deliberately looking for a pun that might be played on the terms that have just been spoken; but puns and wordplay would just spin out of my brain. I would enjoy them so much that I would feel obliged to share them with the company and perhaps to reduce the pressure of whatever serious business was being discussed. Likewise, just about any conversation I have will trigger off my memory of jokes and funny anecdotes that I've heard over the years, and all too often, I've burst out with the funny bit that occurs to me, to every one else's dismay.

Mind you, the humour did tend to be shared within the home.

My father enjoyed the jokes that we had all heard over the radio; and my brother and I would recite and rehearse the comedy sketches that we had heard. The dinner table would very often be the venue for the three of us males to come out with our favourite sequences and phrases to the despair of my long-suffering mother. However, there was a distinct difference between the two NT members of the group, and this AS one. While I tended to be indiscriminate in my tossing around of these pearls of humour, they kept it to the most appropriate areas, and audiences, and topics. I was not very good at choosing my material and, as can be readily imagined, my tendency to toss around this would-be humour at the drop of a hat was frequently unappreciated, and as a small child got me into a lot of trouble. Even the home environment, which encouraged this expression at the right times, was not infrequently shocked or appalled at the things I came out with at other times. Keeping in mind the fact that despite the good sense of humour and the basic kindness and love that permeated the household, it was still an old fashioned environment, of near puritan proportions. And my childish outbursts or impulsive high spirits didn't always match the propriety or limits that prevailed.

One outlet that was used by all three of us Hedgcock males was the ubiquitous church concert. From time to time through our childhood and youth, my brother and I did do the occasional comedy sketch or number, usually based on some standard piece that we had heard on the radio, as performed by some famous British comedian. On more than one occasion, even my father would appear on stage to take a role, and he was not averse to playing the fall-guy comic, who said and did the clown thing.

It can be stated that as I've got older I have learned more and more to take appropriate care. I no longer grab a total stranger and startle the life out of them by delivering childish and embarrassing lines that would have been quite stupid or inappropriate even if spoken in front of friends or relatives. I can still find myself slipping in minor ways; but nowhere near in the appalling fashion that characterised certain desperate efforts of my youth. Some of these memories can still make me cringe with humiliating embarrassment even some 60 or more years later.

With my inherent sensitivity I developed techniques to protect against taking myself too seriously. I got used to pointing out my own weaknesses and failings. I must admit that I'd rather get in first, than have others comment on these things as they would in a more hurtful fashion. As an actor I don't mind portraying embarrassing emotions etc. I make sure that I'm not too vulnerable for the most part. Since the discovery of my AS, I've taken to making relevant jokes on the subject of Asperger's.

In daily life, I can find it hard to refrain from cracking jokes or making facetious comments as I go into shops. When I buy cat food, I'm liable to tell the checkout girl confidentially, that my Pussy sent me out with a special order today; and that "one simply can't argue with a determined Burmese cat". And to the girl in the bank who is counting the notes I've passed over, I might say something to the effect of 'Dammit! Do you have to count it? I was hoping to get away with it today.'

I have to admit that it is with the very greatest restraint that I refrain from making wise-cracks at the Airport check-in counter. I make a point of carefully reading and rereading the notices over the desk, that remind one against making jokes about illicit packages in the luggage. It is literally hard for me! It's times like that when you become all too aware about the inherent risks in this powerful compulsion to indulge in gags and puns.

References.

(1) Howell M and Ford P. The True History
                              of the Elephant Man. P 138.

Chapter 6 FRIENDS AND THEIR COMPARTMENTS

On Friendships

My most comfortable and genuine form of relating is with friends. Friendships are predictable and logical; and they rarely bring about the sorts of problems or conflicts in my life that are all too common with intimates. I would like to say that in the long run, I am my own best friend; though some of my intimates have found this idea a little disconcerting or even improper.

It must be said that my easy-going friendliness has been regarded with suspicion by a couple of my wives. (1) I never have any idea about the genuineness of another; and I can easily be manipulated by the wrong person. But then, I suspect that the 'wrong' person wouldn't really be attracted to me anyway. In any case, I've seen an awful lot of NT folk who with all the right brain wiring in the world still get their friends, advisors and partners wrong. Now if I find that I have managed to get them wrong and duly suffer, myself, I don't complain or jump up and down over it. I allow myself to learn in my own way without having to submit to tiresome lectures from well-meaning friends and relatives about my mistakes.

Even if a person didn't particularly care about me or my life, any expressions of kindness from them, would mean more to me than anything. Peoples' comments have just glossed over my head when they have laughed at me or talked behind my back about the friends in my life.

I've noticed that with all the good will in the world, plus their much vaunted intuition (or insight and 'mindreading' talent) my intimates have so often got it wrong about my friends. I don't think that I've been let down more frequently than most other folk; but at the same time because I trust easily and very rarely take offence it is seldom that anyone has badly upset me and I must say virtually never when they have not intended to. If on the odd occasion I suspect that someone is 'having a go at me', I just put my reactions on hold for a few moments to see if they emphasize or repeat what they just said or did. If they show no signs of either, then I take it for granted that the suggestion of offence was purely accidental.

I can't comprehend the way that NT persons believe that they have some extra insight into other people (which as a species they seem to agree about) and of a type of experience not shared by us Aspies. Is it that much vaunted faculty of mind-reading that makes the difference for NTs? Is it some special trigger that stimulates the chemistry in their brains or hearts that gives them a special feeling of perception and knowledge? Is it some sort of psychic ability that is possessed by 'normal people'? I'm damned if I know.

Obviously when I observe or talk with or interact with others, I am fully aware – or I allow myself to believe that each one is individually different from each of the others. I am happy to treat them as individuals like myself. I try not to be selfish. I like or even 'love' some of them. I treasure my interaction or friendship with a special few; but I can never kid myself that I 'know' any single one of them. I will gladly share with or give to certain of them. I will be delighted to see some of them just about any time, so long as I will not have to be with them for too long a period. I will respect their opinions, their feelings and all rights that they may be entitled to. But my personal experience and knowledge of any of them is for me externally based. I know nothing of their inner beings, but I am prepared to 'believe' things about them, as they act them out or verbally describe them.

I can weep with or for them. I can laugh with them, or feel concern or indignation for them. But this sympathetic alignment with them is based literally on what I observe or hear, but as if from a distance and not directly from the person themselves. In touching another person, (which I am quite happy to do) it can be as if my body is detached or separated from my mind, and is being observed from some distance. Other people are just like images on a movie screen; while my own body seems a bit like a robot that I am controlling from a distance. Of course, I am constantly getting feedback of pleasure or pain from this same body, despite its seeming distance.

The inherent sympathy I have mentioned above is something

I can experience just as totally with or for characters in a film or in a book or play. Of course there are a couple of distinct differences about the character I associate with in real life. For one thing, I will be taking their communications, including their self-exposure, literally and as fact. Then as well, the unique thing about each of them is that they will be reacting to me with demands or expectations, or gratitude or whatever.

The other major difference is in my awareness that the film and other fictional people by contrast are fulfilling a script that is set and fixed, whereas in real life the people appear to be acting, thinking and talking with no direction, and in something of a state of chaos. One just cannot predict anything much about them. Oh, I've never actually been fooled, as it were, by film and fiction, you must understand. I understood in my heart from earliest childhood that the film characters are not of the 'real' world, and that one cannot interact with them, despite the consequent emotions that I might be going through because of them.

Mind you, I can recount one early period in which I got my realities a little mixed. When a small child, I made great use of the old Gramophone in the lounge, on which I played some of the old 78 record disks that were all we had in those unsophisticated days.   I remained quite convinced for years that, tucked away in some sort of studio in a distant land, the artist recorded on the disk was sitting there waiting for me to play the record.   As soon as I did drop the needle on It, the singer or performers would get up and perform just for me.   It really amazed me that these same clever devils were actually able to take up their performance at the exact right spot, when I applied the needle halfway through the track!

Anyway, to return to our discussion, let me assure you again that I have absolutely no doubt that every one of you who happens to be reading these words of mine is real - that you are human and personal (shall we say?).   My problem is simply that this concept of your realness is something of an academic fact and a pragmatic common sense reality. But it is not really for me anything like an inner experience. Aspie brains just don't seem to be geared or wired to register human contacts or interactions in the same way that the brains of NTs do. Some experiments have suggested that we see other humans as objects, and I believe I know what this is like. However I must make it plain that in agreeing conditionally with that finding, I am not implying that most Aspies generally manifest a cruel impersonality or a lack of compassion.

For those of us who were raised in an encouraging and loving atmosphere, it is not too hard to partly over-ride the natural tendency to be completely oblivious of others. But undoubtedly it can demand of us a considerable effort of will and direction of consciousness to consistently break out of the natural self-centredness, and set about genuinely contacting those others. It suggests to me, and I feel a conviction about this, that when we do, it represents something of a considerable compliment to the other person, and indeed, that they are special to us.

It is said that every person displays or offers a different or unique personal face or persona to each single party with whom he associates. For the Aspie, it is not just a way of adjusting to the difficult or impossible world of people about him. It is actually very much a whole way of life. Probably no-one knows the Aspie in any real truth, as the high functioning AS person learns to present a very carefully crafted and distinctive self for each milieu that he moves in. Frequently I read how the wife and friends have been startled to observe just how different their Aspie can be when they first catch sight of him in the work place; while there may well the similar surprise his workmates may feel when seeing him with his family, or out in the public eye.

Our literalness is proverbial. Whatever another says is just what we are most inclined to believe and to accept as gospel. The hard-luck story, the pitch toward a 'con' etc, can be hard for us to resist, let alone for us to even believe that the person involved could possibly be lying or manipulating. We are frequently notorious for our tendency to lack guile. We may, with the best of intentions, all too easily put our foot in it. We speak without anticipating the way that the NTs will take things. How often have I made a comment in all sincerity and straightforwardness, and found that the NT listener had made all sorts of incorrect assumptions about particular meanings behind my words. I guess though, that you can't blame them. After all, they are only poor benighted NTs; and they are so limited by that sad illusion of 'mind reading'!

Another and more unique problem that I've faced on a number of occasions is that I've picked up friends who were subject to mental problems. There was one guy for a short period that I regarded as close, who turned out to be something of a Paranoid Schizophrenic; and another who eventually I recognized as giving every appearance of the Bi-Polar Disorder. Now I automatically believed that everything these folk said to me was completely true. One borrowed money, books and other things from me; - and I'm sure with the firm intention of returning them in due course. However, it turned out that he clearly forgot, and I was never recompensed.

Another confided for years to me about the terrible things her relatives and her ex-husband were doing to her, and I honestly believed every word. I only discovered the hard way after a time that there was not a single word of truth in what she had told me. She was inclined, I subsequently learned, to go into dreams and visions that she believed in implicitly. Subsequently she would follow this up by writing letters to all sorts of people and authorities, as well as the persons she was blaming, duly causing no end of trouble.

I am something of a sucker for the stories that are told to me. Despite a number of cases like this, I still find it hard to listen in a critical or sceptical way to things that others relate. I recall folks I've known and worked with over the years who are by contrast natural sceptics, and who listen unbelievingly to just about anything they are told, with responses of 'Rubbish' or 'Bullshit'. Such responses have always seemed to me to be impolite or disrespectful. Everyone's opinion or story tends to be sacred to me, and if a person declares something in a serious fashion, then I can't find it in my mind to dispute or ridicule it. That is of course unless it is in the form of an opinion or statement of belief on an issue about which I have some expertise or better information.

So a person who has some sort of disadvantage or complaint may well find a willing and sympathetic ear in me. I must admit that I do occasionally wish that I was a bit more careful and disbelieving than I am. The 'lame ducks' that have come into my life have certainly made things difficult or embarrassing for me on occasions. On the other hand, my inability to read and identify the good ones in my life has proven tricky as well. I had an exchange with an associate some years back that left me with issues which I'm still coming to terms with. The particular chap belonged to an organization of considerable importance to me at the time, and he was one that I saw as a close and indeed as a dear friend. This day when we were chatting, I told him I regarded him as one my closest associates. He looked at me as if I were crazy, and told me that I must understand that there was actually no such relationship between us.

He went on to deliver a mini-lecture on the real and subtle closeness that is supposed to develop in such a condition. He spoke with something of an ecstatic rapture about relationships he'd had at times, in which their two minds thought and spoke as one; and he went on to make it plain that this friendship of ours, though a perfectly good one, was for him nothing like what I had defined it as. I was rather stunned, I must admit, since I did regard him as a close mate. But it did emphasize to me the blindness about relationships that can afflict Aspies like myself. We simply don't see into people with any clarity.

It is amazing to me to observe such discrepancies. But I must make it plain in regard to my friend, that I wasn't actually at all hurt about the revelation he delivered to me; and his perception of it all in no way affected the way I continued to experience the friendship for myself.

On Short Term Person Tolerance

Since I rarely spend any extended time with any of my friends, my tolerance problem presents few difficulties there. I do like to be with my friends for just a few hours at a time. But it is any ongoing or unpredictable situation that is my biggest hurdle. Such times with the associated expectation for dealing with the unexpected and the spontaneous can trouble me.

I do best when I've made prior arrangements about things. When I'm with another, I want to know roughly just what I'm in for and especially what sort of schedule is ahead. It's something of a sad fact that merely being with the very closest of friends can be uncomfortable at times. There have been many occasions when no matter how much I've been looking forward to a time with him or her, it has gone completely flat for me. It usually happens that in those moments I've been unable to steer or manipulate the conversation into some exciting exploration or issue which I had literally planned for in order to make the occasion good.

I may feel a distinct embarrassment as I realize how all the hard work that I've engaged in just to be with the person has been a waste; and the further work I've done to stay through the ensuing conversation has proved futile. Such experiences have emphasized to me the impoverishment that can exist within even my very best relationships. There have been many occasions when I've realized that the most familiar and valued relative or partner has become as tiresome as a stranger just at that moment..

The native ability in the regular human consciousness to love one's fellows purely for themselves is something that is not appreciated by me. Possibly the human race has actually only survived satisfactorily because of this very factor; and it may be that a community or race composed purely of Aspies (that some of us still dream of in our unguarded and idealistic fantasy moments) would simply not survive for long. Reluctantly I guess, it is a combination of NT type faculties and virtues that have kept the world spinning on its axis after all. There are clearly benefits and blessings that are endowed upon the NT character that an Aspie can only marvel at, albeit from something of a long (and possibly safe?) distance away.

I must make it plain that the likelihood of my sharing any extended time with a friend or with friends rarely comes about. Now really, I have no major objection to being with a close associate for a holiday or trip, say, just so long as I have adequate advance notice; and particularly if I'm aware of the time that will be involved, AND just when I will be able to get back to 'normal'. I don't like the short notice, and I don't take kindly to the spontaneous arrangement. I want to know roughly at least when it will close. Then as a rule, I won't mind, and will be able to prepare for it.

On Partners and Friends

I find the obligations with a partner are uncomfortably demanding and awkward. And regardless of the way it sounds just so ideal and beautiful, I've never really comprehended the concept of one's wife or husband as being a 'best friend'. The two roles appear to me like incompatible ones. A best friend is a person you rarely live with, and with whom you don't have the loaded emotional qualifications implied by the married state. Just about all interactions with a partner seem to me to be filled with duties, intimate history and obligations. It seems too heavy a relationship to be able to relax with, in the way that you can with a friend; and I guess that somehow the sheer seriousness of it is a major factor that I find most disturbing. By contrast, there is some kind of a freedom in the way you interact with a friend. The friend will take your word for it if you have to make excuses. The friend won't be reliant on you day by day, moment by moment. There will be allowances offered for your short-comings, in ways that are not so likely to be made by a partner.

I would be very disturbed or dismayed by the process of having to switch back and forth between my experience of the partner as a wife, and my partner as a best friend as well. (2) It simply wouldn't make any sense to me. They would be like two separate persons there, with conflicting experiences, and constant adjustments. It would not be easy or natural in my view for the role of friend to be consistent in a partner, without some serious compromising of needs.

This is not to deny that friendship might be exercised or be readily manifested like a specific function or activity from time to time. But an insistence by the NT partner that the other acknowledge them consistently as Best Friend, could be a pressure that I as an AS partner would find impossible. Such demand on any partner, that he hold some sort of particular attitude or belief, may pressurise him into making literally false statements or holding positions against his will. It would seem to me to be doubly stupid to force an Aspie into doing this.

I am not suggesting that good friendly marriages can't occur between Aspies and NTs; but I suspect that when they do, they originally started with friendship, eventually to develop into something else. I can't conceive just how a carer, an organizer, a guide, can truly become like a best friend. I treasure the wonderful opportunity to be open and honest with a friend, in a way that would be virtually impossible for me with a wife. The situation and balance with the latter relationship is too loaded and delicate, and too difficult to maintain.

On Therapists as Friends

Perhaps among my most loved and interesting friends have been certain of my Therapists and Psychologists.

It is some 40 years perhaps since I first consulted with one on relationships issues. I recall how certain of them (and I've been through quite a number of them) appeared to be most disappointed that I didn't break down in front of them, and cry. Perhaps I am only now comprehending why this is. I think that perhaps because my relationship with a therapist is so verbally centred, that when I'm with one, I am concentrating so profoundly on the words that each is speaking that I fail to contact my feelings. It is not a matter of not wanting to or of squashing them; but rather it is as though the situation allows them no room to be expressed. Any question or a theme of conversation, however loaded or sensitive, just grabs my concentrated attention, and demands that I answer logically and clearly.

It must be kept in mind that when going into contact or interaction with another person who is not an 'intimate', the Aspie is moving into a compartment that is divorced from his personal life. He takes on a detached stance and view in which feelings have little relevance. He can pontificate 'from a great height', you might say, almost becoming somewhat computer-like, while he considers the matters under discussion as if they are or have been happening to some third party. Regardless of how personal they may be in actuality, questions that are asked of him in the Psych's office appear to him to be almost hypothetical, and all his efforts are concentrated on analysing and solving problems.

Actually, it is probably what he's been training himself to do all his life; and it demands all the skills that he has developed. So in front of this other party, who represents some sort of authority, he goes into his best professional and intellectual state. He is no longer any sort of personal being, as it were. Feelings and personal wishes or preferences are no longer to the forefront. Here we see one of those situations when the Aspie is at his most Aspergic.

The detachment I indicate may possibly manifest in the Aspie forgetting or ignoring himself completely so that he talks about situations and principles with little regard or reference to any other party in the problem area. This can be excruciatingly painful for a partner in such instance, as the focus of the Aspie's intense concentration ceases to include their interests. And it may in some cases mean that he will take on a dispassionate view, and describe the most intimate and self-revelatory details about himself just as if he were talking about a character in a movie or a book. Certainly it can be totally disconcerting to the unprepared Therapist.

I have realized that there are three types of human contact that mean most to me, and in which I feel most alive and at home. The greatest of all is probably when I'm lecturing, and enjoying an audience. There is the pleasure of talking with a friend, with no demands, no emotional issues, and no obligations. The other and equal one would have to be when I am in tandem with a Therapist or Psychologist. It is here I guess that my self-indulgence is at its peak. I am happy then that just for once the discussion is exclusively concentrating on me, on my thoughts, feelings and experiences.

Heaven knows I've rarely felt awkward or lost when with a Therapist. I've disturbed plenty of them as they've battled to work out just how to deal with me. I've come to the conclusion that I hadn't played the client/patient game properly. I've tended to talk to them from the first session as if I were an old friend and indeed as well, like a professional colleague. According to the conventions and all the rules of the 'game', I understand that it is supposed and expected to take weeks or maybe months for that desirable Break-through or Crisis, when the barriers collapse and the real issues as it were, come out in a burst within the therapy situation.

So with me, our unsuspecting Therapist may get them in the first five minutes of the very first consultation. This has made some of them very suspicious that I am just too glib, and must be hiding something. And then, I recall Psych X literally ordering me to leave his office on one occasion, presumably because he felt that my contributions in the interaction were not authentic or sincere. I didn't take the hint and leave on the spot, being just a dull minded Aspie; and the session actually went on eventually. Another time, the same gentleman told me I was boring, when I was telling him of something that I considered to be a profound and important emotional event in one of my marriages. I suspect that I was relating the tale in the detached or cerebral fashion of an Aspie, and it must have seemed fake or contrived to him.

Of course, there is just the possibility that he may have been testing me out, with the hope that I would get uncharacteristically emotional. I let him down again. Then I recall Psychiatrist N who was completely bamboozled by me. On my very first consultation with him, that same N did a few little 'interpret the scribble' drawing exercises with me. This style of impromptu Rorschach type process is a lot of fun for me, and I tend to let my imagination go into riot mode. I promptly and innocently gave an interpretation of one early scribble we did together as representing a phallic symbol from the Pagan sacred sexuality of ancient Greece or Rome. It apparently shocked him, as he confessed to me some weeks later when he knew me better, that he jumped to the conclusion on that occasion that I must be some sort of a sexual pervert. I found this hilariously funny.

On one occasion the poor fellow felt a bit lost with me, and actually brought in another Psychiatrist associate from her own separate practice to help him get to the bottom of me. She just happened to be a practitioner I had seen before, and was one of the very few with whom I just didn't get on.

Well, together they tried all sorts of tests and questions, and eventually came to the conclusion that I simply did not fit any classification they had ever known. Indeed, I really upset the two of them profoundly. At one point in the session the visiting lady made some sort of comment about me that I can't recall now, and asked me just what my spontaneous reaction happened to be. Well, trust me to be off with the fairies, and to come out with something totally irrelevant! I confessed truthfully to my actual feelings which were quite benevolent, and said that I had an urge to hug her. Their shock at the total inappropriateness of it, as it must have been at that particular moment, was palpable and for me not a little amusing. They hurriedly conferred in something of a state of desperation; and decided to send me to some fellow who was a 'body worker'. Apparently my body/mind relating systems just didn't match the conventional. As it happened, I didn't get around to seeing the guy. I suspect that I wouldn't have made any progress if I had.

Looking back it does seem rather amusing just how often my Counsellors and Therapists were totally baffled by me. If only we'd known in those days about AS! Then there was the time that I went to a church sponsored counselling group, which offered things like Psycho-drama, and Encounter groups. It was during a period when Counsellors in such places were engaging in very trendy pop processes, that were often, to say the least, rather dodgy.

Once, the Counsellor, a retired Minister of Religion, in desperation, called in an associate. (Funny just how often they had trouble with me.) The consultant turned out to be a very sexy lady in a tight short skirt. For one of his tests or experiments with me, he got me to stand and hug this particular lady, and hold the position. He proceeded to ask her if she felt she could have sex with me. Now I was certainly take aback at this, but I could follow what he was doing. I realized that this was no seduction ritual he was playing round with. This interview took place in the mid 1980s, and these were very New Age types of people there. So I came to the conclusion that it was some sort of test he was applying, in order to determine just what sort of vibes that the lady might pick up from me (not to mention the opportunity of seeing just what sort of reaction I might display.)

I must say I haven't decided to this day if it was some sort of compliment to my inherent attractiveness, or just a kindly but insincere word of encouragement to me; but she duly reported that she would be able to have sex with me. And that was that! I learnt later that the particular establishment was riddled with individuals and practitioners who were involved in the notorious group known as the 'Orange People' that came such a serious cropper a few years later.

Yes, my experiences with Psychologists, Counsellors etc have indeed been interesting, though rather bizarre at times. I must confess that for the most part, I have enjoyed it immensely. I recall my good friend Edgar Schneider telling how Therapists and Specialists found him particularly frustrating and strictly beyond help.(3) When you think of it, it must be difficult at times for these poor professional folk to have to deal with us strangely brain-wired aliens. At least it must especially have been so in that innocent AS-free world some 20 or 30 years ago.

Apparently, when present in a group situation, Ed simply didn't match the requirements. He didn't play the game. He didn't conform to the conventions and the expectations of what a patient ought to be or do. What he was able to do was to contribute 'intellectual observations' as if from the outside. I recall a similar sort of comment made about myself when I joined in my one and only group 'encounter' weekend. I was introduced to the assembly of varying neurotics as one who might fulfil the role of a catalyst in the discussion. It must indeed be a disconcerting thing for these specialists to handle us when we are not behaving in the standard, predictable and thereby manageable fashion.

Confessions of an Unashamed Asperger

In all my pleasant dealings with my therapists, it was not with any possessive sense that I clung to them. I certainly felt no jealousy about the fact that they shared with others in the same way that they did with me. Such a thought had no concern for me whatsoever. It was more as though the other contacts or clients simply didn't exist. I was self-centred enough to gloss over those others.

I have been baffled by that horrible sense that some people go through, as it hits them that these Psychs are only seeing them because they are being paid money. This point has never struck me as being any sort of anomaly. The immediate effect of the consultation is the same regardless. I have to confess that I've been presumptuous enough to fantasize that the Therapist found me especially interesting as a case study. For all I knew, I might even be helping to advance the cause of Science by my attendance.

I did ask one Psych. about just how she found me as a 'patient'. Did I represent any unusual case, or whatever? She told me frankly that it took her a number of sessions to get used to me. The stages of psychological therapy that one is supposed to go through simply didn't work, or show up. She described how neither the proverbial 'Projection' or the requisite 'Transference' appeared to be operational in our sessions. Somehow I didn't go into anything with her that resembled 'Therapy' or any sort of healing work.

Come to think of it, I have to confess that with all my reading on Psychology and personal counselling, I've never been able to comprehend the rationale behind the accounts of personal healing that are supposed to happen. Are we AS folk just so terribly different? Thinking back, of course, I think there may well have been a number of instances when I held a blindly cheerful illusion that my therapist felt as friendly to me as I did to them. In any case I don't think I could have cared less about the truth of it. My own perception and enjoyment or interest, was the important thing, not the facts about what went on in their mind. We Aspies can be so infuriatingly self-centred!

On Aspies and Cats

How does one explain the relationship between humans and Cats? If it can be seen as special among the NTs of this world, it is even more so among the Aspies. I have read of surveys indicating that upwards of 78% of Aspies (and presumably Auties) are cat lovers. It must be added that we resemble cats, and cats resemble us! (4)

I am happy about the fact that I cannot engage in a literal argument with a cat. I can't get confused or panic-stricken with a cat. The cat speaks a language that approaches something that I can understand. The cat's lack of human-like intellectualising makes them easier to deal with. And with no arguments being possible, there are no mis-understandings; and what is more, one doesn't have to switch off one's feeling self when with them, either voluntarily or involuntarily. Consequently there is a real sense of genuine and continuous relating that otherwise is impossible to me. Listening to me talking to my cats, one might get the impression that I am intellectualising. But actually I'm going through old and familiar routines of self-centred chatter that resembles traditional unthinking baby talk.

Now our cats can't confuse us, and consequently we feel comfortable with them. I have heard Tony Attwood describe the situation when little Johnny comes home from school in a state of distress He first of all sits down with his dog. He proceeds to tell Doggie about how he's being bullied at school. Dog pants and wags his tail lovingly. Boy feels better. Then he goes on to tell Dog that he failed his exams that day. Dog proceeds again to pant and wag his tail. He further tells Dog that he was suspended for bad behaviour as well. Once more Doggie pants and smiles comfortingly with a tail wag. What a wonderful response, and just how like our experience with the beloved cat. Our pets never sit in judgement upon us.

I don't know that it can be truly said that they love us 'unconditionally', in the precise meaning of the word. For starters, they are instinctive opportunists, but they can take on a special relationship with us that represents a beautiful form of free acceptance. It's a very worthwhile experience to have such love; and I must say that you know that you are achieving something very special when you have the devotion of a domestic cat.

Then there is the smell of a cat. The Pheromone scent on a cat's paws just happens to be one of the most beautiful musky smells that I know. For most of my life too, I've shared my bed at night with the current resident Moggie. There is a distinct comfort in being able to reach out to touch a soft lump of fur, and getting in response the delicacy of a contented purr. And my original definition of a domestic cat? - "A furry hot water-bottle with an in-built vibrator'.

Cat lovers are entranced by the sheer aesthetic looks of a cat. The immaculate grooming, the graceful movements, and then that wonderful meditative relaxation that contributes just so much peace and homeliness to one's abode. So different from the looks of a human being. It is noticeable that a cat, unless mangled by accident or fight, usually looks quite beautiful even up until its old age. Whereas I must admit that I am all too easily put off by the aesthetic distortions of a sick or disabled human body.

As well, I have no hesitation in putting a cat down, when its life has become insupportable due to illness or injury. And that is just as I would earnestly wish that the same might be done for me when I reach the end of a useful and contented life-span. I wholeheartedly support Euthanasia for human beings, and deplore the fact that what we will readily do for our suffering pets is not paralleled by what we might do for our human brothers and sisters.

I can be described as being somewhat deficient in the physical energies of the body and the natural world. I don't like taking risks, and I don't fancy the business of pitting mind and body against the elements. So I believe that cats can become something of a vicarious representation for these more primitive areas of life and nature. Cats help keep me in touch with the primal and earthly part of life. A lovely proverb from the pen of Fernand Mery, tells how 'God created the cat so that man could caress the lion'.

It is a most comforting thing in my daily life to come home and to see one or more little 'four legs' trotting out to greet me with tail up, and perhaps with a gratuitous Meow. At times in my unhappiest or most stressful moments, nothing has been quite so comforting and recuperating for my soul as has the contact with my cat. I lie on my bed... and how well I recall lying there in tears on a few occasions over some shattering experience. Then I hear a Plop Plop on the floor, followed up by a Whomp as four feet land on the end of the bed. Then this little furry thing walks up on my chest and burrows its head into my beard.

I've been only too happy and prepared to spend money on health and other care for my cats, having lived with cats for the greater part of my life. How well I remember old Crusty from my earliest days in a country town. Then there was the beautiful but temperamental long-haired Blackie; and ah, the greatest cat of all, the magnificent Tigger (also known as Humphrey). He lived on till something like 23 years, and he coped with shifting house innumerable times due to the demands of my father's job as he made promotional moves about Australia. He was just a common Tabby, but blessed with a wonderfully dignified and friendly nature. We considered that his capacity for sleeping in a shopping basket in the family car, and being sneaked in and out of hotel rooms at the places we stayed, was admirable.

Over the last thirty five years, I've become entranced by the Oriental breeds, and I well recall with affection my beloved Mysti, a Lilac (or Frost) Point Siamese that I rescued from a cat haven. She was my personally favourite cat of all time; and I shed many tears when I eventually had to have her sent to the 'Rainbow Bridge'. She had been my closest companion for some 9 years, and had a most beautiful nature.

Petrouchka and Gopa followed soon after (Blue and Seal Points respectively) and then Mandy, a perfect specimen of the Chocolate Point Siamese and a very close intimate. Tinkerbell (or Beast as she was commonly called) was another contemporary, and a very sweet natured little Tortie-Point she was too. She was replaced by Missy, a

Siamese/Silver Tabby cross, who just had to be the most annoyingly gentle and affectionate cat I've ever known. It was usually Missy who walked across the keyboard in order to sit on the Monitor while I was reading or attempting to type Email.

My current collection of little 'Four Legs' comprises Felecia and Tamino. The former, known affectionately as Kittles, is my very first Burmese and of a pure Lilac colour. She is fanatically loyal and devoted, but proud and very bossy. You just don't dare to take any liberties with her furry little person, since she is quite prepared to say some very rude things in Burmese, and to follow up with tooth and claw if you take no notice. Different as they were in so many ways, the two of them, Felecia and the late Missy were devoted to each other, despite the occasional spat. And that did happen when Kittles decided that she had to make it plain just who was the senior cat of the household. Tamino, the latest feline arrival in the household as a replacement for Missy, is a magnificent brown Tonkinese with a lovely nature, who converses periodically with the raucous and unmistakable voice of the Siamese part of his ancestry. His face, paws and tail are classic Seal Point. I describe him with the words from an old World War One song that should have run… 'There's a long long tail a-winding…'

When alone with my cats, I talk to them in an extraordinarily parental fashion that I could never really achieve with my human children. On leaving the house, I'm usually telling No 2 cat to do just whatever No 1 tells her to do. 'Kittles is in charge, and there are to be no wild orgies while I'm out.' Neither may they invite any strange neighbourhood pussies in. (So far it appears that my admonitions have worked, because I've never found signs in the house, of any wild parties, on my return.)

When I let them in, I ask just what they've been doing; and being typically vocal Oriental felines, they answer just about everything I ask with a thoroughly appropriate and communicative 'Reow' or more informatively 'Nuh-Row' or some such. I am most likely to comment in return with something to the effect of 'Ah, I see. That's very interesting'.

Talking of cat conversations, I might ask just who but an Aspie would listen to his cat making her standard Meows, and follow up by trotting over to the electronic keyboard, to press a few notes in order that he can determine just what key the cat is speaking on?   Doubtless my readers will find it fascinating, (not to mention profitable) to learn that the late lamented Missy would talk to me in F sharp.   I have to confess too that in my latter married days, if my wife was standing at the basin with head thrown back, doing a noisy bit of gargling for a sore throat, I did precisely the same piece of research on the organ. I seem to recall that she happened to gargle on Middle C.

No, I'm not really going crazy, and I guess there are plenty of people who, living with their cats, dogs or even chickens too, get into conversations with them.   For me as an Aspie, I find that this seeming inane interchange is very comforting and real.   Keep in mind this fact. I can't insult a cat by anything I might say to her.   She just can't or won't argue back - well at any rate, not with any sort of convincing or purrsuasive arguments.   She doesn't have to comprehend a single word that I might say; but that comforting deep throated rumble, or the friendly expression on her tail, is enough to give support and reassurance just when I need it.

For us Aspies, or for many of us at any rate, our animals are the only ones who don't make us work too flaming hard for comfort when we set out to communicate with them.   As well, we even manage perhaps for the only times in our lives, to get in the very last word of a conversation.   Er well, some of the time, anyway!

I suppose that my conversation with the cats get to something of their most extreme states when one of the animals says something rude in cat lingo to the other, and swipes out with extended claw.   It's then that I'm most likely to read the Riot Act, with a lecture on how "I don't want any scrapping on the bed please", or 'That's quite enough from you guys, thankyou."   Then with a rapid pass of my foot beneath the bed-clothes, I shove them both off, until they can return ready to rest in peace again.

Actually I must comment on the wonderfully forgiving nature of a cat. It doesn't hold a grudge against you for your day by day discipline. You apologize to it if you were in the wrong, or for some accidental hurt, and it will be back with you in a trice. And furthermore, it won't be reminding you of some offensive thing you said to it some three or four weeks previously. Perfect company for the Aspie!

(Note. The reader is referred here to the Appendix no.4 at the back of this book, which offers up to date research, indicating that 'All Cats are Autistic'.)

References.

(1)Stanford, A. Aspergers Syndrome & Long Term
Relationships.   Page 98
(2)See Essay   On Roles in Relationships
(3)Schneider, Edgar   Discovering My Autism.   Page 98.
(4)Hoopman, K. All Cats have Aspergers Syndrome.

Chapter 7 A CHEMISTRY NOT TAUGHT AT SCHOOL

On Attracting a Partner

One of my wives demonstrated something of an amused indulgence when several years after the event, she reminded me about the details of our first meeting. We had introduced ourselves over the phone, and met for a walk and a chat in a nearby park.   Apparently I filled in just about all of the meeting time by talking about myself.   I took some hour or more, telling her about my personality, my history, my likes and dislikes and my hobbies.   In my mind, it was the most sensible and even ethical thing to do.   It can be said that I was not choosing the partner.   Rather I was endeavouring to make it practicable for her to choose me. Maxine Aston reports similar accounts. (1)

Almost it could be said that with enough of the right interests along with a reasonable personality and appearance, just about any woman would suit me.   Therefore in my mind, the real business of wooing must revolve around me selling myself to her.   It just appeared like a thoroughly pragmatic business.   So logically, the offering of a full and frank description of me was the expedient thing to do.

The AS literature teams with tales of just such naïve and misguided sorties into the mystical world of dating. I recall the story of the lonely Autistic who spent most of one hopeful dating occasion just discoursing to the poor unsuspecting girl about the medication he was on! (2) Yeah, I know... sounds most romantic! But as my readers will be well aware by now, we Aspies in our mad and youthful days can be blissfully unaware of how painfully inappropriate our conversation can be.

I was very surprised when one of my associates described how in her younger days, on going to outings and social dos, and thus be on display to other young persons with the potential for dating and mating, made a point of deliberately wearing tight jeans and other moderately sexy gear. It had just never occurred to me (and this by my 50s, no less!) that when they went out, driven by their raging hormones, people actually dressed up specifically to attract the opposite sex. But let's face it, it must be understood that I never realized any of the truth about those raging hormones, during the time I should have known all about them.

I can't recall any stage in my adolescence during which I was in any state of confusion or disturbance that could have been associated with those states. I seemed to live through that time in a steady and consistent fashion uniquely my own, that didn't get bitter and twisted. The sexual development that I went through was merely one of the many mental compartments that I shifted in and out of. I never found myself confusing. But I did go through the tortures of the damned trying to figure out the rest of the population, who, of course, I have long since determined to be NTs.

But coming back to the matter of clothes. Oh yes, with my theatrical sense, I could conceive that people may well dress up in films or plays; but I never associated this sort of practice with living people in real life. The only times I ever dressed up, as it were, was if it were a 'posh' event, or if I happened to be personally on show. I never, to my knowledge, ever dressed up to impress individuals personally.

In the same way, of course, I never pictured anyone I was with as having dressed up to please me on that date. How strange that it would always be the most natural thing in the world for a character in a play that I'm portraying to dress up appropriately in this way. What I would do or portray then, might be very different from the way I would behave in everyday life. When I am studying my character, I learn and figure out what are his motivations in the scene; and then I deduce just how he would dress, as well as how he would speak and behave. But, as I say, I would be most unlikely to come to any conclusion in reverse, deciding just what he is like from the way he dresses. Thus it might be speculated that I have a certain efficiency in prognosis, but am sadly deficient in the process of diagnosis.

It must be made plain that I did not at any time in my life, frequent any of the obligatory places where singles are supposed to find their mates. If you just think of it, if you neither smoke nor drink, (and therefore never go into bars of any description, and of course you never join with anyone in the use of recreational drugs;) you never go near a night club or a dance hall; you are not attracted to the beach, you do not drive a motor car, nor are you at all keen on spending excessive funds on dining out, then clearly you don't come near members of the opposite sex who are engaged in surfing for a partner, whether casual or permanent. If you add to this a profound discomfort in any party situation, and even can find the greater part of home entertaining rather unpalatable, then your mating system is sadly inadequate.

Now I did achieve three marriages and at least one relationship, albeit of a brief nature. But it must be noted that my partners in these cases were practically all drawn from clubs or groups to which we both belonged. In one particular instance I met a 'wife to be' in my acting classes. Back in my earliest (and most idealistic) times, I took it for granted that it would have to be within the environment of the church groups I belonged to, that I would find the appropriate sort of potential wife. Even here, it shocked me to find that I still played second fiddle to more dashing and conventionally good looking young guys who must have presented as more desirable partners.

In between marriages, I did make special ventures into the realm of Introduction Agencies, through which I came to meet a very few friendly ladies; but nothing whatsoever got off the ground in these instances. On one occasion back in about the late 70s, I wrote a descriptive introduction to myself which was published in a national magazine that included an extensive advertisement section. I learnt in due course that just about everyone who participated and advertised received up to thirty or forty replies from their ads. For me – well, I got precisely one only. As it turned out, the lady in question was already a member of a group I belonged to, and in a different State.

Looking back, I guess that the content of my blurb had nothing in common with the successful ones. I ingenuously told the exact truth about myself in a way that I determined would have to attract the precise sort of female that I was seeking.   It would never have occurred to me to publish something about myself which was designed in the usual fashion, especially to attract.   Mind you, I suspect that anyone who happened to be of the appropriate sort for me, would not have been looking at such advertising. Don't get me wrong though, this was a respectable and serious magazine, and was not of the sleazy variety.

Clearly my mechanical and pragmatic approach to partner selection was not of a kind that worked in the real world   All the same, in my dreams I still hoped and speculated that a respectable Nerd like myself may represent something of an improvement on a disappointing field of traditional and predictable prospects. - Sigh!!!

On 'Sexual Chemistry'

I have never been 'turned on' by any individual person. I am attracted to any friendly person, and my eventual partners have essentially been ladies who have chosen me, and made themselves available for a relationship.   During the development of affectionate or intimate relating, the one I was with could actually be swapped for any one else, so long as they were equally friendly and attractive to me.   Oh sure, I wouldn't have wanted to make such change, since the unique thing about each of my partners was the surprising and gratifying fact that she had come into my environment and in the process chosen me at all.   The 'Devil you know' must surely be a better bet than an alternative and uncertain Devil that you might swap her for.

An individual chemical attraction has always been unknown to me, whereas a kind of generalized sexual interest or arousal seems to be what I and other Aspies of both sexes have experienced.   This sort of sexual alignment can sound rather shocking to NT women partners, who can well feel that it makes them rather interchangeable in their partnering, as one writer put it, certainly not making or finding any individual at all special in herself. (3)

Morally of course, this characteristic could mean that one might easily be promiscuous, because there is no inherent pressure towards a personal bonding or loyal fidelity to a partner. Thus it could be envisaged as a heavy demand on an Aspie like this, to remain with one partner only, and it must carry a lot of weight. Sure, a lot of the time though, such a decision might be more pragmatic than moral. What I mean is that it clearly complicates life too much, if one mixes one's partners; as well as the fact that it will be diabolically hard enough for an Aspie to keep the attention or love of the one particular partner let alone two or more. Again it is just too difficult for many Aspies to find a partner in the first place. Most of the time, it would simply not make any sense for him to try to deal with these complications.

Clearly if one experienced some sort of chemistry, and got duly hooked on a single special person, then fidelity might well appear a natural outcome for the conscientious person. If as in my own case, one has never felt any particular chemistry, then there may appear no biological need for this special person. This would demand then that one's fidelity has to be a chosen and purely ethical state, and is seen pragmatically as a preferable course.

Over the last 25 years, since I first came to understand something of this business of chemistry between lovers, I have been rather bewildered by it, and have even found myself deploring the idea of such subtle attraction mechanisms at work. I cannot forget the shock I got when certain young marrieds and lovers of my acquaintance explained some of the pleasure (and the effective turn-ons) that they got from just their partner's smells. Body smells???? The very idea just revolted me. As I said before, the idea that sexual attraction is not just a matter of logical choice horrified and puzzled me. And any suggestion of a subliminal bonding didn't make sense.

I have always valued a freedom of partner selection that is based on cerebral issues, that is the selection of compatible persons because of the various desirable features that make them up. The concept that the body and the chemical system prompts or even compels one person to be drawn to another just feels to me so earthy, so non-human. I've had to come to terms with such issues as I've learnt about the way older folk have indicated their loneliness and distress, when after bereavement they no longer have the comfort of the familiar physicality (via smells) of their departed partners.

But now (or rather – So) having watched my own dismal mating procedures in operation (over some 55 years!!!) I have come very reluctantly to the conclusion that sexual chemistry is actually the thing that makes the greater part of the romantic relating stronger, and increases the likelihood of the relationship lasting. Sure, there are naturally some inherent weaknesses in the precedence of chemistry in love choice. But it does have the subconscious effect of suggesting that 'God and Nature' are directing you towards this particular individual. And how can one possibly argue with God and Nature?

I recall one lady friend telling me how she strictly needed chemistry with a partner, before she could participate in sex. As it happened, this same chemistry drove her to a series of affairs with one partner after another, most unsuccessfully. It must be noted, incidentally, that every one of the gentlemen she was attracted to just happened to be a clone of each of the others, and for that matter, including her (unsuccessful and duly discarded) husbands. She claimed that if she essayed to engage in romantic affection with no chemistry, she would be violently nauseated. To her, there was a need, a requirement for that sort of subliminal prodding, as if there was an imperative direction from the higher realms. Does this mean, I speculated, that women (or at least, some women) have no self-motivated sexuality in their beings? Are they unable to find or express a personal responsibility for their sex interests?

Coming back to my problem with body scents, I guess I have to admit too, that the devotion we humans receive from our four legged friends might be at least partly based on their attachment to our familiar smells. And it may be that there are other more subliminal emanations that they are attracted to in us, as witness the instinctive urge our cats have to jump up and curl up on our laps. I have no real difficulty in accepting this fact about our little furry companions, although I can't happily apply it as yet to the business of human to human attraction.

In another case, a particular lady with whom I had a great deal in common, and had some high hopes of an on-going relationship, assured me that I happened to be just the exact kind of male (in body and mind) that she dreamed about marrying and spending her life with. But (and it was the big but), in practice she was never turned on by my type. The guys who provided or stimulated the required 'chemistry' were of an entirely different sort from me in both body shape and habits. In fact, as she confessed, they were inevitably persons who were anything but attractive. This whole matter was just unbelievable to me; and I must say, it still leaves me reeling. What shocked me even more was the fact that the lady admitted that she didn't even particularly like these men that she was thus irresistibly drawn to.

In a further, (and to me unbelievable) revelation, she seriously confessed to me that sexual congress was an experience of 'magic' for her. She tried to explain that she was truly transported out of herself, presumably in that fashion that has been described as 'melting' into each other. With my naïve ignorance of this 'chemistry' at that time, I speculated that she must be in the grip of some sort of pathological hypnotic state.

I can be appalled at the attraction so many women appear to find in those 'wrong' men, who one can only assume must be emanating some spectacular and exciting love style about them. I recall how these characteristics were exemplified in one of the disturbing songs in Rogers and Hammerstein's Carousel. 'Nothing's so bad for a woman as a man who thinks he's good'. And another line in the same song ... 'Be sure you're a bum like your father was, cos a good man ain't no fun!' Not at all the ethic of my upbringing!

Now Carousel is one of my favourite musicals, but I do marvel at some of its content. Towards the end, the young daughter, having been struck on the face by Billy, her dead (and temporarily returned) father, asks her mother if it's possible for someone to slap you, and for it to feel like a kiss! And of course, her bereaved and idealistic musical comedy mother tells her "Yes Darling! It is possible for someone to slap you, and for it to feel like a kiss!" - Heaven help us!

I suspect that as opposed to the more 'normal' males of this world, who show that they are being constantly impressed or affected by their love and their lover with traditional jealousies, passions and mood swings, many Aspies with their inherent detachment can give an impression of being simply unaffected by the partner. And the result is that it is not uncommon for the AS partner to make their women feel at times that they simply don't exist for them.

When I was young, I indulged in all sorts of romantic ideas about love. Nat King Cole's irresistible song 'They Try to Tell Us We're too Young', gave an image that I automatically fell victim to. The incredible optimism over the promptings of adolescent chemistry is beautifully depicted therein. But naturally at that time, I didn't associate it with a chemistry. I just saw it all as a 'liking', and an enthusiastic enjoyment, which appeared to me to be quite enough to make relating work well. It was very largely a cerebral thing, an idealistic mental construct that went on in my being. When eventually it all had to be translated into the nitty gritty of down to earth 'loving', I simply floundered.

With my native obliviousness of chemistry, I have sometimes compared the business of physical sex with the combining of a couple of people in a motor car. The sharing of a car represents the sharing of a bed. The trip together, along with the attendant driving and navigating represents the actual sex activity. Both parties have to combine and cooperate in order to keep the car going well, and without any interruption to the material process. The actual drive has the potential to proceed correctly and happily; while each of those in the car independently does his best to maintain a harmonious atmosphere. The physical driving of the car and of cooperating in the business of fitting into the car, and combining on the actual job of driving, is a separate and independent matter from that of emotionally getting on together, and feeling happy with the outing.

So it would of course be quite possible and feasible for one or other to drive the car alone. Also, either could drive the car by himself, with the sheer passive cooperation of the other person, regardless of any affinity between them. Each may legitimately have a separate agenda for the car trip, and using their separate skills and determination to fulfil the journey, be prepared to do it well and happily. This latter may well be a successful venture, but clearly, the closer and happier the relationship between the partners, the greater the satisfaction will be. Thus the companion is approving of how the driver might be handling the car, and vice versa. The whole business has to be an activity freely chosen by the partners. It is voluntarily guided and decided at each point by the parties, and in the long run, each discovers or achieves their own satisfaction from it.

Sex would be easiest, most obvious, as well as most natural for me with the ones who resemble me the most. No gut feelings ever gave me anything special in feelings about a particular woman and her availability. I suspect that for me, the ideal relationship would be founded on a long term friendship.

Another image that I relate to sexual combining is the practice of recreational dancing. I've always found dancing incomprehensible. You know, it is just so much like a sex act – a mating or courting ritual that is inherently designed to represent sexual coordination, or even to pre-empt foreplay. It just astonishes me that most moral societies in the West do take dancing for granted. Let me make it plain that I'm not expressing here any personal objection to dancing, on moral grounds. I just find it is remarkable that in any Christian community, it is conventionally acceptable for a person to dance with any other person, and not just with one's exclusive partner. One is allowed to come together with another in the most intimate and body centred fashion. I can enjoy watching the dance as a 'spectator sport', but from my biased and theatrical viewpoint, just why anyone should actually want to engage in this strange and complicated rhythmical activity for pleasure, just beats me.

I don't think that the major problem for the Aspie, in initiating sex with a partner, is essentially because he fears rejection. No, it is rather the unspoken and undefined conditions of the activity that are the sticking points. I've come to feel that the sex act can be in itself a very complex procedure for the AS person. In it, one has to deal directly and insightfully with another human being in such a way that the other knows and fits to the occasion. Let's face it, we Aspies can have difficulty in simply conversing with anyone, including a partner. So think just how hard it will be to communicate in a much more subtle and unspoken way with another in the absence of a sexual chemistry. The sheer business of coordinating clumsy bodies, arms and legs together, and making the appropriate rhythmical set of movements could seem terribly hard to organize.

As is often correctly pointed out, the sex of the bedroom is just one polarity or aspect of a total intimate life with a partner. If one like an Aspie finds the give and take of day to day affectionate relating very hard, then when one reaches the bedroom, it is not likely to get any easier. There are so many ways that NT lovers play the 'game'. There are the ways they look at each other or touch, whether in private or public, with the arousing words of desire. When the spouse of an AS partner fails to get these signals and tokens during the times away from the bedrooms, she can feel unloved and unappreciated. See Edgar Schneider. (4)

I can be disturbed by imperfections in other people's bodies. And since none of us is particularly perfect in body or complexion, I have to detach to some degree, in connection with just about any friend or intimate, in order to accept them in their physical selves. I have never understood the down-to-earth, and nitty gritty contact with the physicality of another, that appears to be one of the fundamentals of sexual attraction and contact. Clearly I doubt for this reason that I could ever be a doctor, or anyone who had to work with human bodies. I recall and can completely understand the story given in Oliver Sacks, about the blind man, who regained his sight late in life. Up until then, he had greatly enjoyed his occupational work as a Masseur; but with his new-found vision, he discovered that the visual imperfection of the bodies of his patients distressed him so much that he had to close his eyes while working on them.(5)

Clearly that desirable and subtle chemistry we were discussing earlier can make one oblivious (or maybe accepting) of any outer and naturally imperfect characteristics of the partner. I am a very non-physical person. I live in something of an isolated cerebral world. When I look at couples in the movies, I'm always fascinated and incredulous at just how earthy and instinctively driven their love-making appears. Everything they do together appears like an imposed ritual or set of actions that they have not chosen arbitrarily. This passion, this jealousy, this lustful physicality suggests an experience that is totally foreign to me.

Intellectually I know that all people, including these mysterious female ones, are normal human sexual beings. And yet... and yet, to this day, I can't say that I have ever really been inwardly convinced that women are sexual beings. It is so strange to have an accurate intellectual knowledge about such an issue in the abstract; yet to be unable to believe it, or find it credible when confronted with a woman face to face. It almost appears like one of those alien characteristics, that never feels real to me. Other folk, that is the rest of these human aliens of the world give every sign of mutually understanding their sexuality, of course; but I can not be a part of it. In my Aspie fantasy world, sexuality in women is envisaged rather like an optional extra that a woman may choose; but not as inherently part of her nature.

Oh, I must make it plain that I don't suffer from any neurotic fix on labelling women with terms of 'Madonna' and 'Whore', or for that matter of 'Bitches' and (thereby as well) contrasted against those others, who are 'Non-Bitches'. I regard and treat all women equally. I look at sexually forward women when they are depicted in films or books with a certain disbelief, and with no judgement. I can't quite come to terms with them.

The messages that I gave quite inadvertently in my young days especially must have made some women come to the wrong conclusions. My deliberate but indiscriminate friendliness may well have misled them. You see, if you don't read people, or pick up signals or experience sexual chemistry, you really feel as if you are in an alien world, and you act accordingly. I guess I almost imagined that it was only by accident or even kindness that certain women should indicate sexual interest in me, in those very few and isolated incidents of my experience. It didn't seem to bear any relation to the reality of human life, of the world about me, and of the only kind that I could envisage theoretically.

My friendliness which I always expressed as being directed all around me may well have been interpreted as having a deeper meaning for various women I knew. There was once a class I was running in my own home some years ago. The majority of the attendants were women, with whom I got on very well. In retrospect I guess I have to understand that there were certain women who were signalling 'interest'. It appears that this was actually happening with one or two of them. "You know, Ron" I was told at least once, "You could have had any one of those women you saw this evening." But of course the thought simply never occurred to me.

Clearly when the signals were ignored or glossed over, the ladies in question simply withdrew and came to the conclusion that I wasn't interested. The fact is of course, that a woman would probably need to spell it out in specific verbal terms, or just about undress me and get me into bed before I'd work out what was going on. A woman is always and completely in charge of her own body, and also of her sexual favours, as far as I am concerned. When you don't understand about 'reading' another human being, you simply don't know when they might be expressing sexuality, and for that matter, you would be unaware even if they are sexual at all.

It has only just struck me that recalling my teen years, it is true that up until about the age of 21, I had some three girlfriends, and enjoyed some two or three dates between them. (yes it's true, no more than that.) And it was only later during the more developed courtship which led towards my first marriage that I actually got around to associating sexuality with a live woman. It is absolutely true to say that I never had a sexual thought about any of those previous dates. I never even thought about the desirability of their female figures. Somehow it was nothing that struck me at all.

Ron Hedgcock

These girls were nice companions, and pleasing to look at, and I enjoyed my conversations with them. I held purely 'romantic' thoughts about them, and did consider the possibility of marriage in an abstract and idealistic way.

I recall my sheer naivety with a mixture of embarrassment and amusement. Let me tell you one classic story of an instant when I was about 18 or so (keeping in mind the fact that this was during the early 1950s). To my profound chagrin, my mother pointedly asked one girl I'd been out with (in a group) if I had been 'well behaved' when I was with her. She was pleased to learn from Maggie that I was 'the best behaved boy' she'd ever been out with.

How shocked they'd both have been, no doubt, (and maybe for totally different reasons) if they had known what they didn't know! This very term 'well behaved', until years later, meant for me only one sort of thing. And that was simply that I proved to be 'respectable' whenever I was out in public. I didn't act in a stupid or irresponsible fashion. I didn't drink. I didn't swear. I was consistently polite, and I didn't run about like a noisy idiot. I treated everyone including the girl in a respectful way. The last possible thing I'd have ever thought of was some sort of sexual advance or activity. Let me make it clear, I was not in any state of denial about a lustful interest in the girls of my life. I honestly never ever thought about any girl I was with in any sort of sexual way.

While on the subject of missing the whole point of what I heard about sex in my youth, I can recall another classic tale about my naivety. At the age of 17, I was told once that an official at the church I attended was in the process of losing his wife. 'She is leaving him! – He chases girls' I was primly told, in shocked and scandalized whispers.

Would you believe that this information could mean only one thing to me? I concluded that this despicable man must be physically running around in the streets behind young women and endeavouring to play 'Catch'. Well the whole thing sounded terribly degenerate and improper, although I couldn't quite understand why. It was only years later that I came to realize that my literal understanding of the term 'chasing girls' was curiously inadequate. It was not that I blocked out any sexual connotations of these accounts, - it was just that I honestly had no idea what was implied.

On Kissing and Hugging

When I was young, I had no idea that there was some sort of literal truth in the phrase from the old song, (as sung by the Weavers back in the forties,) that ran "Oh kisses, sweeter than wine". In my late teen years, when I went on my sole two or three dates, I did engage in the odd kiss in the only way I knew, of a mild and rather chaste sort. I didn't get to experience any 'heavier' kind of kissing till involved with my first potential wife. But you see, kissing, despite being a very important aspect of young loving, was essentially then, and still remains for me an action, a shared activity that bears no implications other than mutual 'liking'. It represented something of a gift that a girl bestowed on me - that is, the permission to kiss, and the fact of her obvious respect and trust for me, that she would actually kiss me back.

But I must stress, and I must say again, kissing was always, and to this day, is still a physical ACTION to me, and one which varies only according to the enthusiasm with which the girl so engaged participates. It is more than anything, a demonstration that one is 'fond' and respectful of the other. Again, I never conceived of it as being a sexual contact. I was never conscious of any such thing as a taste or a smell that went with an exchange of certain hypothetical pheromonal oral fluids. It was only later when one of my wives mentioned something about the erotic impact of the mouth chemistry, that I came to understand, albeit with sheer astonishment, that kissing represented much more than just such a shared activity. And the proverbial subsequent process of 'falling in love' due to a kiss leaves me to this day in something of a state of incredulity. Does anyone today recall the old popular song of the 30s or 40s ... 'Just a Kiss in the Dark', and how it triggered off love's young dream?

I'd be most interested to know if it could be that the naivety of the Aspie's sex life is partly due to an inability to detect or interpret physical sexual input? Is it some deficiency in his

Pheromones, or maybe his reception or interpretation of them that is the problem, and not merely that proverbial AS inability to read body language?

Popular songs like Peggy Lee's 'Fever' were totally meaningless to me. I had no conception that being turned on by a particular person could become some sort of raging energy of desire. I honestly was convinced that to speak of 'Fever', and 'Kisses sweeter than wine', represented nothing more than just romantic hyperbole, and thus became part of the repertoire of 'lover' talk that made sex a lot more fun. Then that word 'passion' meant for me nothing more than a word for a strong interest or 'love'. And it meant too, that the person who was particularly jealous or uncontrollable in his love nature had to be something of a disturbed and pathological case.

Actually as a curious anomaly in view of my foregoing comments, I have always found kissing in principle as being a far more intimate act than the practice of sex itself. There is for me, regardless of its inherent and particular pleasure, some sort of remoteness or disconnectedness about purely genital contact, which occurs one might say at a considerable and isolated distance from the brain, that crucial site of thinking and observing.

Kissing, on the other hand, is for me a closer and more potentially intimate sort of act with a partner. Just brainstorming here, I suggest that in kissing, one is primarily engaging that organ (the mouth) which is the means or centre of verbal communication. And since it is through talk that I am mostly aware of the presence and indeed, very existence AND sexuality of the other person, it might not be so surprising. For that matter, it is true that some of the most important highlights of my sex life have been during the times of intimate verbal communication with a friendly and open partner.

But now, I would return to the business of physical engagement with a beloved, for the Aspie. Keep in mind that it can be hard for him to gracefully hug and kiss another person without some of the oddest collisions going on. (6) I look back on a lifetime of peculiar ones that I've achieved, when attempting to kiss various ladies. And here I'm not speaking of romantic contacts necessarily, as I have no objection to briefly hugging or pecking in greeting on those occasions. So many of these encounters have been simply clumsy. While successfully and discretely avoiding a mouth to mouth connection, I've also missed the cheek, so often finding my lips to be attaching to a projecting ear-ring, a collar, or an awkward section of the lady's head-gear. I've come away, just wondering where I went wrong, and for that matter, just what the lady in question must now be thinking about me. I guess you could say that I do not know how to communicate effectively 'body to body' with another person. My relating is very cerebral in nature.

I can't say that I've ever had any conflict or problems when it came to hugging, except when I am upset, or specifically alienated from the partner. I wouldn't want any physical closeness then anyway, but rather to be as far away as possible. The one exception may be that if I am in a state of fear, wherein I'm actually scared of just what the partner might say or do, and there may be demands or pressures on me, that I'm getting agitated about. Then I might actually seek out a hug, or such physical closeness in order to properly assess the danger situation, and perhaps to manipulate the situation in order to avert the danger. This would of course represent a very pragmatic action. If the partner is to be appeased, then whatever action is needed to achieve this must be done.

My mother undoubtedly socialised me from youngest childhood, so I had no trouble going through the motions of affection. It's probably a good thing for my profession of acting, wherein I do have at times to come close to others on stage or screen. On stage one does have to do a whole lot of things that would be uncomfortable with a stranger in everyday life. In the profession, one has to be able to take them very much for granted. Of course, it must be understood that when it comes to a simple clinch of some kind on a stage or film set, there is little difficulty for me, because it is designed and choreographed specifically to work gracefully; and of course to be thoroughly rehearsed. It is not necessarily left to the two parties to determine for themselves.

Interestingly, I realized recently that through my family life, and my three marriages, hugging has never actually brought me a special sense of intimate closeness to anyone. The experience of hugging a willing and friendly individual either male or female is a happy enough business for me. I can say with the greatest sincerity that I do like hugging. Oh sure, I trust that the other party will be enjoying it, as she receives comfort or encouragement from the action. But for me, it is essentially a very self-centred thing. I'm not really aware of another 'person' being there, except that intellectually I know that I'm touching an alien body, and if that body be female, I'm uniquely enjoying the same. In this NT world, it appears that hugging is as productive and welcoming as a verbal greeting or hand-shake, so I've long since made it part of my daily human repertoire.

AS persons probably go to their typical extremes when it comes to matters of physical contact. They can be either too restrained and remote in their personal touching with an distinct sense of repulsion when close to another; or else they are embarrassingly 'promiscuous' in their indiscriminate approaches. Both responses probably stem from the very same cause, which is a lack of empathy and insight into one's fellows. The inner state of non-bonding and non-intimacy may cause some Aspies to find close contact with other human bodies painful and unnatural. They are simply not drawn to be close to others, because all those others are aliens. On the other hand, and maybe depending on upbringing and parental love-styles, they may simply take it for granted that one can come close to other bodies without any discrimination. They may fall into that obliviousness that characterises many AS folk who show no sensitivity to other people's personal space. Closeness may then be unthinking and certainly lacking in any depth.

In some cases the 'affection' processes may well be based on political considerations, in order to maintain whatever shallow relating with others that may have been developed by the individual. He may have got into something of a habit of close hugs and kisses, since he has observed from childhood that it 'oils the wheels' as it were.   People take you as being more natural, real and spontaneous than you really are.   It can relate back, I suppose, to the old bit about pretending to be normal.   Oh yes, the sensation of cuddling and hugging a body can be sexually pleasing in itself.   But from the sensation itself, I'm not aware of the person.

I tend to think that if I am in the position of happily and freely giving a reassuring and comforting hug to another person, regardless of their relationship to me, or their potential intimacy with me, it is rather like me being a professional carer, or father figure, rather than having an intimate personal experience.   Just about any pleasant person hugging me gives me the same experience as any other, unless the aim and purpose is specifically sexual.

I may need to explain a bit about my feelings while I'm in the process of sharing a bed with another.   My experience of her presence is very much of an academic or practical kind.   I am aware that there is a body taking up room in my bed, for example.   But when they open their mouths and I can hear their voice, then I'm aware that there is a person present.

I notice that it is most uncomfortable and very unpleasant for me to attempt to have any sort of intimate discussion, or for that matter, almost any talk, when close together with a partner, or even when just holding hands.   Physical contact tends to dry me up from spontaneous talk.   Somehow the contact distracts my mind from the major object of the closeness - that is, the process of the words.   Words are for me the most profound part or expression of intimacy; but to look into the partners face and eyes, while I'm talking, makes the practice terribly difficult.   So long as I have a couple of feet distance between us, I can manage okay.   But in closeness or specifically in hand-holding, I can't concentrate for the talk.

The same applies in the case of eye contact as well.   I remember how it was drawn to my attention, when last I was given IQ tests, that when I had to explain the meanings of words, I was inclined to lean back and close my eyes, as I searched my mind for the proper answers, and the details I wished to convey. Then still with eyes closed, I launched into an extended little lecture for each word. This was described to me as pretty typical of the (Aspergers) 'Little Professor' syndrome. I have to separate myself from the material situation, and from any connection I might have with my companion or protagonist, in order to be able to come to grips with the verbal issue at hand.   It is always in a verbal and head-centred fashion that I contact another person.

This is a situation that drives poor 'New Age' proponents absolutely wild with frustration.   According to them, one is supposed to be 'right there' – 'In the Moment' as they call it - in some sort of real contact with that other. To approach another in a state of head-centredness is regarded as the very height of spiritual failure and shame.

References.

(1) Aston Maxine. Aspergers in Love.   Page 16
(2) Ratey J & Johnson C. Shadow Syndromes   Page 228
(3) Stanford. A   Asperger's Syndrome & Long
                      Term Relationships   Page 115
(4) Schneider   Discovering My Autism.   Page 88
(5) Sacks. O.   An Anthropologist on Mars.   Page 135
(6) Stanford, A. Asperger's Syndrome & Long
                      Term Relationships.   Page 88

Chapter 8   LOVE AND THE ASPIE

On Love as Basis or Result?

The literature and the teachings of psychology and religion tell us that love is the thing that brings people together. It is the glue that binds. When a couple fall in love a foundation is laid that will hopefully enable the two people to gain a very great deal from the association. In difficult times, in arguments or loss, the redeeming fact is that this quality or foundation called love is there to fall back on. It can over-ride the differences and the difficulties, and the two can find themselves again.

When I started studying the literature on love and considering the things people said to me, I realized that I had a totally different idea of what it meant. For me, love is not a specific force that underlies a relationship. Rather, it is the dynamic that flows between the persons when, and only when, the relationship is actually working and the pair are blending. Love in my book, is the smooth flowing ease that I feel (or expect to feel) when I'm with a loved one. It is of the moment only, and it bears no inherent permanence. It depends entirely on what is happening, and on what is being said or done at the time

This does not mean that I lack what might be described as an ongoing humanitarian love; but this is hardly a personal love or commitment. The way I can best detect and interpret love from my partner, is when I experience politeness, respect and kindness from her. The peak of my conviction about her feeling for me would show because of her obvious enjoyment in my company with a minimum of reservations.

How do I know if I love a person? Well, it is probably by the bare fact that I want to be with the person at all, with any consistency. As I write elsewhere, I have a limited tolerance for being with anyone, and I can conceive of no specific hypothetical called 'love' which would motivate me to desire to live with anyone.

So when it comes to my closest associates, I would want to

Ron Hedgcock

be with them in two sorts of circumstances. I want their company during certain relaxed parts of my spare time. And I also want them when I have 'business' to engage in with them. By business I mean the particular or unique activity or study and discussion, for which I've chosen them. But the fact that I do want to see them, and do enjoy being with them under the right conditions, is the proof for me that I do 'love' them. I may well convince myself that the temporary enjoyment is enough to warrant a longer term association.

I consider myself to be a highly emotional person; and I guess I've got no problem with emotions per se; but the emotions that seem to centre round love in the romantic sense, just don't sit well with me. They are too illogical and unpredictable. They can change frighteningly in a split second, and bring about the opposite of what is wanted and intended. It is the intrusion or imposition of another person's will and emotions that disturbs me. When I have to deal with this, or support a partner through it, it can be truly frightening. I can assure the reader that I am naturally sympathetic; and when in the grip of this sympathy, I tend to be taken over by the emotions that I see the partner going through. I'm not aware of any such thing as Empathy so I can't 'share' with her in the real sense of the word.

However, the Sympathy experience in itself, is limited in its benefit; and can prove frightening in instances of the other's distress or anger. The emotional NT person appears to me to be temporarily in charge of the world; and when I'm observing a person in an emotional state, it feels as if I am losing contact with my own self for the time being. To repeat, it can be said that for me, love is not any sort of basis but rather a Result, an eventual consistent sense of confidence with and about the other party. The degree of happiness, harmony and trust that I develop then, will constitute my version of a love that I can feel.

It can be very informative, and indeed may represent something of a shock for the NT partner to ask her tame Aspie to define just what love actually means to him. In her book, Barbara Jacobs asks Danny what he intends by the word. After thinking for some time, he answers "I feel safe".

Confessions of an Unashamed Asperger

(1)   Note that he had to carefully consider it before he could say. Now I know exactly what he feels. Love for me is based as I said before on a similar factor. It is a state of confidence about the other party, with attendant feelings of safety, trust and relaxed comfort. It is a sense of being okay within my own mind, DESPITE the presence of the other... rather than of states achieved BECAUSE of that other. I suspect that NTs would feel some shock of horror about this.

I can't say for sure just what it means, but I believe that I am capable of caring strongly ABOUT another person; but this appears to be distinctly different from the process of caring deeply FOR another person.

On Commitment, Desirable Negatives and my Limits

I've never understood the insistence on commitment. For me it would appear to be only some sort of guarantee that one will always 'be there' exclusively for the other. Any other requirement or desirable quality in love would seem like a totally separate compartment of human interaction. To specifically like or love a person is surely another thing altogether. But then, just how in the name of heaven can anyone logically and truthfully guarantee to 'love' another person in a future period?

You can promise to dedicate yourself to another in perpetuity, and to their happiness and welfare. You may promise the technicalities of fidelity and dedication. You can guarantee to maintain this other person through all sorts of conditions, just as the marriage vows suggest, for better or worse, for richer or poorer, etc. But however, to promise to LOVE or even to like forever just doesn't make any sense to me. Scott Peck gets around the issue by entirely rejecting the definition of love as a Feeling. He wants it defined as something in the way of a dedication to that other. (2)   I simply cannot go along with his definition.

One of my philosophical mentors, the incomparable Edward de Bono (he of Lateral Thinking fame) states, and I believe it is true, that one can't be expected or forced to love consistently, and for all time.   But, he says, it should be possible within the bounds of most normal human conditions, to develop and retain the state of respect for another person. (3) And while love will fluctuate, - in fact as I see it, simply must vary from moment to moment, and I think, is singularly unreliable, a genuine respect should be far more practical and permanent as a contribution to the marriage. De Bono makes no mention of Asperger's Syndrome, of course, but to my way of thinking, he could well have written many of his books with AS people in mind.

The rules that NT people claim to live by in marriage just don't make any sense to me. The truth is that I can't really picture just what those rules are. I've not been aware of any inherent need for another person in my life, since reaching adulthood. And fundamentally, experience has taught me that there are relatively few benefits or necessities via a partner that seem to display any great desirability. Furthermore, I never had any particular desire to have children, thus eliminating one common motivation for joining in a relationship.

I am simply too much of a self-sufficient person, and can look after myself pretty well. I find within me something of a child-like (or childish?) innocence that is not prepared for the business of dealing in a down to earth way with another person. Call it self-centred perhaps. ... Is it simply that incapacity to read or know other people? (4). Well, I work, think and emote at my most efficient and in my most balanced way when by myself. I don't seem to be able to find any major personal fears tucked away inside, when by myself. There appear to be no 'black spots' or particularly dark corners either - and heaven knows, I've looked, and for that matter, so have more than a few therapists. It is only in my dealings with others that any of my negative worst side tends to show up. Maybe some would suggest that this very fact just proves how much I actually need, (for my 'spiritual growth') to be in an intimate relationship???

I describe my state as being like a condition of innocence. But this desirable state is delicately balanced. Other people and especially partners disturb or upset this state all too easily; and intrusion or interference from a partner can tilt me right off balance. And the worst result, at least for the health of a relationship, is for me to be thrown into a state of fear. I discuss this matter elsewhere. (5).

I have thought in detail about my personal code of ethics, and of the things that I may more readily forgive or adjust to. But I do have limits. With the loss of the innocence I mentioned and the development of fear, I find that there is really nothing much left for me in any situation or relationship. Certainly I can forgive, but not in such a way as to want to live again with the partner. I no longer have the childlike trust that was there. And that childlike trust is the crucial factor and indeed the only factor that keeps me near to a partner with any comfort. If the relationship has lost its innocence, then I never feel the same about it again.

Particularly critical remarks or emotional outbursts that come from an over-wrought partner are likely to bring me to the conclusion that the marriage is finished. I've been accused of being a 'fair weather friend' for this reason. As I see it, the utterance of a truly hard or cruel thing is far far worse than a destructive action like infidelity; and should be impossible for a committed partner. And thus for me, it would just have to signify the end. If a pair actually remained together after such talk then it would be out of a sense of responsibility only, and in my mind, what follows would be just a routine fulfilment of the same.

As I have said, this is nothing whatsoever to do with forgiveness or lack of same. Now if the partner immediately and very quickly withdraws, or modifies her comments, then I might be able to adjust. But it would have to happen very quickly, before I've been too badly damaged and gone into something approaching a traumatic breakdown of trust. However I've never had a partner who did this. In certain cases I did have an apology offered some time later, and in one case a few years after. But that was too late. I recall occasions when I was pleading over and over with the partner to stop the pressure and make peace. It was only when I tried unsuccessfully with no response that I exploded with something like a screaming fit, or a meltdown.

I have always been bewildered by relationship living. I can't comprehend just how other people's marriages succeed. I didn't manage at all well with mine. Marriage brought me only a small range of desirable benefits, since there were so very few things that I expected or desired from it. None of these few things appears to me as being worthwhile at any cost. As it stands, I don't want anyone to cook, wash, sew, housekeep, shop for me. In fact rather than me wanting positives or specifics from a partner, I have realized that what I appreciate most is an absence of Negatives.

In other words, my dreams of happy relationship will be most disturbed if they are contaminated by on-going intrusions or emotional pressures from even the most valued of intimates. When the negatives occur, then there may well be nothing much left in the union that can make up for it all. I am quite aware that such a negation of positives is not at all flattering to a partner.

I recall an occasion when one of my wives asked me just what I might really like to get from her, to enhance our life together. Perhaps she was expecting possible requests like displays of affection or special experiences of sexuality. Or maybe it would turn out to be some outing or activity that would be special to me. Or again some special service I'd appreciate like special meals or home appointments. My truthful but rash answer did nothing to benefit the relationship, as I indicated a desire for her to reduce considerably what I considered to be her intrusiveness and her depth of involvement with me. I guess that in her eyes, my demand appeared as if I wanted her to deny her own humanity, and become only half as natural and real with me. She was certainly shocked and distressed by my answer.

Common wisdom tells that one of the traditional and natural joys of marriage should be the way that each partner gets involved in the business of the other. It must seem something like a permanent vote of no confidence for a loving partner to be asked simply to reduce her involvement, to refrain from interference, and indeed to refrain from too much intrusion in the other's .life It would surely represent a denial of all the very reasons why she wanted to get married in the first place. And sure, I can honestly see that!

A book from the 80s that fascinated me was called "Love Styles'. (6) It was an interesting study of several different ways in which people experience and pursue love. Each type was given a Greek label. The Eros type was the rapturous pursuit and worship of an ideal beloved. Ludus was the playful enjoyment of a sophisticated and uncommitted relationship. Storge was the contented and companionate friendly sort of love. Mania offered the definition of extreme and passionate demanding and jealous love; while by ultimate contrast, Agape (as commended in the New Testament) was the unselfish, dedicated, or God-like sort of love.

The one that interested me most was Pragma. This love style was described as a shopping list variety. It is, as the title suggests, pragmatic, unromantic, and thoroughly conditional in its approach. With the Pragma approach, the emphasis will be on agreements, and day by day efficient relating processes. So, neither passion nor ideals, or for that matter Romantic attachment will be the key issues keeping the parties together. Pragma does not discount them entirely from the relationship, but the major factor is always the on-going satisfaction of the partners. The description of course reads very much like my ideals.

For the Pragma type, it is taken for granted that various faults and misdemeanours can show up in just about anyone and in any marriage, since all are human. Now many of the common faults may not worry the Pragmatic person, because they don't unduly intrude on his life. However, the crucial problems that will disturb him are specific direct and unpleasant interactive words and deeds. It sounds very much like my own main worries over the three 'Unforgiveables', which as I mention elsewhere, are Interference, Intrusion and Involvement.

So in the case of the Pragma type, it is suggested that though sexual infidelity might hurt, and may well need work and forms of adjustment and reconciliation, nevertheless, it might not be of such serious account to the pragmatist, as a savage row would be; or the deliberate delivery of critical and vicious words. Now, I am perfectly capable of forgiving such 'sins', in fact, I guess - most sins for that matter. But the problem for me is not a matter of forgiveness. It is, as I've stressed previously, the business of 'living with' afterwards.

I have to acknowledge that regardless of either my childlike romantic inklings, or the idealistic dedication in the back of my mind to an unselfish Agape ethic, I think I can say that my biggest want or need in marriage would be to remain as comfortable in my wedded life as I would otherwise be in the single life. Strictly speaking for my present life, apart from the issue of survival, as in the case of linking up with another through necessity during fire, earthquake, famine, foreign occupation or other emergency, I cannot now think of any advantage or benefit that I might derive from marriage that would make it truly crucial for me or as comfortable.

Another thing, - I must admit that I have never understood the benefit in, or for that matter, the process of 'making up' after a fight. Getting together in intimacy following any sort of violent row seems to me virtually incomprehensible. I recall in those fascinating books on 'Romantic Love' by Nathaniel Brandon, the author was asked if lovers should make it plain to each other from the start just what sorts of behaviour or attitudes will be considered finally unacceptable; and thus would warn of a potential finish to the marriage, or at least the occasion for some serious ultimatum. His answer was that he would certainly hope so. He argued that we all have not only our principles, but certain absolute cut-off points which are crucial to our integrity. (7)

Every last one of us has his limits of tolerance, almost as a manifestation, you could say, of his integrity. For one, the limit may concern the question of whether he or she has been lied to by the partner. To another it may be sexual infidelity. To another the very slightest hint of physical violence. Another if the partner took up smoking or started drinking inappropriately against all previous agreements and guarantees. Obviously we have all seen instances among our friends and colleagues of people who were perfectly willing to accept individual combinations of these behaviours from their partners, but who would regard it as a total breach of faith if one of the others occurred.

Confessions of an Unashamed Asperger

Now I am a non-drinker, a total abstainer, who never has a drink even at the Christmas dinner table. But I had no worries or concerns about my second wife who did enjoy a sherry or a whiskey in moderation. Though I tasted a couple of drinks with her out of curiosity, absolutely nothing appealed and I remained a non-drinker. But smoking would be a totally different matter. I could never tolerate a partner who smoked, or who indulged in any variety of recreational drugs. I guess that all too many relationships have failed just because lovers have not made it plain to each other from the beginning just where these barriers of finality actually lie. I guess though, for many romantic lovers, to lay down such a standard or law would sound just too un-romantic, or cold and calculating. Just in passing, I feel I must confess to an addiction to one particular recreational substance - Chocolate!!!! (I hang my head in shame.)

I would presume that with many of the factors I mentioned, it is probable that most couples already share certain of the habits involved; and indeed these may constitute some of the attraction that helped draw them together. In such cases of course, neither can really ever complain about the other's practice, unless indulged to excess. In my own case, all else being equal, with none of the habits I just described, it would still be the case that I could never cope with a partner who indulged in unnecessary or illogical abusive talk or interrogation that was cruel or destructive and pressurising. For me, my delicately balanced interest or enthusiasm for the relationship would simply evaporate at that point. Not having or never having found a unique sexual bonding with any lady during my life, there would be nothing left other than convention and duty to tie me to her, not to mention any pressure or emotional demand that she might apply.

In my young and headier days, I blithely imagined that marriage/relationship was a pretty simple sort of thing. I must have taken it for granted that partners metaphorically 'waltzed' around each other in daily life, and easily avoided conflict and even unnecessary contact.(8) My dreams of a relationship without the latter factors (which I have since come to recognize reluctantly as being integral parts of intimacy) were totally unrealistic. A relationship for me simply represented a process that worked to order, not something that was lived through on the spontaneous moment by moment interaction. It also avoided those same three unforgivables - Intrusion, Interference, and Involvement.

I did have all sorts of dreams in my early days about what I wanted in love. I was definitely caught up in imaginary ideas fed by movies, and indeed by love songs. Love was just fostered and motivated by good will, and by the search for happiness. I suppose that because my family life had been so stable, and so secure, I grew up with the idea that love was an easy thing. I recall asking my mother what it felt like to be 'in love'. She put on an ecstatic face and told me how it was like walking on air. I guess the image remained with me for years, with the accompanying assumption that nothing need ever go wrong. I was sure that in a marriage, everyone just automatically fulfilled their separate little jobs. No-one ever complained about anyone else. Husbands and wives got on very well; and they achieved their happiness and fulfilment by the things that they did whether separately or together.

Since I could not detect any inner depths in my relationships, I haven't really been aware of what others may be able to feel. I notice that I've often gained considerable reward from what NTs would see as shallow or superficial contacts. Since I haven't known any different, I'm not aware of missing anything. The same thing can apply of course in sexual activity. And in the best of those old days, sex to me meant that I was doing enjoyable things with a cooperative partner who was hopefully gaining every bit as much from the exercise as I was. In the process, I felt a natural gratitude. But I've never felt any mystical unity in it all.

I don't know if this is true for other Aspies, but fundamentally I've never had any interest in being understood by a partner. If I feed her information about myself, it's largely as a self-expression job. This material will be limited to just what I want her to know at the given time; and I'm just pleasing myself in doing it. As far as a process of 'understanding' is concerned, I can't imagine just what it might mean. I don't want to be understood, rather to be respected, liked and believed. Similarly I make a sincere effort to both respect and believe my closest friends just as I do my partners.

On a Language of love

Those who saw Peter Sellars' remarkable portrayal of an autistic man in the movie 'Being There' will recall that telling and hilarious scene when he was faced with the problem of love making with Shirley MacLean. He simply didn't have the foggiest clue about what he should be doing; but it happened that over her shoulder, he was able to view a relevant love scene on the TV. His mimicry of the action he was watching, proved sufficient; and the lady in her besotted state, simply didn't know the difference.

Now, the natural procedures of love and sex, dating and courting, don't come easily to the AS person; and he may well fumble, stutter and falter through his attempts to promote himself to the ladies that he likes. If he is fortunate in having certain natural qualities of attraction, like the right physique, a pleasing boyish smile, perhaps certain athletic skills or maybe a beautiful voice or sexy smell, then he may just have enough to draw women to him without trying. Some of these factors are depicted in the person of Asperger Danny as related by Jacobs. (9)

But having certain features that may draw the ladies won't be enough for long.. He will find there is a need to use appropriate words no doubt, and to follow up with initiative and decisive action   There comes the crunch, and his deficiencies will quickly show up in large measure. Many Aspies may well have learned to mimic (like Sellars) the words and phrases that are used appropriately in films and in television, and which seem to be the right ones for the job, in the short term at any rate.

Those who have read Temple Grandin will recall how for the whole business of getting on with people, and dealing day by day with them, (and in her case, not in intimate relating) she developed something like a series of tape recordings in her head. These were essentially observations of things she had heard and seen people say and do, in all kinds of situations. Thus, when faced with an interaction, or a communication time, she could virtually just spin her inner tapes until she came up with the right sorts of words and reactions or questions that would satisfactorily cover the particular moment.

A procedure like this will be well recognized by many Aspies; but regrettably there will prove to be down sides of the practice. Not being aware of the subtle nuances, which may come from facial expression, or body language, it is all too easy to omit the particular demand of the moment that is not so routine, and is not typical of just the surface meaning. Our Aspie's clever and carefully chosen words or actions, and indeed his very decisions may be totally unsuitable. If for example being unwittingly confronted by sarcasm or irony, he may naively show up in the conversation in a way that will have him labelled as stupid or impolite. Surely the intimate part of life and its love demands must be the most difficult and complex area to understand. The Aspie is not well qualified to surf through these difficult waters without pain; and subsequently lands himself with many disasters.

A favourite personal story concerns an incident from my very early days at school. In a fit of romantic interest over a little girl in my grade, I wrote her a mash note, in which I stated that 'I cannot live without you'. Luckily my mother saw it, and turned out to be very understanding over the matter. She broke it to me gently that the little girl's parents 'mightn't like it'. So it didn't get sent. Sigh!!! Ah, just what happiness was thus denied me. Just what might have been????

But seriously, the point is that I had no idea of it being unsuitable to say such a thing. To me at that early age, just as throughout much of my later (and hopefully more mature) years, I literally believed that this was simply the correct way one spoke to or addressed the person one liked (for 'liked', read 'loved' as I understood it). Even to this very day, I feel occasionally the urge to speak to friends or 'intimates' with hyperbole that is not appropriate. Luckily I generally manage to restrain myself. It is not deliberately dishonest or insincere. It just feels like the correct terminology to be used.

Something within still tries to tell me that it is legitimately the crucial and official Language of Love.

On the Expression of Passion

There is a very old joke that describes the enthusiastic young lover telling his girl "And remember, I'll go through fire and water for you". She asks him "And will I see you Tuesday?" He answers quite naturally and unthinkingly, "Yes of course, darling, - so long as it doesn't rain."

Since I never understood love or passion, I could not see past the superficial side of love- making, whether vocal or physical. For me, people just contrived to 'act out' the urgency and the fiery nature of sexual or desire love; again because it was essentially the conventional language that one adopted or employed, in order to emphasize that one really liked the other party. It appeared to me as a language of hyperbole that was just deliberately chosen for effect. I did realize however that one side benefit of this 'language' was that it enhanced the sex excitement between the partners.

The fact that some people take the matter far more seriously and duly become jealous in some drastic way, seemed pretty strange and indeed horrific to me. I felt sure that they must have some sort of pathological defect. The idea that one might get literally carried away with passion and simply couldn't exercise restraint, was something that I couldn't understand. For that matter I actually tended to believe that it rarely ever happened - well, in real life, at any rate; though for the sake of drama or fiction, we must take it for granted in books, plays or films.

I recall a song by a favourite Western singer, Marty Robbins, called - 'Devil woman'. Here is a guy with a wife he loves desperately; and yet he's entranced and held captive by a fiendishly seductive woman that he can't leave alone. He begs her in the song to let him go. I still don't get it. I can't imagine that sort of passionate fixation, unless perhaps the designing woman happens to be actually blackmailing him.

References.

(1) Jacobs, Barbara   Loving Mr Spock.   Page 74.
(2) Scott Peck, Dr.   The Road Less Travelled.
(3) deBono, Edward   The Happiness Purpose.   Page 132
(4) See Essay on   Knowing another Person.
(5) See Essay   The Fear Factor.
(6) Lee, John   Alan Love Styles.
(7) Brandon,N.   Romantic Love Questions
                       & Answers Book.   Page 206
(8) See Essay On   Marriage as a Stage Play.
(9) Jacobs, Barbara   Loving Mr Spock.   Chapter 1

Chapter 9. MARRIAGE OF ASPIE AND NT

On the Attraction of NT Woman to AS Male

As I've mentioned before, Barbara Jacobs gives a most interesting picture of her boyfriend Danny, in 'Loving Mr Spock'. Danny has a childlike charm and a disarming openness that captivates her against her will and despite her better judgement. But then she finds that the touches of immaturity that appeared so novel and endearing at the beginning prove to be the warning signs of irresponsibility and a haphazard life-style; and she is forced to bring the association to an end after just a few years.

Sure, not all Aspies deliver an immediate boyish charm as Danny does; and many find it hard to exhibit a sociability that can give them any kind of sex appeal. I expect that many Aspies decide to drop out of the dating/marriage market altogether, because it's proven to be just too hard for them. They think as well that no woman would ever find them attractive.

All the same, I don't feel that there is anything extraordinary about the preliminary attraction that occurs occasionally between AS males and NT women. The accounts I've read and heard in person from many cases tell very similar stories. What the women are attracted to are probably not the AS peculiarities possessed by the male, but rather by the gaps - the absence of other, and very specific things that are seen as undesirable..

Now, there will be a range of Aspies who are not immediately distinguished by signs of Asperger reserve or immaturity. Some of these may look and sound reasonably normal, and even significantly attractive. It is only later, when the lady begins to observe or come up against quirks and habits or blanks in the guy such as she has never observed before in the opposite sex, that she starts to think she is going bananas.

So the Aspies who do appeal, are probably not consciously motivated by the urges and instincts of predatory sexual behaviour. And since they are so unschooled in fundamental masculinity, they give the appearance of being unusually decent and thoughtful. 'Ah', thinks the woman, 'for the first time I've found a guy who really respects me. He is not out just to make use of me, and I can take a suitable time to develop intimate feelings and confidence with him'. She is likely to find him reticent about taking the initiative in the relationship, and thinks that this is a pleasant and relaxing change, despite being a little disconcerting.

The differences about him might well be striking. This Aspie may not want to spend time out in boozing, and knocking about with the boys. In fact he may show an interest rather in hanging round quietly at home; and perhaps he pursues some of those 'higher' things - Music, Literature, Mathematics, Religion or the Arts. This can look very impressive, as he expresses a surprising expertise as well, in the area of his 'special interest'. He gets to look like a person of quality and depth; and one who can be relied on not to behave like the typical male with whom she is disillusioned through dire experience. The lack of initiative he exhibits may perplex her somewhat, as he lets her decide just what she wants to do in their time together.

She may find herself having to gloss over the fact that under his dating patronage, the relationship shows no sign of moving forward in any way; and she attributes this to his unselfishness and reserve. But, she assures herself, he will change; and any poor habits of untidiness or hygiene will give way under her encouragement and capable handling. A good woman will certainly fix things up for him, when they are together. Unfortunately - he just doesn't change for the better (well not automatically anyway).

He may just go through the process of exchanging one set of dependent behaviours   for another, and she finds that she has to take on a mothering job that she wasn't counting on. The guy who was just so attractively naïve and easy at the beginning is now a burden and saddles her with a near full-time job of care and encouragement. A brand new set of problems, questions and confusions hits her in a way that she could never have anticipated. The child temperament, so cute before, becomes difficult and unpredictable. He doesn't seem to mature after all, or to grow in any sense of responsibility. A whole lot of curious habits and routines become apparent, and disturb the smooth running of the household.

She now sees him in a much wider variety of situations and problem areas. Then, for him, living in close quarters to another person full time, may not prove quite so congenial as he naively expected; and his occasional or frequent demands for 'time out' for retreat or whatever, will take her by hurt and surprise. His fumbled interaction with any pre-existing or subsequent children will be likely to complicate things still further, as he shows a surprisingly incapacity in being a normal parent or father figure.

A select number of women may be attracted to men of AS nature, for rather practical reasons. Perhaps this Aspie, because of his ranking in some well-paid profession, such as in the halls of Academia, will represent in her eyes a ready ticket to 'Society'. The lady may be of profound intellect herself, for whom only a partner of equal or higher learning will be desirable. On the other hand, perhaps she is motivated by some sort of 'Red Cross nurse' fixation; and will feel a sense of fulfilment in the job of looking after and encouraging a bright and unique talent to flourish in his chosen field. But eventually growing out of this primary and maybe blind enthusiasm, she may well find that she no longer copes with the responsibility and the undue demands put upon her. Certain of his childlike propensities get to represent a burden, and hold her back in her own aims and ambitions.

On the Aspie marrying the NT

I feel the greatest sense of awe at the way successful marriages work. And when I express this feeling to those who are contentedly wed, the impression may be given that I'm in a state of envy. However, this is not what is actually going on. "You are just so lucky", I might say to a happily married guy. But my sincere comment is intended in just the same way that I might say how incredibly lucky a footballer will be when he is able to indulge in his favourite sport. Or perhaps just how fulfilling it is for the photographer who has just had his best work exhibited. As I comment elsewhere, marriage appears to me rather more like a hobby or a part-time occupation. But I'd never been able to come to grips with the actuality of this thinking in me, until my later years. All too late, I learned to regret my relationship failures; just as I profoundly regret the corresponding pain and disillusionment that were inflicted on the ladies involved.

I suspect that in many cases the Aspie wants to treat his wife in much the same way as he does his computer. And he is confused and maybe rather shocked when she fails to respond to metaphorical Start and Stop buttons, eventually reacting, as she must, like a human being (and an NT human being, to boot)! You see, when an Aspie sits at his computer, he expects the machine to take his word for everything, and never to answer back. He knows it won't be 'reading' him for sub-text or inner meanings in his entries. The machine won't be expressing puzzlement at his motivations, or for that matter, at his quirks and habits. And so it just has to happen that when communicating with a human partner or potential partner, he becomes confused and pained when she seems incapable of simply taking him literally. And quite extraordinarily too, she also appears to develop opinions about his habits and life style.

('Good Heavens', the Aspie in him thinks about this with wonderment... 'Just fancy, she actually has OPINIONS about me!! Very odd. Why should anyone bother having opinions about another?') Clearly, in his birth family, just as with his working associates, it can't be expected that he will have got all of the understanding and acceptance that he craves. He didn't have the free choice about who would be there. But when it comes to a life partner, he calculates that he has selected her in a pragmatic way, believing that she will be something like his human computer, and proving to be every bit as non-intrusive as that companionable and programmable machine. With his keenness to be accepted, his lack of gut reactions and his weak faculties of discrimination, he probably hasn't, strictly speaking, chosen the partner in any significant fashion at all. As I've said elsewhere, he probably has done all he can, in order that this girl, maybe the very first girl to have paid him any attention, will choose him.

On Infidelity and AS

According to most assessments, it appears that AS males are not so likely to stray from the regular marital straight and narrow. This is partly because of their restricted social movement and their dislike for mixing in groups or making new friends. The Aspie wants the familiar and manageable status quo to be maintained, and is never keen on changing his routines and habits. It will be realized too, that the business of womanizing and picking up new or casual sex partners does not come easily for him. It was probably hard enough for him to achieve the goal of his current relationship in the first place. His antennae of sexual chemistry are not readily activated, and so he is not likely to calculate or recognize the sexual potential of the females that he sees. I might imagine that the sophisticated complications of running a marriage plus a mistress at the same time would be much too stressful and demanding for the average Aspie. He would not be likely to consider it for a moment as being worthwhile.

Now I suggest that in a perverse way, it may turn out that many an NT wife does actually have a rival for her affections from the start; but she may never suspect the fact. It will not be in the form of another woman. With the self-centredness of the AS nature, the Aspie might demonstrate that his primary relationship is truly with himself. In the long run no-one else, and not even the most devoted intimate or family member, might get a look-in.

If all Aspies are like me, then they do a lot of talking to themselves –silently, or aloud when alone, and find a unique relationship within, that can't be shared with any other. Thus, as I would describe it, the only one who really knows me, is me! The only one who won't disturb me with demands or questions and pressures is me. The only one who never distracts me from my thoughts and my profound inner world is me. Very very hard for the poor woman who comes up against that extreme self-centredness of an AS male.

I presume that there is always the fantasy, the idea in the heart of the Aspie, that somewhere out there in the big alien NT world, there will be one person at least, or maybe even a community, who would never represent any threat, any puzzlement, or distraction to him. The dream is doubtless a fantasy; but nevertheless I, (and I guess so does many an Aspie), do constantly keep up our antenna, looking out for such a one, and duly anticipate the extraordinary comfort and refuge that would have to result.

If we are realistic (and maybe typically desperate) we give up hunting for the ideal, and settle for the very rare ones (as we picture it) who will actually have us. And I understand that research indicates it is only a minor proportion of Aspies who do succeed at the business of marriage. Apparently the divorce rate in unions involving an individual on the Spectrum is very high indeed. Some, these days, quote that about 80% of Asperger marriages are likely to fail. The Aspie male is frequently a needy person, and whether he realizes it consciously or not seeks for that one who will look after him, and who will allow him to be the 'himself' that he desires to be. He rarely sets out with any desire to be changed.

But as the old saying probably should say … 'Scratch an Aspie, and you'll only find another Aspie underneath.'!

On Roles in Relationships

I didn't deal at all comfortably with any of my partners, as they swapped their day to day roles around. Quite appropriately and predictably, as is the proverbial lot of woman, my partner had to move easily and naturally from being a mother or wife one moment, to become in quick succession cook, hobbyist, driver, book collector, sex partner, mother, gardener, home decorator, companion, communicator, etc etc. Logically this is just as one would expect it to be. But the process didn't sit easily with me. I actually tended to get confused, when she switched and duly changed from role to role. For example, if she were driving a car, I couldn't at the same time experience her as being a wife. I would only feel comfortable with a partner being one thing at a time. If she were cooking, I couldn't think of her as mother. And so on.

After some time together I lost contact with her in the personal sense altogether. She no longer had any reality for me as a partner. I could only see her and experience her in one or other of the many roles; thus she became quite remote from me. I would go through the routine and the motions of the relationship, but it was artificial and contrived, and thus very uncomfortable. If she happened to be fulfilling any of her designated roles, I would want her to look after them without consulting me. This does not mean in any way that I would refrain from helping when it was necessary. But at least, I felt, let her make the decisions, without consulting me about them. Really, I hated the obligation to discuss the concerns and issues that belonged to those varying roles; and I never felt comfortable joining her in the activities. I felt ineffective, and quite irrelevant to them.

It must be understood that there was no double standard for me in this, as I have always wanted to do my things by myself. The major reason I might engage a partner in to my stuff, would either be as a concession to her, or because there was actually some sort of unique situation that I couldn't handle myself. As I've said, I went through the motions, but it was all largely contrived and patiently polite. It must have been lacking in conviction for my partner, ultimately to leave us both with frustration. Many years of this business of pretending to be normal took their toll, and helped to destroy each of the relationships.

It must be understood too that I engaged in each of the various roles that I undertook, and one of those roles was of course that of the husband. When I was in any of the others, it was with a genuine wrench that I detached myself and had to force myself back to being with my partner. Marriage, as I have described in one of my lectures, was actually very much a compartment that felt unnaturally isolated from all the other things I did in my life.

On looking back, it seems just so odd to realize how unreal my marriages were for me, at heart. It was difficult to fulfil the day to day routine of home living; and at times it could even feel unnatural to speak the very words 'my wife'. I don't know that I was ever truly 'there' for any of my wives. I always had preoccupations going on inside me. The surface acquiescence I gave to the marriages was simply never adequate, but must have given some appearance of relating. I just didn't know how to do it.

I'm not aware of wanting a partner today, and I live on my own with two pussycats, and get a great deal of my joy from them. I discuss my friendships with fellow humans elsewhere in these essays. (1) It is interesting to note that each of my friends and associates seems to hold a single or limited function or role in his association with me. Generally, I don't mix them together, or overlap their roles and involvements nowadays if I can help it. This policy has tended to prove itself by the fact that seldom do my friends actually get on well together, if and when they do happen to meet.

Just while I think of it, another matter concerning the sort of partner one might want; I have been amused and shocked to observe the horror with which both psychologists and lay people have reacted to one of my fantasy dreams. I have envisaged how my ideal partner or companion would be an exact duplicate of myself. And I must make it plain that for a heterosexual like myself, the desirable person would have to be a female. I stress that since one supercilious Psych asked rather coldly, "I presume that it would be a person of the opposite sex???"

I gather that such a vision of an identical twin-type ideal partner represents one of those unaccountable NT 'No-Nos', that are regarded as pathological by relationships specialists. I gather that mainstream Psychology regards such as a narcissistic fantasy, bespeaking something of an over-blown satisfaction with oneself.

I realize that at no time in my search for a partner, did I have any concept of a female companion who would literally fill some gap or deficiency in my life. I didn't have any thought in mind of someone who would look after me. Nor was I ever looking to marriage for some means of escape from an unsatisfactory life. This is of course apart from the natural sexual requirements. In looking for a partner, I merely held the dream of adding to my otherwise full and fulfilling life that added presence of a female who had the necessary communication skills. I never really had any proper understanding or idea about the business of 'sharing' for its own sake.

On Bonding and the Underlying Qualities

I've never had that classic sense of 'owning' one's wife. Oh, I know that one never actually owns another person; but surely there does have to be some sort of possessiveness at heart when one speaks (or even thinks) about 'MY wife' or 'MY husband'! To me, a wife was still an alien, but one who had voluntarily and curiously come into my life. And in the long run, it seemed that it was she who would automatically come to control the association, and its content. It was the wife who understood the nature of marriage, and who knew what it meant to propagate the essential investment in it.

I started each of my marriages with an attitude of naive confidence. Just how could I possibly ever go wrong, I felt, in a wedded life? I'd grown up in a happy united family. Two years after the death of my mother, when I was 21 my father remarried and enjoyed no less than a further 26 years with my step-mother. Then my brother engaged in his marriage, and that has lasted for over 50 years. So, I took it for granted that marriage had to be an easy enterprise, and even automatic in practice and experience. It depended, I believed, on little more than decency on the part of each partner, and an on-going good will. I had no concept of the real meaning of principles like intimacy, love and bonding. I still can't understand them, I must admit. They are clearly human gifts or attributes that I, with my vague Aspie brain, still cannot fathom.

One of my Psychs must have been endeavouring to point this out to me many years ago, when I was enthusiastically showing him references in a popular Psychology book that claimed to give useful and logical techniques for achieving intimacy with a partner. At the time, he was not able to get it across to me that these glib and simplistic sets of rules or procedures just can't be effective when taken in isolation. A crucial empathy or bonding has to be there for these to work. There must be something extra there, that underlies the techniques otherwise   they are simply empty.

Marriage for me is still something like a separate compartment of life.   I don't really understand it as a committed vocation.   As I've stated, it seems more to me like a hobby, or an optional extra which may be added to an already full and satisfying life.   Clearly, for the greater number of the NT population, such an image or concept is not acceptable, nor would it be seen as moral or natural.

On Disillusion and Disappointment

With the illusions and misunderstandings that are natural and endemic among Aspies, it's only natural that life will make little sense to us from our earliest days.   I guess that what we Aspies do is to create our own unique world within, and hope to find or create a world outside that matches it.   We constantly search in the big NT system, eager to locate and recognize patterns, processes and activities that will give us some impression of having control.   But the lack of that control in life and destiny, outside of our mind, is probably the big disappointment that plagues us through our whole life.

But the Aspie's deficiency, when it comes to self-knowledge, can make things worse again.   Looking round at our NT colleagues, and being unable to comprehend their ability to use the normal human faculties, we try to emulate them with disastrous results.   We think we want what they want, we try to get what they get.   We are so sure that it's just a matter of trying.   All we have to do is to imitate these others.   Looking back now, I can thank my lucky stars that I did miss most of the things that appeared so desirable and appropriate for me.

There were occasions on which I made application for jobs or responsible positions for which I would have been embarrassingly inadequate.   I recall applications I submitted, without the slightest conception of what would be required of me.   But it was not only particular activities and vocations for which I stuck my neck out.   In friendships as well as intimate relationships I could make every bit as many blunders.   I was thoroughly careless in getting friendly with many a lady whose interests and whose ways of living life were incompatible with mine. I could not see the importance of mutuality of interests, or of sharing a common life-style.

Then there were the occasions on which I was approached or befriended by others, only to realize later (and sometimes years later) that I had actually attracted men of the Gay persuasion. They had misinterpreted my naivety and non-masculine appearance as denoting me to be one of their own. Fortunately things never took a turn that put me into any unsuitable or compromising position.

One classic instance of my blithe miscalculation was during the time I was faced with the unhappy business of determining the appropriate custody of my children, or at least my daughter, when the first of my marriages hit the rocks. It took years and years for me to become aware that it had truly been the best thing for the child to remain with her mother, even though I fought like mad at the time to keep her with me. At the time, I simply floundered through the whole business of the marriage split, constantly lost in bewilderment at the chaos that it appeared to represent.

So many spells of disillusion in my life were based on unreal expectations, as well as the vain fantasy that I was far more capable at fulfilling certain things than was the case in reality. Look at a couple of major roles that I coveted during my years in amateur theatre, and particularly in musicals. Despite the fact that with my short stature, I could never be seen as an imposing Matinee idol, and also that I could neither dance nor sing properly to save myself, I went through the greatest disappointment when I was not chosen. I didn't realize it at the time that though I had the capacity specifically to do the acting in any of these roles, it didn't mean I would necessarily look right for them, or be possessed of the other requisite skills. I can now say 'Thank Heaven I didn't get there'. Of course, there was no conceivable way in which I would have been chosen in the first place.

I did frequently let myself down, when I essayed for certain qualifications, or to tackle subjects for study. My time at

University was a good case in point, despite my being a high functioning Aspie. I had no idea until I started in my first year that I would be completely ill at ease in the University environment. And as far as my ability to comprehend and master textbooks in higher learning - well I soon discovered that my brain appeared to go soft when confronted by the material, or when I was expected to draw intellectual sustenance from the lectures of the Dons. I proved to be a lousy Academic But above all it must have been the disasters that my various marriages became, that represented my biggest disillusionment. This just couldn't happen to me! Through the collapse of my first marriage I was devastated; and I have since had to do a lot of thinking and analysing, in order to determine just what exactly it was that triggered off the big hurt and the terrible pain

Let's be clear - I had not been unduly dependent, either physically or emotionally, on a partner's care and presence. I had not experienced any sort of unconditional love with my wife. Just what exactly was the source and root of my despair? I have come to the conclusion that it was not essentially the personal loss of the female partner or even of my infant children, at that time. But the fact of her leaving me was something more like an affront to some ethical principle of what was proper and somehow cosmically appropriate, or 'meant to be'. It was a good and necessary thing that had been destroyed. Just about everything I believed in had been taken from me; and to top it all off, I was letting down my family and its standards. Divorce was almost unheard of in our circles; and maybe my own particular sort of pride, for what it was worth, was sadly shattered.

With my prosaic and pedestrian Aspie mind, I could not come to terms with the idea that people could just uproot, or chop and change at will, in this business of 'falling in love', when to my mind, such actions merely appeared like vain fancy. But many of us Aspies have little of the romantic and impulsive capacity that may lead one to lust or throw away everything, in order to follow a dream. For the most part, we seek for consistency and changelessness, without the desire for stimulation.

Relationships don't seem to us to be predominantly sources of excitement. Although there is for the minority of us perhaps, one big exception, when for the first time in our lives we discover someone who actually appears to like us enough to be prepared to throw in their lot with us. Up till that time, we tend not to believe that such a thing could be at all possible. Our relations with the opposite sex all too often turn out to be confusing disasters, with disillusionment galore. And as Maxine Aston points out, many married Aspies find a great inner conflict going on during their relationships. (2)

On Marriage as a Stage Play

There is a proverbial saying which circulates among theatricals, and is attributed to the late Mr Noel Coward. When it comes to the rules or the secrets of acting on the stage, he tells us, it is very simple. "Learn your lines, and don't bump into the furniture". Now The Master, as he was known, was certainly speaking with tongue in cheek, as he doubtless recalled innumerable theatrical blunders that he'd witnessed over a lifetime.

Be that as it may, I have to state that I have only just realized that Noel's instruction is rather like my own survival mechanism within marriage. As I see it, marriage is extraordinarily like a stage play, in which I (like most Aspies) am virtually unacquainted with the script. It is rather like being put into a tricky job position, that turns out to be as uncertain and unpredictable on the 1000th day of employment as it was on the first or second day.

We Aspies resemble innocent laypersons who are unwittingly thrust into this play-like situation, with little idea of the 'language' to be spoken, or the rules to be followed. "If only I held a copy of the script," we seem to be crying, - "and knew the lines". AND, it might be added, if we can be alert enough not to bump into the furniture (oh yes for sure), but as well not to bump (metaphorically) into the other person - or into the standard routines of daily life, and (maybe later on) the children. As well we might add, into the expectations of the partner, and the responsibilities of home management and usage.   But above all we plead over and over again, - "PLEASE tell us those lines"

Now what is humiliating and confusing is that our resident tame NT actually appears to know them already; and frequently gets away with what appear to us to be totally random and inappropriate lines. This becomes obvious to us when we Aspies try the same ones as the partner, and find somehow that they don't work for us.   Oh sure, we will probably not be saying them at the correct time.   We may not anticipate the proper receptive mood of the partner for them. We may well be just repeating them in imitation of the partner, in the absence of the accompanying body language or facial expression. And horror of horrors there may even be lacking some other required subliminal or psychic quality, which alone might make them acceptable and legitimate.

What I'm saying here is that marriage can be likened to a stage play. But perhaps I might add that a stage play, when provided with its proper and natural accompaniments, is a bit more like what I might want marriage to be.   But please, please, I would add – be sure to supply me with a script, with a director, maybe a stage manager, and then a Prompt! How very much more practicable marriage would be for me as an Aspie!

When you think of it, in this current 'stage play' of marriage, you have two characters or persons who are flung together onto the stage of the big wide world (largely without experience or training), and they are told or expected to play the roles of husband and wife. They have to perform a series of intricate moves and situations together, and deliver lines at and to each other over an extended period.   There is no Prompt looking on to help. Each successive scene enacted between them appears as unrehearsed or unprepared for as the very first.   (And I must confess here that I hate having to improvise lines in theatre workshops, every bit as much as I hate to improvise them in the domestic setting of real life.)

These expectations imposed on the parties are alarming at least, to put it mildly.   Each one has his own part to play; and there is the demand that each will allow the other to take centre stage equally often; and furthermore will allow them to shine in their role. No-one knows just what will be the high points in their story, and no-one can anticipate much about the other characters that will enter, and eventually become key players with them. The supporting roles are to be played by in-laws, friends, bosses, tradesmen, and who knows who else. And I might add, - Heaven help that marital partner who has difficulty playing his role against those most unyielding co-stars – children! (Oh, and animals as well!)

No-one knows anything about the total impression of their tale, whether it will turn out to be tragedy or comedy; and none knows just what will be the denouement or moral at the end. The vagaries and uncertainties based on the unknowability of each partner, with the accompanying possibilities of ill-health, mental disturbance or bad habits, makes it a most difficult task. And yet, for the conscientious NT majority of our society, it would appear that it can be this very uncertainty that makes it so very human, so exciting, and therefore expressive of the soul, as it were. Also it is the sort of factor that promotes that desirable achievement of 'growth' in people. But for me, and I suspect for most AS folk, it is just these same things that make it so insupportable and potentially unpleasant. If only one could know at every point just what is expected, or just what the other is going to say or do!! But it is all so peculiar and demanding. To me the business of tackling the world and daily life is difficult enough, without adding the complexities of an unknowable and unpredictable partner to the equation as well.

It will doubtless be a very strange thing for the NT reader to understand, as I affirm quite truthfully that an acting job on stage, with another acting person, is for me more real than is interacting with a real person in daily life. This living and presenting of myself on stage is more natural and less confusing than the real life activity. Just think of it; on stage there is a mutually known and understood SCRIPT, that is permanent and which tells the whole story, allowing full cognisance of the past and the future. There is none of the confusion or the uncertainty that is to be experienced in daily life.

With a play script in hand, everybody knows the outcome of the story or the scene. There are no unknowns here - no spontaneous acts, and no unexpecteds. Sure, the audience may be primarily unware of what is to occur; but regardless of what might be written into the plot, the individuals depicted in the script are not tossed about by a careless fate; and a clear finish is ahead. For an Aspie like me, it is reliable and predictable, fair and satisfying. If a person watches the play a second or third time, he will see the same outcome, and won't be confused.

I must repeat, - for me, a stage play is far more real than the ongoing sorts of interaction in everyday life. Those latter, thrust at us by an unfeeling fate, and without a script as they must necessarily be, are painfully unreal, unbelievable and undirected. My times on the stage on the other hand have always felt so real, so predictable and so ordered and established that they have been satisfying. They made sense; and as well they were duly restricted or bordered by both time and demand.

References.

(1) See Essay on   Friendship.
(2) Aston, Maxine   Aspergers in Love   Page 160.

Chapter 10   RELATIONSHIP PRACTICALITIES.

On Loyalty in Marriage

I have a great deal of difficulty in understanding just what constitutes loyalty in marriage.   Just how is one supposed to deal with the strong opinions and firm demands of a partner?

My second wife was a lady of the very greatest integrity and honesty, but she was capable of going well overboard in her intuitive/instinctive thoughts about people.   If I had been strictly loyal, and had taken her insights on board consistently in my practical dealings with people, I would so often have been sadly wrong.   I would have lost some wonderful friends, and further spoiled many important activities in my life.

It has always been a worry to me about the 'insight' that some of my NT associates and intimates claimed to have into others, in such terms as... "I just haven't trusted him from the first moment I met him", or "She'll let you down one day, you see if she doesn't" etc etc.   Well, my experience indicates that if you wait long enough, there is scarcely any person in this world who won't eventually slip up, do some sort of 'wrong thing' and let you down.

When this happens, our intuitive NT has been triumphantly proven right.   Of course, when the blundering individual happens to have been liked and trusted by the same NT, the problem   gets   overlooked   pretty   readily,   and   the misdemeanour quickly forgiven.   Naturally by the sheer law of averages, this same intuitive NT will and must be right in her assessments in a reasonable number of occasions.   But the Aspie is terribly vulnerable to the essential pressure that is part of it all in the relationship system.   He can't tell the difference when he looks at his fellows, or else finds that the 'rules' don't make sense, especially when different NTs seem to be able to come to totally opposite conclusions about the same person or situation.

I recall a classic line in Noel Coward's one act play Fumed Oak, when the obnoxious old grandmother, while pontificating at the breakfast table, states concerning a local acquaintance, that "Everybody knows, you only have to look at her; I'm a woman of the world, I am, you can't pull the wool over my eyes ---". (1)   Now this sort of folk wisdom just truly frightens me.   And this sort of self-righteousness can be convincing, and seems to demand that all listeners will take notice and be warned.

It is perfectly true that one or another of my partners has demanded 'loyalty' of me, when they were fighting some battle in the outside world. An Aspie spouse, with his inherent lack of sophisticated vision, when confronted by such a demand can be thrown into a state of chaotic confusion. Again the supposed rules of intimacy don't seem to make sense. NTs are not always as infallibly 'right' as often as they believe themselves to be, (any more than any Aspie might be); and in a particular case, I might side with the parties on the outside against my wife's judgement.   Is loyalty to the partner demanded of one, just regardless?

It might be said that we Aspies have to look more carefully and consider things a bit more deeply than most NTs do, since we don't have the sort of immediate insight or response and gut reaction claimed by them. So in the long run, our socialisation may actually prove to be more efficient than theirs. The problem though, is that when we are practicing or exhibiting these skills, we don't look very 'real' about it.   We don't appear natural enough.

The NTs get on so well and convincingly in their interactions or assessments of others because they all seem to go about it in a similar or parallel way. Each NT recognizes the familiar process going on in their fellows, regardless of whether they finish up with the same (or the right) conclusions.   NTs, therefore tend to trust other of their kind in a way that they find difficult or even impossible when dealing with the AS person. And on those occasions that they happen to disagree with the other NTs, it seems to be still with the unconscious recognition of 'well, at least they went about their process of assessment in the normal way!'

I spoke before of my second wife. So often despite being wrong, it is true that by the   sophisticated standards of the world she was on the right track in her observed procedure; and so was highly esteemed and loved. She maintained that it was all to do with other people knowing 'just where you stand' on issues. Thus if a person appears to be using the standard NT processes of Intuition/Judgement/Assessment, then other NTs will recognize a colleague, a fellow NT processing things in the same way they do. It spells CHARACTER. It doesn't seem to matter if this person came to different or mistaken conclusions. The important thing was the familiar self-confident process.

Now, I've been singularly deficient in intuitive assessments of my fellows. Occasionally, it's been days or even years after an incident or discussion that I've come to a useful or correct interpretation, and probably much too late to influence my reception of the person's input. But that is if I have eventually come to a correct interpretation at all. Sure I've made my blunders, and been manipulated or 'used' in a few cases. But let's face it, I've observed many NTs (for all their much vaunted intuition) getting into loads of trouble and getting sadly let down in the same way. I've observed as well that because they are so reliant and sure on their inner faculties, these NTs are more inclined to be shocked or devastated at the things that go wrong in their relationships or dealings. Actually I pride myself on the fact that my own record has not been all that bad. And maybe because I have no inherent sense of intuitive certainty about the cases involved or the character of the persons concerned, I've tended to come out pretty philosophical about it all and generally less damaged than most when things have gone wrong.

Now I desperately want the freedom and privilege to come to my own conclusions about things. I don't object to a relevant input or suggestion from the NT partner, but I resent the pressure from her when she feels that she has the prior right to press and insist on the rightness of her conclusions. But what I so often discovered was that I was judged as disloyal when I failed to take notice of what she told me, and further, when I neglected to act on it.

Yes, loyalty is a word that is hard for me to comprehend. I don't understand the issues of relating to another with its inherent component of emotional involvement, and this accompanying quality of loyalty. And the power of any other person's emotional appeal or pressure can tip me right off balance, regardless of where my own personal priorities lie.

Some years ago the weekly column written by a Psychologist in the daily newspaper had a most penetrating article on Self-Centred Persons. Though it was pitched at and about the regular NT persons in our midst, I had to recognize that it could be very specifically applicable to the Aspie. Her thesis was that self-centred persons find it very hard to retain their loyalty to other people with any ease or consistency. In the case she described of such a man who happened to have both a wife and a girlfriend, who were competing against each other for his affection and commitment, the Psych said that the one of the two who succeeded in making him feel the biggest heel would 'win' the battle. Loyalty and love would not have half the power over him that emotional pressure would have. And loyalty would not be anywhere near as influential as the pressure and pleading from the person who gave the appearance of being under the greater emotional stress.

Regardless of my own independent thinking and observations, if I'm confronted by a person in emotional pain, or who is exerting powerful pressure, I can be overwhelmed by this, and find that their demands will take a certain precedence over any other person or their needs. I rather guess that if I were placed in the position of having a wife and a girlfriend, or for that matter two girlfriends fighting for me, I would be in a pretty pickle, to put it mildly. If as I suggest above, one was emotionally more powerful than the other, and made me feel worse, I would be inclined to go along with the strength, and pick her. However if there was no significant difference and both exerted equal pressure, so making me feel equally bad or guilty, then I would most likely collapse in a nervous breakdown.

Because I don't understand the rules of human life and interaction, I feel that the heaviest emotional pressure must take priority. It seems to me that this person is expressing the strongest and most pressing 'truth' of the moment. I don't have any inner conviction about who is right, when it comes to emotional and relationship issues, and the other person's conviction can totally sway me. Thus a particular girlfriend, new or old, might bear every bit as much conviction and truth as a present partner. It can make one vulnerable to emotional blackmail or manipulations as you could imagine. My own wish and need in such a case would always be to be left entirely alone, with the chance to choose freely in peace between the alternatives or alternative cases with no appeals or pressures.

The following example of the problems of loyalty is based on a real case. Certain of the details are hypothetical, but I did face the situation in a fashion. This is not a world shattering issue. But when you're confronted by a passionate and determined intimate, you can get to be uncertain of your priorities.

Picture this situation, with the influential input of three successive spouses. Wife number 1 has an old fashioned fad of referring to every female as a 'lady'. In her conventions, and as trained into her from early life, this is the respectful and proper way to talk. You are committing an impropriety if you call someone a 'woman'. And thus the word 'lady' expresses something of the respect you will be demonstrating when you are with her or in talking about her.

"Ah," I say to myself, "I've learnt something significant here; and I can see no reason why I should argue about the matter, or do any different from what has been asked or expected of me". As it happens, the whole issue of this terminology in such a case has never occurred to me before, and I feel that the logic of it seems right; and as well, it gratifies the partner. The matter has been settled in my mind, and I take the new 'rule' literally.

Then it so happens during my next marriage or relationship, that I am matched with an equally honest and respectable lady, who is of a more modern thinking disposition. She happens to be a Feminist, and simply detests the word 'lady' with a vengeance. I am duly reproached sadly and severely for my usage, when I say the word 'lady' in her presence.

"No," she asserts, "All females are 'women', and you don't use this antique and sexist term nowadays."

Well to put it mildly, I'm rather shocked by this reproach, and start doubting the instructions I'd previously been given. I feel a bit foolish to boot. So I try to put her precept into practice. I feel after all, it must be correct, and as well, from a pragmatic point of view again, it must please the partner. Since she is so adamant about it, and it is something that I'd never looked at before philosophically or morally, then she must be right. Then on top of it, I'm only a poor male (and a poor benighted Aspie to boot) so what can I be expected to know?

However some years later, I'm married again. And somehow this plaguy issue raises its ugly head again. My third wife insists on the term 'lady' all over again, - and now I'm really confused. Okay, it's not really a crucial matter; and a tactfully passive partner might just try to please each of these strong minded women while with them. Perhaps the whole issue doesn't actually worry me at all, and perhaps it makes no real difference to me just which of the two terms that I use.

But consider this. What if I've actually had strong views of my own, whether linguistic or philosophical, on the matter? How do I deal with the wife or wives that I don't agree with? Why should I necessarily be the one who has to automatically give way when a partner has a different view? Is this a matter of the vexed commodity of loyalty? Why can't one of the wives demonstrate her loyalty to me for a change?

I have to confess to being flummoxed by the matter. My own thinking would automatically proceed along these lines. In debates of this kind, the ideal thing would be to resolve them in a state of Aspie conceived 'fairness' and respect? Perhaps the parties can simply agree to differ. But what if either one happens to get offended by the other's immovability? And then as another alternative, it would be the shot for the partners to have some sort of pre-agreement to give in to each other alternately, when dealing with matters of principle that bear no emergency. That would make sense to me. Otherwise just how can a pair ever come to an agreement about anything? Surely one is supposed to be able to stand firm when holding a strong conviction, while giving ground from time to time. One should surely be able to demonstrate that he is not just a walkover, all the time!

I've read more than once in the literature on Asperger's syndrome that a great deal of the ethics engendered and pursued by AS folk is based on their passionate belief in the principle of fairness. Like the child who feels overwhelmed and dominated at every turn by their huge and superior parents, the Aspie screams for fairness from the world.

Funny, but I recall one of my Psychs who just astonished me, when I tackled him on just this issue of fairness. In all disputes I had with my partner of the time, I found that I was never able to win any argument at all. I always turned out to be the one to give in, and it confused me very badly. To me it suggested that my partner was a very inflexible person, since she insisted on getting her own way all the time. And this happened both in verbal disputes as well as in practical arrangements. I brought the matter up with my Counsellor, and told him I would desperately like to have a situation wherein my partner and I agreed to win arguments in turn by rote, or roughly so that there would be a balance. In the long run then, each would 'win' roughly as many debates as the other and duly so with a good grace.

I explained that consistently my wife 'won', and duly got her own way. Well the Psych pulled the most horrible face of disgust, and made some comment to the effect that I was being just too inflexible in my requirement. I was really shocked, and didn't pursue the matter; though I did lose just a bit of respect for that guy who happened to be one I really liked.

On Working at the Relationship

Through much of my married periods, and even during the subsequent years of separation in one case, it was a great distress to me when I was told by my wife, with a show of grief and disappointment, that I was not 'supporting her'. This might be on occasions when she was in some sort of depression, or ill health, in a state of loneliness, and maybe also over the phone.

 Well I would try to switch off my own inner world – hard for an Aspie - and listen in a growing state of agitation, putting in the occasional "Yeah", or "Uh huh". Periodically after racking my brains, in order to express my interest or concern, I would calculate out some innocuous question or suggestion to put to her, but it was obviously inadequate. All too often then despite the length of time I'd devoted to the conversation, I'd be told that I was not showing her any support, and that in fact I was making things worse. For me, of course, that 'very little' I was doing was the most incredibly hard work; and it seemed to me that I would have to be doing an enormous amount to help, and, for that matter, to 'work' on the relationship.

Actually because of all the stress, this very business of working on the relationship came to mean little more to me than a process of gritting my teeth, squashing my feelings, putting on a calm outer face, and pretending to be interested. It is something like the extreme of being self-consciously 'unselfish' or even like martyrdom. Naturally I'm perfectly aware that this is not a hoped for attitude; and would bear no resemblance at all to St Paul's description of love (or charity) in 1 Corinthians 13.

As I see it of course, it feels profoundly unselfish because while I'm putting my own needs and feelings on hold, I am giving the partner the total right of way in the interaction. Since anything approaching a disembodied or ideal dynamic of love is unknown to me, I can't find any way of offering some sort of atmosphere wherein she might feel loved or cared for. With the feeling of agitation and confusion I'm then going through, I can't imagine how I could offer anything at all. It can well be pretty impossible for many of us Aspies to understand just what is meant by atmosphere or vibes flowing between people.

Perhaps the reason is something like this. The emptiness or so -called lack of support which is claimed by our partners is based on the fact that Aspies like me are not aware of that real person in front of us, and therefore with no awareness of her emotional needs. We go through the process of just being bombarded with words, and we are waiting in an intellectual and practical way to see just where those words will lead. But this can be destructive, and so I have often found myself switching off as the emotional and pained talk drives me into confusion, and eventually into a state of resentment. In my mind I'm convinced that I've already given so much and been so supportive with no recognition of the fact, so that I finish up badly hurt when the complaints come.

Now, simply recalling the words of the other party in the abstract, I can conceive that I've not been adequate. But in the actual situation, when I'm concentrating on the words I'm hearing, I am actually out of touch with any inner knowledge. It all makes no sense, and no course of action that I can think of makes any sense either.

The other issue is that with all the goodwill in the world, one is likely to provide to the person in distress only such help as one would want for oneself. Aspies notoriously have been through a lifetime in which they desired and sought respect, fairness and space, rather than emotional comfort. Because we are frequently incapable of indicating clearly to the NTs of the world just what it is that we personally need or wish for, we rarely get it. And I must say too that on many occasions when I have frankly expressed my wants, the NT partner or listener either doesn't believe me, or may even determine that it would not be in anyone's best interests for me to have them granted. In fact the way they have appeared to my partners, my pleas have presumably not been based on the sort of love and bonding that they believed in or were hoping for.

I'm not sure that our partners actually appreciate us Aspies for the particular qualities which we believe to be our greatest attributes. It may then be understood that the occasional special person who in kindness or patience does listen to us receptively or who allows us our unique and unorthodox space will readily gain our individual variety of love or devotion.

So when we see a partner who according to the conventions

is our primary responsibility, and so long as we actually recognize the fact that this partner is in distress, our first tendency will be to do for them just whatever it is that we've always been so desperately wanting for ourselves.

We might work hard to listen and to pay respect. Quite possibly we won't understand a word of what she is saying, and will look for a very quick solution of what can only seem to us as an essentially practical matter. It will not make sense to us to be pursued for some obscure desired dynamic such as love or empathy. And thus our contribution so frequently does not work; and eventually we are left in a state of unbelieving frustration, finding ourselves in a state of unwanted, and from the NT point of view, unwarranted anger at the charges of inadequacy and unconcern that are being thrown at us.

On Politics in Relationships

There is a perception that persons with Aspergers Syndrome are usually inherently honest, and that they will consistently speak their minds with blunt abandon. Certainly many among us do engage with our fellows in this way, but it will depend very much on the temperament of the potential partners as to whether the resultant 'truth' will be acceptable or not. Will the particular wife for example really welcome it when in answer to the question "Does my backside look too big in these trousers?", the straight speaking Aspie replies with "Yes it does!"?

But evidence shows that this somewhat admirable but disconcerting honesty is by no means universal among us. As usual the Asperger's brain wiring appears to manifest in extreme fashions. There is a strong tendency with some Aspies to act and speak with their partners in a political fashion, rather than in a real or authentic way. Now when a Politician speaks, he is calculating the most productive way to go. He can't be totally real or natural. He is obliged to say just whatever the Party wants him to say, and to enlarge on it in the way that the Electorate want to hear. This process in a politician is deliberate and well trained in him

Confessions of an Unashamed Asperger

The Aspie frequently does a similar sort of thing; however it is not because of anyone else's deliberate training but rather because he is too uncertain or afraid to do anything else. Our NT partners assume that if they ask a question or make a comment then the Aspie, just like anyone else, will answer honestly and directly from the heart. More than one Aspie has made it plain that even in the most relaxed and intimate moment with his wife, his comments and conversation will still not be totally open, relaxed and spontaneous. (1)

The Aspie has very little confidence in the status of his own opinion while under the scrutiny of other people. So he will frequently look for the most acceptable and peace producing answer or expression that he can give. So repeatedly, we deny and disregard our own feelings, in order to come out with what appears to be the 'right' thing to say. We thus suppress our honesty and our realness just so these interactions and the resultant conflicts or mis-understandings don't get out of hand. We feel that the sooner they are put to rest, the quicker we can get back to the familiar and comfortable daily routine.

This same daily routine, it must be pointed out, can be difficult or unnatural enough, but it may fast become intolerable if it is confused by the introduction of NT questions or problems that are non-routine. I think it is true that many years of accommodating the unpredictable and unfathomable quirks of our NT partners have the effect of making us lose sight of certain of our own feelings and needs. Keep in mind that the things, the issues and questions that seem so natural to the NT mind can appear to us like gobbledegook. So rather than ask just what is being said or questioned, we will often choose to shut up and risk missing the point. Then we feel obliged to indulge in a process of fudging, rather than to get into a complex and confusing discussion on the spot.

Another thing; when you have a literal mind unaccompanied by the NT ability to carry subtle and unspoken dynamics with a partner, then it may be desirable to have a series of pre-arranged systems in place that can obviate the need for on the spot confrontations. But this doesn't necessarily go down particularly well with the NT partner. I recall just how shocked my partner was in one relationship, when I suggested that I would like a whole set of hypothetical agreements set out from the beginning like a contract that might obviate many of the shocks and misunderstandings later on.   Apparently many NTs consider such pre-arrangements as destroyers of spontaneity and realness, and they seem to define it as a prime virtue to face difficult issues only when they come up in real life

Though AS folk can come to the conclusion that other people actually do have needs of their own, nevertheless the urge to fulfil them might not be so spontaneous and pure for the Aspie as they would be for the NT.   So NT partners do not get the appropriate feeling when their partner is responding to them.   A lot of our relationship gestures are chosen and delivered for those same calculated or political reasons rather than from any sense of love.

On Fair Fighting when the Partner has a Gun

Just what are some of the weapons that NTs seem to wield against us? Well, I suppose, above all, their awareness that we Aspies are vulnerable and uncertain about things human and social. We indicate surprise or perhaps shock about the things people do or say, and consequently we appear inadequate among our peers.   Therefore that person who displays some sort of certainty - that one who 'knows' human nature and can utilize an intuition and worldly wisdom, (or Folk Psychology, as Baron Cohen puts it) - that person will naturally feel and appear superior or as the supervisor and mentor. This facility, this confident sophistication will arm the person with a powerful gun that is wielded constantly and right in our faces.

I think it is true to say that the Aspie in his naïve imagination tends not to anticipate the ups and downs of a relationship. And when he enters into marriage, he is dumfounded at finding himself forced to conform to the expectations of a system that he doesn't understand.   He turns out to be the uninvolved one of the pair. He is the one who doesn't discern the feelings and needs of the partner. He doesn't see the things that need to be done, the attention needed by the children, perhaps the rubbish disposal, or the latest pressing bills or whatever. He is the self-centred one who primarily knows only how to look after himself and needs constantly to be brought back to reality by that other one who is always on duty.

Of course it just doesn't look that way to the Aspie, who can't see the difference between the things that the NT tosses him to do, and anything he might want to do. Both look just like the separate decisions and impulses of an individual. Since however these come from the other party, therefore they appear like nothing other than her personal quirk. So any quick explanatory comment by the partner in which she explains just whether the request is personal or outwardly important and significant would be a big help in order to help him to adjust and understand.

Naturally he relies for the regular running of a household on the astuteness and efficiency of the partner. But the inevitable let down occurs as his personal Aspie expressions and wants come into conflict with the practical and more cohesive demands that are recognized and conformed to by the partner. He is frequently hurt by this. On one hand, he may find himself to be compelled eventually to acknowledge the apparent appropriateness in what the partner says or expects; but he will throughout be feeling a sense of inferiority. His unique personal sense of logic and right just doesn't seem to stand up in this world of the NT, and he can get to the point of dreading to hear the statements or reasoning of his partner. The partner becomes a catalyst, a source of information and expression that is typical of and identifiable with the big alien world outside. By contrast, when we Aspies try to put our needs and feelings forward, our wants appear not to be legitimate; and this leaves us with little alternative but to squash the things we want to express.

Probably we restrain ourselves too much, and give too little indication of the feelings that go on within us. When we show emotions, it is frequently in chaotic bursts, when pressure has built up too far. We tend not to express them routinely. But these alien NTs seem to indicate their emotional fluctuations just at any time of day or night. They seem to be tossed about in an unpredictable fashion at any time; and the pressure of their emotions, with their irrational sense of urgency over the smallest things, can leave the poor Aspie in a state of wonder and shock.   It must be appreciated that our blank and simple talking at these times represent an honest expression of our feelings just the same.

For me, I don't show much of the emotion and feeling states when I'm talking about my needs, or when expressing my disturbances. And as well, my carefully chosen words would be distorted or ineffective if I did not keep the tightest control of the feelings. I feel that the simple fact or the truth should be sufficient. There is no need to rock the boat by emotions. In childhood I remember, my emotional expressions caused just so many serious repercussions and reactions that I learnt to restrain myself to the utmost. Stick to blank facts and unemotional explanations or complaints, I concluded, and one can't go wrong.

Since I'm disturbed by the emotional expressions of my partner, I try not to speak or think the same way that she does, as it would not only intensify my pains, but would trigger her off the same way.   This is not easy, as I find myself emoting in resonance with the other. There is as I see it, room and relevance in any given moment for only a certain limited degree or amount of emotion and chaotic talking, and if it must be expressed at all, then it's safer to leave it to the other person.

So the expressiveness of a passionate and convincing partner may make the Aspie feel that he has no choice but to go along with her.   Then it will appear to the NT onlooker that the Aspie has now had something of a welcome change of heart that is taking him well away from the point of view that he previously espoused.   The Aspie will give to her the appearance of having a vacillating nature; and the NT will logically come to the conclusion that she is fully justified in guiding and mentoring the Aspie. She will feel sure that she is giving him a much needed confidence and a sure path, and duly congratulates herself on proving to be essential in his life.

The danger is that the Aspie will just feel that he has been hustled or bullied or bluffed. He has been overwhelmed by the reasoning or intensity of the argument of the NT partner AT THAT MOMENT, and he feels he has had little alternative but to conform... to go along with the superior thinking and decision making power of the other. He will, it must be understood, frequently resent this, but will fall in with it all, being unable to find or formulate the sort of argument or certainty that would be necessary if he were to maintain his own views against the opposition.

Part of the trouble is that in offering his own opinions, wishes or needs, the Aspie is just not convincing to the NT world. He can appear half hearted and uncertain. In my own case, I frequently cant formulate any specific reasons for my opinions and preferences, and thus I can't justify the things I'm putting forward. To the reasoning and commonsense practical NT this shows an inadequacy and even a regrettable dependency. This Aspie, she thinks, must be clearly needing guidance and decision making from a well meaning and properly informed partner.

So the many and fluctuating emotional expressions of our partners are rather like a gun held at our heads. And for me they represent pressures that I just wouldn't feel right to utilize in return. It is almost like an emotional blackmail that is hard to resist. I might add that any one emotional expression or plea sounds to me exactly like any other. I can't tell the difference between a demand or request that is legitimate, right or moral, on the one hand and one that is selfish, immoral or inappropriate on the other. Somehow NTs seem to have some instinct or maybe lack of inhibition that enables them to judge the demands and impositions put on them by others, so that they appear to be perfectly justified and right when they refuse. NT demands and expectations are certainly like a gun pointed at us.

Then too, the quoting or flaunting of their intuition represents a gun. This very certainty that they appear to have, due to their native insight, is strong. They have a confidence that they can 'read' us and other people for that matter, and the conclusions they come to frequently appear so decided and certain. They may make the special plea that 'this is my inner truth' and that you can't argue with that. It appears to be related to that proverbial empathy that NTs toss about so freely. And empathy being a special knowledge about the inner states of other folk, must inherently be authoritative, and thereby can arm the person with extra force and authority.

Honestly, it almost appears like cheating, when this same empathic and intuitive capacity is applied in the middle of an argument. And a poor benighted Aspie like me is inwardly protesting in bewilderment 'This is simply not fair. She's wielding a gun, while I'm having to make do with my fists.'

Probably the other and tremendously powerful gun that is wielded by the NTs about us is the commonality of understanding that NTs seem to share. Everyone, just everyone seems to have the same ideas, the same demands, the same principles, and expect the same from us. These are frightening things to have confronting us. How can a poor ignorant and confused Aspie stand up against the accumulations of folk wisdom and the obvious agreement of the masses? He must indeed be deficient. He must be morally bankrupt - he must be helpless. And therefore there seems no alternative for him but to submit to the 'gun' or guns wielded by the NTs about him, and just give in.

From time to time, it will hit us very hard and hurtfully as we wonder just how come that the battle, the debate, the interaction is so one-sided and so unfair? Why does the other party seemingly have this freedom and moral permission to wield a 'gun'? It is again so much like the battles we faced so inadequately when we were children, and had to confront the powerful adult superiors that we totally relied on with no alternative but to trust and obey. Somehow the NTs in our lives don't seem to suffer from those uncertainties and confusions that are inherent in us.

I guess it feels like the old complaint... You just can't fight City Hall!!

Confessions of an Unashamed Asperger

On The Fear Factor

Research has detected a conflict that goes on inside Aspie partners of NT wives, even when a successful relationship is resulting. On the one hand there is commonly a profound gratitude and relief they feel, to actually have someone who is there for them, and who acts at appropriate times of need as a necessary minder, or carer. They may know that they could not afford to be deprived of this marriage. Somehow there is a 'love' experience that they couldn't do without. But anecdotally it is understood that they can still find the experience painful and confusing, as Maxine Aston found in her research. (1)

Probably my biggest inherent weakness is fear. I mention elsewhere about the three things that disturb me most in relationship – intrusion, interference and involvement. At the drop of a hat, I can become deeply nervous about a partner, just as much as I can about any other individual. And she like all others is unknowable, and represents unpredictable possibilities. Ultimately I am not aware of truly trusting anyone that I know, even a partner. But as a principle, I make every effort to treat the people about me as if I do appropriately trust them.

The way that others know and apply the rules of life is deeply worrying. Ultimately, safety exists for me only when I'm by myself. Once I've experienced a strong sense of fear towards a partner, my confidence in her is gone. I might go through the motions, but I can never really trust again. As a young person I wondered why I felt lost so often. I recognized little of this, approaching people and prospective partners as I did with a naïve unthinking trust. I learnt in the long run that consistent close proximity to anyone else is disturbing and somewhat frightening. I now choose to be with selected people for limited periods of time only. That is a major reason why with my more recent discoveries and observations I can confidently assert that there is no way I would have got married in the first place, if I had known then what I know now.

In the process of attempting to deal with the more delicate

issues that a partner might   bring up, it can seem like being obliged to watch the dial on an electronic device which monitors some dangerous functioning. Thus the attention stays riveted on the dial, with the concern that the needle will move further over to the red danger zone, leading inexorably towards some almighty explosion. Such a 'blow-up' would have repercussions far bigger and wider than those around my own petty concerns. It is as if the whole world looks on breathlessly as I fasten my gaze on the dial. It is a big responsibility. To me, any other person, being as they are - a total unknown, is capable of anything. But the buck stops with me as I seem to have the responsibility of making sure nothing happens.   In practice, the worries fears and complaints expressed by the NT partner become of grave concern, and I find that metaphorically I cannot afford to take my eyes off the 'dial', or to allow my attention to be distracted from what is being said.

Again we feel/I feel that we just don't know the rules - these rules which are the stock in trade you might say of an alien world that constantly hurts and oppresses us. We learn from an early age to be afraid of doing the wrong thing. While NTs appear to express themselves honestly and openly, we learn to deal with others in a purely political and wary fashion. Again, it's a bit like being lost in the jungle, as I describe elsewhere. For the Aspie, the world of daily life can be just like a foreign jungle.

Think about it this way; if you know you are surrounded by wild animals and potentially savage natives then you take the greatest of care to treat every situation as being dangerous and unpredictable.   Your communications with those natives will be cautious and conciliatory. You endeavour constantly to discern the local rules and the conventions that keep you from getting into strife. But you never feel even after years that you have satisfactorily learnt the language. You recognize yourself to be a stranger and foreigner no matter how you have tried to fit in. You never cease to be vulnerable.

I might be sticking my neck out here incidentally, but I don't really feel that an Aspie can be truly taught to feel particularly free of vulnerability, even with the most attentive and concerned partner. Vulnerability is so ingrained into us, that most of the time we don't realize that we are dealing with it, or making use of our habitual defences.

As I've stated many times, we can be easily manipulated. We don't readily detect the little voice or the gut feeling that can tell us that this or that is wrong or inappropriate. So this is one strong reason why we are so damned vulnerable. The NTs in our lives have been the virtual authorities about this world of theirs all along, and we can too easily train ourselves into taking them as being automatically right, and thus to be obeyed or yielded to. This habit of automatically yielding can blow up in our faces as almost inevitably we can get to be resentful and suspicious. We may well also learn to deny our own initiative in things, too. The resultant loss of trust in our fellows and indeed in our partners, is not thus to be taken as being critical of them, but rather as a symptom of a lack of confidence in ourselves.

We can feel intense guilt in our interactions, a guilt that we don't seem to observe in the natural types of outpourings that come from the NTs. We substitute a contrived ethical code of behaviour that would seem most peculiar to the NTs. We rely on our routine systems rather than on the moment by moment assessments and gut feelings that are common among the NTs. When we are taken by surprise, we get agitated, and can fly into panic, because once more, we cant mind read - we just don't know the rules. And so it is usually wise and practical for the NTs to speak simply and directly with unemotional explanations in order to get some of those rules across to the AS person.

But it doesn't always work as one might expect. Stanford describes how sometimes the simple straight and logical sort of comment which would normally be most appropriately used to explain to the Aspie the cause and effects of his actions, may bring about an unexpected resentment and pain. The case she describes is revealing, and bears a strong resonance for many of us. Neither party could determine for a time just why the wife's appropriate warning didn't work.

Normally one would expect that the more simple and direct the statement given to the Aspie, the more comfortable he will tend to be. But here was an unexpected anomaly. The AS partner indicated that he still felt resentful or uncomfortable despite the warning having been delivered to him in the agreed on way. Eventually, after a close discussion of the reaction, the couple determined just what was going on inside him. On these occasions, even though she explained simply and precisely the consequence of a particular action, he couldn't help but see her as the actual originator of that consequence and thus personally to blame for it. He stated. "I know the consequence is a simple law of nature, but it EMANATES FROM YOU." (2)

Warnings directed at us by wise and wary NTs have probably delivered an unintended pain to us from our earliest years, and we interpret them as personal threats.

The business of modifying the fear syndrome in my nature will depend a lot on the skill and the insight of the NT partner. She may learn to recognize certain danger signs in my demeanour and maybe determine ways to reduce the stimulus she is delivering. I have had to learn all sorts of defensive mechanisms in order to shut off certain of the painful things delivered by the partner. But they can only go so far. For the most part, I do need to be left alone after the exchange, and to be given the opportunity to re-centre myself.

The fear I go through might be of several sorts. One would be the fear of hurting the partner, either getting so angry I might actually get physically aggressive, or of saying things of an extreme kind. With my characteristic and ultimate lack of trust, the fear may well be that she could do me harm. I have had as well a great fear of the sheer chaos that is being created. Then there was a fear of my own panic, fear of having to give in and making promises or guarantees that I could not keep. Another issue of course would be a fear of emotional blackmail, with the concern that my anger or defence may exacerbate the partner's depression, loneliness, suicidal feelings or whatever

I believe that an Aspie's involvement or bonding with another person is rather tenuous at the best of times. Of course, if he lives with a profound dependency on his NT partner, then there may develop a real bond of necessity, and the inherent need may force him to stick with it. In this case, the Aspie will be fearful of tilting the relationship off balance, thereby endangering his security, as well as, for want of a better word, his metaphorical 'meal ticket'.

I would suggest that it is all too easy to misinterpret the motivations behind the Aspie's emotions or reactions. One lady told me of how when she fell seriously ill, with the likelihood of a long spell out of action, on telling her husband (now known to be AS) he went into a hysterical state of distress or panic. She logically came to the conclusion that he was simply devastated from a selfish point of view, and felt inadequate about the prospect of having to look after himself, in her absence.

I got a strong feeling that it is more likely that he was in this major panic state at the thought of being required to say appropriate caring things, and of having to offer all the right supporting things for her in her neediness. She would thereby become something drastically alien to him, in a way he would not be able to deal with. And he would literally have to 'become' something different himself from then on!

It is hard for an NT to interpret just what the Aspie is thinking. If you the NT are in pain and the Aspie seems to be echoing what you are going through, there may be some sort of compassionate sympathy at work. But it may as well be that he is just feeling confused. He is in a state of desperation that he is unable to modify what he observes of the partner's feelings and expressions. And his most desperate need is a personal one – selfish if you like – that those feelings and expressions of hers must be modified - they must be stopped. His every expression of concern may be composed of calculated words that are being thought out logically as a desperate experiment. He feels that just anything is worth trying in order to cease her stream of desperate commentary. Her profound need may make him fearful that he will be totally unable to do anything to help. Eventually a panic state may come about.

Gisela Slater-Walker tells of asking her Aspie husband about how if she injured herself in the kitchen just what would be his immediate fear and feeling. He answered that his instant reaction would be the worry that he might find himself doing the wrong thing. His first thoughts did not primarily concern his wife, and her welfare, but rather his concern about his performance. (3)

Yes, we will have learnt that others have needs, but we can be fearful about how to go about satisfying them. We know that with all the best will in the world, those gestures we make and the words we murmur can look so contrived and so political that our partners describe them as phoney. We watch our fellows in the NT community, and endeavour to emulate them with their words of comfort or reproach. We try to do the same things that they do all the time. But they don't work. They don't come across as real or spontaneous. And as a result, with an increase in our fears, they tend not to be appreciated by the recipients. We retire hurt and humiliated and with a sad reluctance to ever attempt the experiment again.

And experimenting is exactly what we have done through a great number of our actions and words. A lot of what we Aspies do in our human intercommunication can be described as attempts just to see if we can get the same results and achieve the same approval rating as the NTs. However, when it comes to the opposite direction of working I suspect that with our literal thinking and our mental receptors, Aspies will appreciate any sign of goodwill or caring that we might get from another. Of course we are not so likely to be looking below the surface for anything else that is deep and meaningful. But I guess that it might be said that the simpler the sympathy the better. A matter of fact approach will probably work the best for us, and we won't appreciate the sort of panic fuss that others might display.

In Stanford's book too, the wife said that she was shocked when her Aspie husband confessed that he was still not being spontaneous, even during their most intimate moments of talk. (4) Typically we don't really know how to be spontaneous about anything other than the topics and activities that are natural and interesting to us. We are afraid when confronted by those demands and problems that NTs appear to take in their stride. We just retreat into our shells, with our tails between our legs, in order to avoid putting our feet into our mouths with both hands. (Sorry, that's a lousy mixed metaphor, but it does give the picture.)

So in my case, I tended to collude frequently with my partners, and endeavoured to give them what they wanted (or more accurately what I thought they wanted). All too often it simply didn't work, or else I couldn't follow through with the appropriate appearance of conviction or whatever happened to be the necessary accompaniments. I often had to give up halfway through and convey the impression that after all I was not prepared to keep my word. It didn't do my image or my reputation any good.

No wonder the Aspie can give the impression to the unwary NT observer that he is either Mad or Bad!

References.

(1) Slater-Walker, G & C. An Asperger Marriage   Page 67
(2) Coward, Noel, One Act Play, Fumed Oak.   Scene1.
(3) Stanford, A. Aspergers Syndrome & Long Term
                          Relations   Page 164
(4) Slater-Walker, G & C. An Asperger Marriage.   Page 53.

Chapter 11   COMMUNICATING IN RELATIONSHIPS

On Interpreting Words

My literal thinking causes me quite often to speak naively and unthinkingly when talking about my own issues, and it means that the comments I make are simply not trusted by the other. I may be duly accused of lying or of implying something different from what I'm intending. This result may often be triggered off by some discrepancy between what I say and what shows in my facial expression or body language. Since I have to work hard in order to join in a conversation, it is possible that the process of deliberate contrivance of my contributions instead of having them simply pour out naturally, will seem suspicious to the other.

Although I can start with a thoroughly sincere and truthful thought in my mind, it doesn't pass straight from the heart to the mouth, as it were. It goes up to be filtered first through the head, as I may be pondering consciously on the most appropriate way to express the words. So by the time it's actually expressed, it is not going to be perceived as spontaneous; and that to the NT, bears the hallmark of something untrustworthy.

For the NT the involvement and interest of a loved partner will not generally be disruptive. And it may be that she will actually welcome another viewpoint or input that will improve the activity or the thought process. Now for the Aspie, it may be that he actually does need help or input; but this same input can bring about a certain deflation or humiliation, just as he's felt so many times before throughout his life. And thus to have to confess his insufficiency once more might be a blow to his pride.

Another possibility is that the other's input, however well meant, may be delivered in such a way as to confuse him. Very frequently I will not comprehend what a partner is trying to convey to me with her words, and I will find it most difficult to determine, even when I've had it explained to me with more words still, just what is wanted or expected of me.

Sometimes the sarcasm or coldness of the partner who is

angry or hurt will simply not be apparent to me. So that a wife playing a punitive game of 'No Speaks' for a day, may well appear very pleasant. On one occasion, I went through this very scenario, as I had inadvertently hurt my partner's sensitivities over some particular issue. We had to drive through the country for the day, and she made a point, as I later understood it, of being cold and distant for the whole outing. I subsequently found the day to be quite relaxing; while my wife herself came across to me as being just so wonderfully easy to get along with. And this was all without her saying a word. How frustrating for her to find that her method of reproach simply didn't work!

It is a critical problem for many of us Aspies that we don't have the immediate and suitable response to common things that are said or done in our presence. Lacking the faculty of 'mindreading', and if we don't have access to a useful 'gut' feeling when we see or hear things, we are at a considerable disadvantage, especially in disputes. It is not so surprising I guess that all too frequently the Aspie in his panic and bewilderment resorts to an outraged protest.

At times I must admit to some degree of envy or admiration when I observe my NT friends who have learnt to rely on their intuitive responses to people, with the assurance of "This person is safe!" or "This person is dangerous". We Aspies are not so typically responsive. We feel that we have to wait and listen to all that is being said, and may need to concentrate on things for hours or days before we can determine in retrospect just what happens to be or to have been our real feeling about them.

On Missing the Message

When I miss some of the opening words of a communication, it can prove to be very embarrassing. Sometimes the other person talks to me without first drawing my attention, and I think that they are saying something that they are not. More than once I've fallen into the trap of half hearing something imparted to me, and I've given a pat reply of "Oh, that's good" or some such. Unfortunately I found immediately after that the other party was just telling how a family member was just admitted to hospital for an operation, or that the butcher had just run away with the cat. Since I can't interpret or detect some sort of underlying mood or message, it happens that if they don't spell out the details in words, I may well miss completely the essential message. As I've had to explain so often to my poor long suffering wives, unless I'm starting with a full focus of concentration on her voice, I have to go through a sequence of switching on my attention, so I can listen and respond.

In keeping my eyes on the other's face, it is not for the purpose of intuiting her intent, but rather just for the purpose of ensuring that my mind doesn't wander from that job of listening. And it must be understood, as I've said so often, it is actually a considerable job for me to be engaged in. First I have to register that the partner is actually speaking, and then that she is specifically speaking to me. Strangely enough this is often necessary, even if we are alone, since I may not be aware at the time if she is talking to herself or to me, - or maybe even on the phone. I can be totally oblivious of any reason a person may be speaking, and thus may take no notice. I need to have her draw me in, by catching my attention. This may be best done by speaking my name, or catching my eye, or even by touching me.

Then I have to determine just what she is saying and follow up by calculating just what sort of answer is required, and work out an appropriate reply. There may be some level of anxiety in me as I concern myself with determining such an answer as will be satisfying to her. I say again, unless she actually calls my attention before she starts the necessary details, I will have taken up the period spent on the first part of the sentence, just coming to grips with it. I may only catch the middle and latter part; and if what I hear appears to make sense, then I will feel no need to inquire about the earlier part. And it means that not infrequently I will have missed key words from the beginning. I'm reluctant enough to ask what she's already said, as there is the impatience and irritation that will be triggered off then; so since I'm already convinced that I have picked up the essence of the message, I don't check it out. Of course if I haven't picked up any understandable message at all, then I have to bite the bullet, and ask for a repeat.

I think this is an important thing that occurs to lots of Aspies, so I'll describe the process another way. We hear what is being said... we don't have an instinctive understanding of it, and unless we are unthinkingly reacting with rejection or whatever, we are inclined to just hang on and listen, hoping that what is being stated will become more understandable or practical. If we are not taking a hint, for example, then we will get confused, and may wait for some clear cut message or request. All too often we give the appearance of being dumb or slow, as we express our puzzlement, or indicate our incomprehension. The temptation is just to jump right in ahead of the understanding, and indicate prematurely that one is getting the message.

How many times have I fallen into this trap? And the other party has not had the slightest idea that I hadn't understood what was being said or asked. Then at a later date or moment, my misreading of the message comes back to haunt me, with some sort of mistake or blunder that I've committed. Then there is no way for me to explain just what went wrong, or why I made the inherent mistake. Any attempt to explain will only make me look sillier, as I realize for the first time the process of understanding that I have fouled up. The explanations only bring about greater humiliation. The NT will look disgusted or shocked, and will query in disbelief just why the mistake was made. I of course just retreat in hurt dismay, and will feel forced to make myself an idiot in such exchanges in future, by delaying and delaying, as I try to get the real message a lot quicker. On the other hand, I may not try at all next time, and in a vain attempt to retain some sort of temporary dignity, go through the whole sad little plot again and again.

Ah, how often a partner has brought about a crisis in my trust and respect for her, because she has placed the communication of some particular topic she was pressing in importance above our relationship. I do need just one thing at a time. As I explained to one partner, if she wanted me to do a few jobs for her, she would do best to quickly sum up all the various things first, so I can get a general idea of what I'm in for, and the time span they will take up. Since I will carry no memory of all of these in my head, I then need to have the jobs dished out and explained in detail one at a time, just as I prepare to actually do them.

Now I rarely ask a favour of another, but I am usually happy to do a favour for others. But with my literal mind, I do see favours AS FAVOURS, and specifically as rare and relatively exceptional expectations. So when the partner who wants me to do a favour on Monday, then wants another one on Tuesday, I get a bit shocked as I would have expected each to be the last one required for a long time. I imagine it must be due to the way that I cannot envisage with any clarity the continuity of relationship interdependence.

Talking of instructions, I know that I'm not alone in finding technical booklets or papers on electronic gadgets nearly impossible to follow. Any document on the setting up of a computer for example, (or even the assembly of the desk it sits on) will likely leave me in a state of confusion and distress. I am certainly not one of those Autistics who would sit well and successfully in Silicon Valley. I have barely the start of an idea of how to work my digital camera or my mobile phone. I look at the wording and the diagrams, and my mind just goes into chaos.

I'm not too proud, thank heaven, to ask others for help in these things; and luckily I have a tame computer guy, a close friend who is kind and tolerant enough to provide assistance and advice just whenever I need them.

On Talking to Me

Ideally, what I would most want to hear from a loved one would be phrases like "I like being with you" or "I feel good/safe/comfortable when you're near." Or again.. "You don't represent any difficulty/intrusion/problem/danger to me." Such words are much more important to me than protestations of 'love' and devotion.

The following suggestions would make for greater ease and efficiency for an intimate in talking to me...

*Please when you speak to me make sure that you have my attention from the beginning.

*Don't commence your message until you know that I am listening. This may possibly need the calling of my name, and noting my reaction.

*Please don't get impatient if I am slow on understanding just what you are talking about.

*Please don't ask the question "Why?" unless it is really necessary. And for that matter, don't ask for explanations of anything, unless necessary.

*Please don't praise me at all extravagantly, if it happens that you might also at any moment have cause to criticize me just as strongly; and that comes as a horrible shock.

*Any time you have a request I would greatly appreciate it if you could make it plain whether the matter is a personal quirk, a genuine emergency or a routine daily need, or again simply a special favour for you.

*If the subject and context is serious or confrontational, please don't combine reason and emotion in the one sentence or message.

*If you have a serious complaint or lesson for me, please deliver it relatively briefly, and don't go on about it for more than a few sentences. And please do offer an acknowledgement of anything I say in mitigating explanations as the confrontation continues.

On Secrecy and Privacy

It is very common for women to complain that their menfolk don't readily share details of day by day matters. If this is frequent among NT men, it is certainly normal and natural for the Aspie male. Day to day issues tend to be quickly forgotten or ignored by the Aspie, as they bear very little relevance for him especially if they concern other people. Literally, it is hard for him to recall them or describe them to others, almost as though he can't find the relevant words, while the most interesting details have completely escaped him. As I see it, the big and real world that an Aspie inhabits is the world inside himself and uniquely it makes sense for him - in fact it may be the only thing in his life that does!

From an early age, he has learnt sadly that others are not interested, they don't appreciate any adequate discussion or description of this inner life. Of course, the factor that makes it unpopular will be its irrelevance to anyone else, and the lack of sophistication in its details. The content may be in the form of childlike images and thoughts; or it may centre round obsessions or occupations that others will find stupid.

The typical request or demand from a female partner for information on what he is thinking about, in the hope that she will learn more about what goes on in his mind, will, if answered at all, probably be very disappointing or may even be a bit shocking. So he doesn't match the normal, and his views on his intimates may be peculiar and disturbing. He may rarely be thinking of them at all. He may be spending key moments of the relationship time just dreaming about his hobbies. So he learns discretely not to commit himself in words about his inner world.

Is this to be considered as secrecy? Well, I guess it could be described so. He may possibly have no opinions at all on certain of the vital things that a partner would want him to be considering. It will doubtless be intensely painful for a loving partner to observe that our Aspie is so self-centred. He is a 'things' person, and not a 'people' person.

The pre-occupation he maintains with this whole unseen world can appear horrifyingly selfish, and is certainly not conducive to a regular married relationship. When things are bothering him, it is likely that he will say little if anything about them. His central coherence is weak, and he can exhibit an inability to distinguish one sort of obligation or restriction from another. And so he will probably feel that since he has been discouraged from talking about issue (a) in front of other people, as mentioned above, therefore, he can't talk about issue (b).

The sad conclusion has been forced on him from childhood that HIS personal topics and worries don't carry the same sort of importance or significance that other peoples' do. The demands or expectations of teachers might possibly have been worrying; and since he was discouraged from displaying certain sorts of reactions and emotional displays, he has continued through life with a protective habit of hiding behind a blank face.   Behind it may be a seething mass of painful brooding, or maybe even some sorts of mental stimming (or self-stimulating and comforting procedures).

He will probably be anxious to avoid being questioned in depth by others about matters that he is keeping quiet; and will do his level best to give little indication of what goes on beneath the surface. Yes, you can say lots of us Aspies are secretive; and it must be admitted that the tendency and habit is not really conducive to a free and happy sort of adult relationship.   This blank look accompanied by the lack of communication will probably give the spouse, or prospective partners, the impression that nothing much is going on beneath the surface.   But worse still, they may suggest to the uninformed intimate that the Aspie is cold, cruel and unfeeling.

On Me as a Private Person

I am convinced that everyone is entitled to their privacy. A partner who demands that each must be absolutely and totally honest, is surely being unrealistic. I have to admit that I can't conceive how anyone can be totally open and honest about all his inner thoughts and dreams. My own mind and consciousness is so far reaching and free ranging, that I tend to think it is definitely non-communicable to others. I am happy enough to examine and admit to myself the various manifestations of my 'shadow' self (as per Carl Jung). I feel I've usually been very realistic about my weaknesses and my less desirable possibilities. I don't reject these parts of myself, though I certainly draw a line between those aspects of myself that I am prepared to act on, and those that I regard as unsuitable, and thus to remain undiscussed.   Besides I have so many (how shall I put it?) reserves, problems, worries, or whatever concerning absolutely everyone I know, that I fancy it could demolish or shake just about all relationships that I maintain, if they were known.

I have always been a private person about my moment-by-moment decisions, thoughts, feelings and actions. And I feel a distinct resentment about any intrusion or interference. All my partners had this perfectly normal habit of inquiring into issues that were of no real consequence to themselves. Let's think of an hypothetical. In an unguarded moment, I describe to Partner X how I just met Joe Bloggs while I was out shopping. The fact that Partner X doesn't like Joe, or objects to something he did ten years ago, may trigger from her a prolonged commentary about that gentleman that I find distressing. Almost it feels as if once more, I have to justify my association or friendship with Joe. And anything that he has told me or advised me about is automatically suspect. So I am plagued by the implication that since Joe is a problem, then Partner X's comments just have to represent a reflection on my discrimination - that is, a criticism about the very fact that I chose Joe to be a friend in the first place.

Another thing; in many cases, the details that I convey to my partner might draw unexpected criticisms that lead to profoundly upsetting arguments. All too often the partner can get hooked on her own hobby-horse (some pet peeve or hate or feeling of personal expertise) and she would proceed to press me to undo or change my decision in accordance with her own views.

My three 'unforgiveables' may perhaps better be described as 'unjustifiables', and I must say that an excess of them will certainly bring about the loss of my trust and confidence. Maybe they could be described as agents of disorientation. Probably in 75% of intrusions that took place in my marriages, I did not agree with the demand or expectation, or had already taken some suitable action to avoid the sort of problems that I was being warned about. This sort of pressure for explanations and counter action was painful to me; and I realized, as I had learnt early in my life, that if I kept quiet about the 'truth' or rather the 'facts' in such day to day issues, no-one would have been any the wiser, and no harm was done. I was duly left alone, and all was sweet. Where questions and confrontations about subjects that had clearly no relevance to my partner or our mutual interests would inadvertently surface, I might simply hedge or 'lie' in order to deflect unnecessary discussion. Thus any tedious or moralistic lectures would be averted - lectures that appeared to me to be nothing but self-indulgence on her part.

I guess that there would be very little about my 'secret' self that ultimately needs to be and remain secret in principle. But any openness that I allow will be dependent entirely on the attitude of the person who hears or scrutinizes them. It is not that I am inherently ashamed of my inner life; but rather that it is in the capability of other people, especially intimates or other close associates, to sneer or to laugh down ideas or dreams that I have. Virtually any person is capable of making me feel self-conscious or embarrassed. If anyone stares at me pityingly or patronisingly as I explain a point of view, then I can be made to feel uncomfortable. It is in this way that I can be highly susceptible to teasing. I suspect that a certain amount of this is due to the rather naïve or childlike attitude I might express.

My real life and I mean that one which is most fully natural, real and comfortable, is something I engage in when I'm by myself. Naturally, I don't find this is infringed on when I have the company of cats. Those little animals represent something of an extension of my own self, so they can rarely represent any interruption. My natural tendency is to constantly stay in or shift into my own inner world, moment by moment. So unless there is some sort of demand on me to concentrate or focus on other people, I will revert to my fantasy world of adventures, dreams and speculations. It is purely the subjective world of my thoughts, my plans, my ideas, lectures or other projects.

I recall one ex-wife observing how I appeared to express no initiative, no get-up-and-go while she was around. She deplored the fact that it seemed to be only when she left my company that I came alive and appeared to be able to tackle things that I needed to do. My alone time is vitally important and productive. When alone, I am likely to be talking to myself, perhaps even delivering serious lectures aloud to myself. Some will be rehearsals for discussions that I am anticipating or maybe that I would desperately like to deliver to someone (or maybe am wishing that I had delivered at the appropriate time!). I frequently repeat key bits out of conversations I've actually had, as I think back to them, - and I might just repeat them over and over again.

On Truthfulness

Persons with AS have the reputation of being (uncomfortably) direct and truthful. Many can find it near impossible to lie, especially in view of their inability to read the minds of their fellows, with the attendant weakness at knowing how to successfully manipulate them. A love of fact and accurate data characterises much of the communication that they engage in. But obviously a person who tends to keep silence about all sorts of things, and who lives deep within himself for a greater part of his life, will hardly be coming out with anywhere near the whole truth that lies within him. Some Aspies may have learnt from an early age to keep a lot to themselves, and their devotion to 'truth' telling may be very selective. You will probably for the most part get 'the truth' from an Aspie - and maybe even 'nothing but the truth' - but perhaps you are not quite so likely to get 'the whole truth' from him.

Overall, I will resort to prevarication in order to keep private such matters that as far as I'm concerned have nothing to do with the other party. These things are none of their business. My literal Aspie mind says to me that I will inform them when there is something that truly concerns them; just as I take it for granted that they in turn, will happily tell me ONLY those things that they want to tell me, or that I genuinely need to know. As far as I'm concerned, virtually anything else is essentially private. I pride myself on avoiding any double standards. I never expect or demand things and explanations of a partner that I wouldn't offer myself.

I don't tell a partner about stupid things I've done during the daily routine; and I won't generally share about minor objects for example that I've mislaid or lost. I don't really feel that I require the other's scrutiny over such issues. I am perfectly capable of learning my lessons over routine mistakes or losses, without having to put up with lectures from a partner on the issues. The relationship will just suffer and degenerate if I'm subjected to this sort of pressure.

It's not as though I ever want to lie. If treated with respect, and my privacy respected, I don't need to lie or avoid the truth. Since I've been living solo for some 20 odd years, I guess that my own case is a bit different from many other Aspies, in that I don't share my house and private routine with anyone, male or female, old or young. And therefore any relationship for me is not a 'sharing' sort of issue where an intimate other needs to be involved in my day to day affairs, with the accompanying requirement of knowing my every move or activity. I am self-sufficient, and have never since my twenties needed a minder or care-giver. I do look after myself successfully, and like it that way. Doubtless, if I had partner needs, I would want to deal with a lot more sharing and interaction than I do at present.

I must make it plain that if a matter being discussed with my partner clearly deals with important personal matters, or some essential issue about a current pursuit, such as on an Aspie line, or again with a Psychologist in a deep and meaningful sharing of life and thought, then I do not hold back and am very frank and truthful. I just want others to keep out of anything that is simply not their business at that moment. And in the process, I endeavour to refrain from referring to matters that may draw criticism from the other.

On Compliments and Sharing of Confidences

You trust me enough to tell me of your troubles, or perhaps your secrets and inner pain. For the most part I'm certainly happy to listen, so long as it is not for too long; and I can assure you that I take it as a great compliment when you do. Now it is not in the contents or the details of your discourse that I find any gratification. What pleases me is the very fact that you have confided in me at all. I may have no interest at all in what you tell me. I'm certainly not storing up material for gossip or for holding against you at a future date. It is likely that I won't even remember very much of what you told me and I certainly would not exploit any of it. The point is that your confiding makes me feel for the moment almost like an honorary and respected NT. I will be gratified or flattered at the very fact that you have allowed me 'in' at all, and entrusted me with the information or confession.

With the typical Aspie obliviousness to subtext, and with little insight into people's inner life, this process of confiding represents just about the only way I could gain any of the subliminal information that is well-recognized in the NT world, and I'll have forgotten it all pretty quickly afterwards, especially if the material embraces gossip, or concern folks with whom I'm unfamiliar. Not uncommonly if the person is describing the intricacies of his or her relationships, and any resultant neurotic conflicts, I probably won't have understood a single word that they have uttered.

The result, at least in the mind of the other party, may well be that I gain the reputation of readily keeping secrets, and of being trustworthy. But the downside will be of course, that my inherent disinterest in the matter or my inability in remembering the all-important human details may appear unflattering to the NT mind. Taking on board the thoughts, experiences and truths of a friend or intimate may seem like the appropriate action of someone who really cares and who has empathy. But on the other hand, it may indicate the self-centredness of the Aspie who isn't really interested in the other for their own sake, and as a human being. I can't really make up my mind about the priorities and ethics of it all.

Now, another compliment you can pay me is to encourage me to talk. And the most important thing for me to talk about is myself, so long as and especially when you will listen non-judgmentally. And that can make me feel like the respected Aspie that I would most like to be considered as.

At such times, I'm not particularly concerned to question your sincerity or genuineness. For the greater part, I will take you literally, and not be bothered with the business of searching you for hidden meanings or inner motivations. I will not be aware of any kind of 'heart' that lies behind your words. Also it will be of absolutely no concern to me if you recall little afterwards of what I was saying. What I appreciate most is the respect that you pay me in letting me talk freely.

My self-centredness means that I am not out to manipulate

you. Just a few years ago, a Psychiatrist I consulted indicated that he was dubious about the diagnosis of my AS status. He fell into that classic trap of judging me by my ability to retain eye contact, along with some other atypical abilities. But ultimately despite the fact that he found the claim about my mild AS condition to be a bit unbelievable. Nevertheless, at the end of the interview, he did express a genuine appreciation or even admiration at the directness and honesty of Aspies like myself. He commented that in general, Aspies just don't 'play destructive or evasive games' with a therapist. It is interesting to recall that there are Aspies (like myself) who just love the opportunity to talk in an unrestrained fashion (and maybe for the first time in their lives) in front of a Psychologist. (1)

I sometimes feel that the greatest gift you can give me or at least the greatest compliment you may offer is when after an extended period of association, you have instilled in me a genuine trust. If I feel no particular fear or apprehension when I'm with you, then you have achieved a great breakthrough. Such feelings are much more significant to me than any words of love, commitment or intimacy, which by comparison don't really mean a great deal to me.

So consequently, a declaration of love from a partner may convey to me and mean something a bit different than was intended. In the absence of any reserves or worries, I would translate it automatically and essentially into something like a 'vote of confidence' as it were, and thus a most important compliment to boot. Any avowed love in itself might not be particularly important to me, but the fact that the other party is actually expressing it - well, that would be the big thing.

References.

See Essay   On Therapists as Friends.

Chapter 12 SELF SCRUTINY SINCE DIAGNOSIS

On What it looks like to me.

I'm not sure about whether this chapter should be thought of as a summing up, or as a speculation on my future. But I want to share some of my thoughts about where I am going and just what is happening with my AS classification.

Among members of the Autistic community, endless arguments go on about the question of whether one's AS improves or gets 'worse' with age. Certainly with age and experience, not to mention due to the long and painful learning of processes and short cuts, doubtless many of us Aspies do give the superficial impression of 'improving' or getting 'better' in our later years. But I would emphasize that experience might be just making us more careful and discriminating as we age. It certainly has been like that for me. In my own case, as well, as I've dropped from one marriage after another, I've had to become more self-sustaining and less reliant on a partner in handling the day to day practicalities of life. It would of course always be most useful for any Aspie to develop routines and regular systems for daily life, as he is not particularly good at confronting and handling the individual issues that come up.

In regard to the issue of married co-habitation, I am a much older person now. Let's face it, the pressure of sexual arousal and the mating urge is greatly reduced in the older male. The interest is calmer, and less urged by the body. I know that my basic sexual capacity is not in any way what it was, seemingly so short a time ago; and though I occasionally go through the odd regrets or niggles in my masculine psyche, there is no real problem or feeling of having been insulted by nature. I am being aware and honest at last about the problems that marriage always brought me, but which I somehow never seemed to see clearly enough at the time. Was it some sort of masochistic urge that allowed me to go three times into relationships just for the sake of sex or romantic attraction? Who knows! Anyway it is no longer applicable or pressing. I'm indulging my love of simpler living, in a way that is uncontaminated with the obligations to share all my doings with another person.

Just what symptoms and forms of the characteristics are showing in these latter days? What can I point to, to indicate the ways I'm manifesting AS into my 70s? Am I giving myself permission to feel and indulge the real me these days without guilt? I have got over the early compulsion to live with someone. Is it because I no longer feel that I ought to - that it is the correct thing for me to do? It did take me a long time to realize that co-habitation simply did not work for me. And it was hard indeed to admit that this most normal and desirable of human occupations was ultimately unpleasant to me, and decidedly disruptive to the way I wanted to live. Though I have been made to go through uneasy touches of guilt by well-meaning ex-wives, nevertheless when by myself, and considering the matter clearly and soberly, I finish up with no doubt about the rightness of my stance. I could not have felt so right and appropriate about it earlier in my life.

Like my good friend Ed Schneider, I look back on my married life with some regret. Ed says at the end of his chapter 'Retrospect'... "If I were asked to name my biggest failure, it would have to be not being able to give at least one woman happiness with my close companionship over the long haul." (1) I know what he means. Mind you, as he makes plain in his later book, his second marriage has been decidedly successful. He selected a lady this time of compatible talent and temperament, and indeed, it must be added, one who is on the Spectrum with him. But I can look back to only very brief periods of good relations and companionship, and then mainly in the early days with each partner. It is certainly a matter that gives me a severe feeling of humiliation and sadness.

But the closure of each marriage or relationship in my life just had to happen. It was not a situation in any of the cases that could have been readily or realistically corrected by counselling or therapy. For a person like me, who prides himself on his skill or technique at getting on with people, the discovery that I could fail so dismally at the business of marriage was hard indeed.

It is most interesting to read in that very sentence an attitude characteristic of many Asperger persons, and it struck me immediately I'd written it. Just look at it. I did not bemoan the loss of people. I did not wail for the lack of love and companionship. I didn't grieve for a marriage that failed. My major thought is almost insult, or humiliation, to think that it didn't work; and for that matter, that I failed in something that I had felt sure from the start I would be an expert.

Now, what is this thing called love? I comprehend it less and less, I must admit. In earlier times I think I must have taken it for granted that I understood it, and that others held pretty well the same view of it that I had. In later life, as I've got round to observing people and their behaviour more and with greater care, I've actually understood it no better. Somehow though, I have been able to detect a special kind of truth and sincerity in my NT peers as they appear to come into contact with the real 'being' of that other one who is beloved. I admire it, but it still baffles me. I suspect that the nearest thing to it in my life is the affinity I have with my cats. Maybe too there is some way that I can approach towards some equivalent of that beautiful and desirable 'people' feeling, in and through the love and adoration I have for works of art or for certain pieces of music.

I suspect that in my own case, despite getting better and better in many ways at handling the practicalities of daily life, I may be getting more AS as I age. But I vary in the ways I might be exhibiting or revealing the AS to the people about me. Let's consider some of the possible reasons for my feeling more and more AS. Especially since my diagnosis, I am more comfortable and self-assured with the classification. I feel a certain freedom to be myself, to indulge the various characteristics of the Asperger's. In telling my friends and intimates about the condition, I feel that the native peculiarities in my being are no longer quite as worrying or puzzling to them, and I don't have to apologize for them (well, not so often perhaps). And with the confidence that has ensued, I'm assured of the appropriateness of more of my choices, and I'm not so likely to allow myself to be influenced against my will by other people's opinions and pressures.

In coming 'out of the closet' (if you'll pardon the expression) by duly admitting my AS and detailing its complexities and issues in front of audiences during my public presentations, I'm allowing much of it to show. I'm recognizing resultant issues and factors that I've never clearly seen before, and that I am not ashamed to live with. My participation within the Internet discussion and posting lists has been of tremendous value in the process of learning about and sharing this most intimate of all things in my life.

Now I've rarely been shy about confessing all before my therapists and Psychs. The fact that these persons of authority and insight have accepted me and certain of my bizarre characteristics was always a great boost to my confidence. The fact too that some of them have claimed to have been able to learn from me is flattering too. I realize that being free and encouraged to live as an Aspie is proving of some value in the world.

Now for the first time I'm expressing myself in the text of a book. This is something that I always resisted to the utmost. But I must say that crystallizing my thoughts and conclusions on paper, while a little scary, and leaving me exposed and vulnerable, has been an exciting exercise; and perhaps just tops off a process that has gone on irrevocably since my diagnosis.

Certainly the fact that I find no great necessity to fight as much against the inhibitions that I had to live through as a young man both in the work force and within the admittedly limited areas of society that were my fields of being is a relief. Whether in school, work, church, and even within certain of the hallowed halls of the clubs and societies that I frequented, I had to live something of a lie. Those telling phrases... 'Living as if'... 'Pretending to be Normal   ...'Dwelling among Aliens'... etc, I believe, speak volumes in a way that few but Aspies can appreciate. The people of importance in my life are all aware now of my AS diagnosis, and I am happy to say that the greater number appreciate the fact and still seem to like and value me.

In this survey of the possible reasons for my heavier expression or manifestation of the Syndrome in these my later years, I guess I can't leave out the possible reasons that may not be quite so respectable or complimentary.   Is it because I am more self-indulgent in these latter times than I would have been earlier, and am reasonably happy to be my age and take its advantages?   Do I ever exploit my Aspie title unduly, and to the detriment of my integrity and responsibility in life?   If my earlier wives could observe me now that would probably be the verdict.

Thinking back, I can think of at least two of the professionals I've consulted in the past, who would be sceptical of the diagnosis, and who would doubtless point the finger of scorn or disgust at me for hugging a convenient label to my heart, in order to claim some supposed special privileges or exemptions.   I don't bother protesting now, though I did do a little of that in the early stages following the first suggestions that I was AS.

In older age, I haven't got so much of the urge or the pressures to live the 'lies', the pretend life of the Aspie within the alien NT world, that was the natural and of course the necessary accompaniment of living through earlier times.   I can be myself pretty consistently, and no longer have to engage in torment just wondering 'what the heck?' or 'why me?'   I don't have to conform so much.   I don't have to mix so much with folks I don't like or who I feel awkward with.   I don't have to engage in so much of the conventional things with friends and relatives that seemed so important and demanding before.   I can now live out the role of the Elderly Eccentric with impunity, and enjoy it.   I don't feel obliged to seek out the social activities, or to fit with so many of the conventions of the groups that I do belong to.

One thing too, I guess, is that I am not so desperate to seek o from other people the affirmation of myself.   Their approval is not so crucial to me.   If it happens that I manifest some naïve or stupid innocence, then so what?   I can live cheerfully with a reputation that is weird or eyebrow- raising.   I've always had to in the past, but now perhaps I am not so concerned about it.

I am not so compelled to submit to the emotional pressures

from a partner or intimate. I am certainly still vulnerable to other people's emotions, but now I guess I'm more out-going in expressing my feelings about it. I will take more of the initiative in displaying and telling of my Aspie difficulties in dealing with daily life and people problems. It has certainly been of the greatest benefit to express myself in this way; and I have found new freedoms and relief from letting others know what I really feel.

But all the same, as I grow older, I still watch with amazement, as I watch people about me, and especially my own friends and intimates, interacting with their fellows and their relatives. I remain just as puzzled (and maybe even more so) as I observe the apparently very real feeling that is expressed between them. Just what is this beautiful warmth that pours out of one person towards another? I watch in wonder when I see people, whether intimates, friends or just acquaintances chat with a simple spontaneity and relaxation, and with no apparent self-consciousness or reserve.

The very simplest of scenes can make the deepest impression on me. I recall how several years back at the wedding of a close friend, I watched with fascination as the bride walked round in total composure and relaxation, chatting to all and sundry at the tables, and what is more, whether she actually knew them or not. It all looked so natural and spontaneous, and it remained so inconceivable to me.

Speaking of the qualities that may show up in one's presence, I'm reminded of a very interesting thing that was said about me some 20 years ago. I auditioned with a community radio station to do volunteer work on air. Apparently the assessment that was produced gave me top marks in all the necessary attributes for acceptance. Well, that is all except one item got top marks! My voice, it stated, lacked 'warmth'! This I find very interesting. It is quite normal to find that the Aspergers person may speak with a flat tone, and with other dull or uninvolved characteristics. I would like to think that I'm too much of a professional to lack enthusiasm, appropriate emphases or involvement. But apparently I came across on air as lacking in warmth!!! This must surely represent some aspect of the unreal or the unnatural that is often just so Aspie.

Thinking over my career and the various performances that I've delivered, I have to confess that I think this may well be right. I suspect that there is some subtle thing missing in my speaking that would normally express naturalness, intimacy and spontaneity. It may well be one strong reason why I have enjoyed my greatest successes portraying character roles on stage. Straight roles utilising a natural voice and everyday appearance I tended to reject because I experienced them as boring and undemanding. Probably without realizing it, this same 'lack of warmth' made these real and common roles unconvincing both for me and my audiences. Anyway, at the radio station, the deficiency did not deter them from taking me on; and my contributions were well received and appreciated during my tenure.

Apart from the bullying and teasing etc, that I've been through over the years, both within the school setting and even on some occasions in working life, probably my biggest distress on looking back would be to recall any number of embarrassments that my impulsive actions or words have brought me. From my earliest years, I was likely to stick my neck out and make comments that could only be described as naïve, stupid, unfitting for the occasion, and childish. I would make the most outlandish statements or weak jokes, or deliver irrelevant questions even to poor unsuspecting bystanders, that still make me cringe to recall.

Yes indeed, the Aspie tendency to do or say things that don't fit the occasion or the company, was an awkward little habit of mine. I lived deep within my own fantasy world, a world which would be just as likely to burst out at times and in an inappropriate fashion, with outlandish things. Wishing to be recognized as sophisticated or witty, I would try in desperation to be funny, but all too frequently succeeded in being merely stupid or childlike. (2) Heavens above, my attempted cleverness all too often turned out to be thoughtless and embarrassing to all. My reputation was near shattered on a number of occasions, only to be eventually rehabilitated by subsequent actions or words when my good faith and (hopefully) my basic decency was duly recognized again.

I am finding more ways now to utilize my own special talents and creative urges than I ever did before. As well, quite obviously, I've found that more of these urges relate to useful things in the world. Looking back, it is really astonishing to observe just how many of the odd and apparently useless or irrelevant things I studied and tried out in earlier days and that were duly discarded, have become valuable resources either in understanding or in specific skills, that are used regularly and uniquely in these latter days. The greater number of my Aspie inclinations and likes have proven useful, and are utilised today to good purpose.

Sure, I've never been particularly physical in orientation or keen to be constantly 'busy' in the way that many are compelled to be. Still, as an older man, I have had to slow down. I've cut down on activities that were terribly important a few years ago. Even, it must be stated, the vital theatrical interests in acting and directing have been put on hold; and I no longer have a knee-jerk reaction grabbing at any opportunity to perform that might come up. It must be admitted that my declining memory for learning lines is a further reason for not acting on stage any more. My unwillingness to go through the tiresome and frustrating business of directing plays is a turn-up for the books that I would not have anticipated a few short years ago.

Come to think of it, one reason for an apparent increase (or as some well-meaning intimates might describe it - a 'worsening') in my AS, may be the discovery that the pursuit and exploitation of AS, is proving to be a new hobby or even like a vocation and a community service.

With the freer expression of Aspie characteristics, I've released myself from some of the obsessive attempts of earlier times to force myself on other people, or for that matter to deliberately seek out their company. I've made a considerable effort to require as little as possible from others. But this doesn't mean that I am living as a recluse or a hermit. I do have a close circle of a few friends, and these valued ones represent a set of compartments that fulfil certain definite needs in my life. I doubt that I show any signs of developing the skills of 'folk psychology'. I am no closer to being able to 'read minds'. I have no greater empathy. I am no better at comprehending social cues; and I can still flounder embarrassingly when confronted by persons engaging in small talk.

In a crowd, no matter how appropriate to my interests or how closely affiliated they may be with me, I am still lost. The party situation, the reception or opening night gathering, despite the fact that it might be even in my honour, or engaging me as an integral part thereof, is still painful. I still feel, and maybe even more deeply than ever, that I am lost at sea in a fleet of aliens. The business of having to talk, no matter on what subject to any other person, even my best friend, while in the middle of a large and (deafeningly) murmuring crowd, is painful in the extreme. I put on my best artificial face; and through the ensuing inability to hear or understand a word the other person is saying, I'll utter vague generalities, or hide behind a comic or facetious façade, with the prime purpose of getting through as quickly and as safely as possible.

My big worry is whether any of the persons I talk to, is saying something that I strictly ought to know about. Because all too often I come away without the slightest idea of what has been discussed. I just hide behind the "yeah", the "Okay", or the escape route of "sorry, but I've got to grab So and So before he goes. Good to see you", and then a hurried departure in relief.

It's a fact that a large proportion of conversational material that I hear from others comes across to me as unintelligible, so I make no more effort than I ever did, to understand or to run with it. Perhaps I do hide a bit more deliberately behind glib phrases or vague answers than I used to. In the older times, I worried a bit more when I couldn't grasp what was being spoken about. As part of my repertoire, I have a modest but automatic resource of rote talk. If I can divert the conversation into humour too, it is a big relief as I proceed to perform for the general entertainment. But if I can cause the subject of discussion to swing into any of my own areas of expertise or interest, then I have some chance of becoming to some degree real and natural.

It is true to say that I make a point of approaching my friends and associates very much for the purpose of getting my own needs met. In the old days, I would make a bigger effort to please or placate other folk. Sure, I'm not hesitant in stepping out to do someone a favour, or to offer help and sympathy. I don't think I can be classed as being selfish. But I certainly select my chosen interactions and also my friends themselves with the prime purpose of getting the things I want most in life

Strictly speaking, I tend to have less interest in cooperating or sharing with others, nowadays. The difficult and painful business of interacting with other people on small or big jobs has become more awkward for me. Many routine conversations can be boring as hell to me, and it's difficult for me to register or take in every word or idea an associate has uttered. For that matter, I hate to have every word of my own scrutinized critically, and discussed by the associate. I rarely find any desire or need for extra closeness with an intimate.

The Nitty Gritty of my AS Alienation

One of my close friends, who I shall refer to as William, is a retired gentleman from the legal profession; and he has indicated a great deal of interest in my Asperger's condition. Just recently I was telling him about some of the rather bizarre manifestations of AS, with a concentration on the difficulty I have in ordinary everyday conversations.

Now I watch him with friends and with strangers, exhibiting a striking warmth and a fluency of interested talk. He is happy to converse with just about anyone for maybe half an hour to an hour or more; and I look on with admiration, and wonder at his appearance of genuine involvement in the other's issues and daily life. He is obviously being spontaneous and genuine in his interest.

Now in the same situation, I will fall back automatically on my standard questions, phrases, jokes and pat comments. I feel no interest spontaneously bursting from me, as I converse; and barely four or five minutes will have gone by before I'm scratching the bottom of the barrel, as it were, and looking for something further to say. Sure I know a few of the 'right' things to say or to ask; but they are definitely artificial and probably political in their intent. If I didn't have them to repeat by rote, I would dry up after the first few words

Obviously since some of the things I say in these circumstances are echoes or rehearsals of the things that the natural NT person would be saying, others appear to take me on trust, and don't offer an obvious rejection. But in company as for example with the aforementioned William, while confronting or just chatting to strangers, I find myself freezing after those first few obvious and well rehearsed lines, and watching with astonishment or admiration at the contrasting way he keeps on going with a clear relish and a natural flow of interest.

So as it happens, William seems to need regular reminders of the difficulty I truly experience moment by moment; and I have had to work really hard to convince him again of the various stresses I have to cover up in the simplest of conversations. Despite my natural reserve or embarrassment over the business of confessing that even in talk with a close friend like himself, I'm battling these difficulties, I confessed to him that it is literally WORK to engage in everyday conversation. I put in quickly and reassuringly that I am very keen to keep and propagate a good relationship with him as I am with all my closest friends; and thus I am freely prepared to go through this process despite its awkwardness, in order to talk to him.

A look came to his face, and a tone to his voice of immeasurable hurt and tragedy it seemed to me, as he murmured something to the effect of "Oh, it shouldn't have to be like this!" On one previous discussion about the same matter, he suggested that I should just be totally honest and really myself when with him; and duly asked what that would be like for me. I told him frankly that relaxing down in such a fashion, with no effort exerted to keep in contact, would just have the effect of my losing communication altogether. It's perhaps a little bit like needing to fall asleep, but forcing myself to remain awake in order to be able to hear or learn some much needed information.

My third wife once asked me as an exercise, to just be totally myself for a little while and talk to her only as I felt, and as I would respond to her communication without any of the usual 'political' agenda, and without this constant forcing of my attention. Well, it was hard to do, but on getting lost in my self as usual, I took two or three times the usual period to fasten my attention onto her. I found myself getting rather disoriented, as I had to wrench myself out of my inner world. As far as my verbal response was concerned, there was nothing much in my words that would come out spontaneously or naturally. The greater part of what I answered was constructed out of habitual and formal phrases, and was designed to satisfy the demands of the moment and to put a stop to the interruption. There was certainly no sense of genuine communion with her.

It seems extraordinary to me that my NT friends and 'intimates' have just no conception of how I have to fabricate or construct the most common and basic sentences and appropriate words in my discussions.

I am reminded of the fact that in the act of sex, I have never been guided or led by anything that could be described as passion or lust. It is simply inconceivable to me that in the profound states of sexual intimacy one may expect to be carried along by something of a mindless excitement and impetus. It was hard enough to get round to the technicalities of the positioning of body and limbs, let alone to the spontaneous and mad expression of love and passion. I would have to be thinking at any point about just what I needed to do next. ...Well now I must kiss... Now I must touch, now I must start to move here, etc etc

I recall one young woman (with whom again, I had no 'relationship', I might quickly add) asking me incredulously "But can't you just let go, and allow the body to take over?" I told her immediately that if I attempted to do that, I'd most likely just go to sleep. The act of sex for me is a totally voluntary and calculated thing; and doubtless not liable to represent a very satisfying thing to any regular woman. Almost a 'sex by numbers' routine, perhaps?

Another area of non-conformity in me is in my feelings about children. I've written elsewhere about my ambivalence towards children and even aspects of it regarding my own offspring. I do go through a considerable discomfort when confronted with the demand or expectation of dealing with small children. Babies are not too much trouble because one can get away with briefly making just the usual rote comments and an appropriate 'Goo Goo' or 'Boo', with the expected murmurings of congratulations or admiration to the parents before moving on. But small children that can talk and take an interest, represent a very great difficulty and embarrassment, making me dry up very quickly. It seems that I am very attractive to little kids, and I'm not really at all sure why.

As it is, I feel a certain distinct fear when I have to talk to a small kid for more than a moment or two, especially if it happens to be asking me questions or engaging my interest in its activities or observations. I get not a little nervous I must confess. My fear is of course, not of the child itself, but of the obligation to communicate. The very business of understanding just what the child is saying is bad enough; but having to dispense with the processes of adult thinking can be a sheer nightmare. Of course, I cannot discuss with a child any of the matters that interest me in life; and I have to painfully rack my brains to find things to say.

Strictly speaking this floundering state is not terribly different from what it is like when I'm engaged with an adult. The essential difference would be that with the latter there is always the chance, however slim it might be that the exchange will bring up some topic of interest, or lead to an activity that will skate around that tricky business of purely human talk. In tandem with a child however, you have to literally forget yourself, and implant yourself into the world of the little one. This is desperately hard for a self-centred Aspie like myself.

Confessions of an Unashamed Asperger

Some thirty odd years ago, in view of the ready fertility I had exhibited during my first marriage, I became a donor to a Sperm Bank. I saw nothing strange or anomalous in the decision; and felt that the activity could represent a humane and public-spirited offering. I must make it plain that there was in those days no remuneration or material reward of any kind that came back in return to a donor. In my enthusiasm I made something of an attempt to interest other males of my work-place in the matter. It just shocked and bewildered me to hear the responses they offered. None gave any assent to the proposition, and most appeared unable to explain why they demurred. At least two or three with their refusal, presented something of an agonized expression, along with the protest that they simply could not let themselves father a child which they could not personally raise. This instinctive devotion to, or possessiveness over a child born under these conditions, was totally inconceivable to me.

It has been of great fascination to me to observe a few of my closest male friends in recent months, with their attitudes to their children; and I explain this in another essay. (3) Well to put it mildly, I have to admit I was stunned at their testimonies. And let's face it, these were just among my immediate male contacts. Just how could I have missed out on these profound and presumably rewarding devotional experiences? Several times I was asked whether I felt at all sad or deprived at never having experienced anything like these. I thought about it for a time, and eventually had to confess that I've never felt any actual sense of loss or missing about the matter. It seems a bit like being asked if I feel pained because I can't fly like a bird. The answer of course is absolutely No! What I haven't experienced, and further what is not at all real or conceivable to me, won't cause me any hurt.

I can see so clearly now that it is difficult in the extreme to explain the real problems that I face in these human connections. There appears to be no way to describe my conception of the faculties I don't possess. So the NT reader must forgive my clumsy explanations here. Some may well find these thoughts somewhat offensive or shocking.

I'm fully aware when I have difficulty with people, that I am like them. I'm confronting someone of the same species as myself. Intellectually and objectively, I know that they have gone through much the same experiences, problems and emotions that I have. But all this knowledge is merely a detached and intellectual process. As I've tried to explain elsewhere, when I'm confronted with another human being, I am seeing, hearing and feeling a collection of separate and disconnected bits of information. This collection of data does not combine to make a person for me - well, not in any total and coordinated fashion that I can be aware of.

Perhaps I could even put it this way; apart from the fact that the person is clothed in a living body that shows self-motivated motion, the major difference between this individual and a printed description on paper, (like a CV for example) is that the real individual is totally unpredictable. He is capable of responding to his environment or to his companion in a multitude of ways. Naturally this leaves the person as a source of uncertainty, and, I suppose like all people, as being potentially dangerous or threatening.

I've had some individuals confront me with the suggestion that I've deliberately avoided facing my 'demons', and that I need to confront the things that cause me discomfort. I've been told that if I had actually done some of the things I dislike, and dealt directly with people in the way that is hard or embarrassing, I'd get over many of the inhibitions or quirks that I manifest, and that I identify as being AS in nature. I don't think any of this is particularly true. No-one can actually accuse me of shutting myself away from people. The very fact that three marriages and in the process living in co-habitation for some 21 years altogether, must show that. I have managed in a fumbling and peculiar way at times to deal with most people that have come into my life. But it HAS been a matter of fumbling, in a way that most strangely other folk don't seem to have been able to detect. As I said small children seem to like me; and there have been really a good number of adults who have appreciated and commended me throughout my life. Just why and how has this happened?

Well, I think that from my earliest years, I've been

brainwashed and trained (or programmed) to assume the general facts about other people. It's rather like the way that a computer is fed a lot of data and information. I know how other folk eat, drink, sleep, work, love, recreate and etc. I have read about human psychology and I have absorbed a technical repertoire of human conversation. And that is about all.

When I look at another person, I see a face with its degrees of attractiveness, along with its changing expression. It may represent an object of curiosity. If a woman, it may bear some degree of sexual interest or curiosity. Simply 'being' with another person for its own sake brings me no particular pleasure or human satisfaction, regardless of whether the person be male or female, young or old. I hear a voice and I observe a series of actions and gestures. I hear the voice telling things, or asking questions. But I do not directly detect a person underneath. (4)   Like a computer I have been programmed to have a repertoire of questions and comments that I can call upon in order to fill up some of the conversation gaps.

That person is essentially like a body that is housing another collection of data, to which I have to offer feedback. And in doing so, I have the hope and expectation that he or she will exhibit some degree of comfort in my presence, and just maybe express some degree of interest in my pursuits. Then any friction or conflict will be avoided, and some practical benefit might be achieved. When I meet someone new, I'm calculating from the first how they may fit into my life and how they might contribute to my interests.

If I think that I might be of service to the other person, perhaps just providing them with information, a useful introduction or an action of simple kindness, then from my point of view, I'm happy enough about it all. My own natural sense of compassion, mixed with respect and sympathy, may motivate me to offer more to the individual than just a bit of talk.

A larger part of the way I deal with others can be seen as a self-centred pursuit. With those merely pragmatic day by day contacts, it keeps the wheels turning, and guarantees the maintenance of good relations. On the other hand, with the achievement of mutually advantageous 'business', my personal enthusiasms are propagated and fulfilled; and it will be taken for granted that the other will found a satisfaction and progress in the same way. Fundamentally the contact one has, must be based on the detection of the person beneath the facade - the real being.

But you can't have an intellectual and remote or detached conversation or engagement in a sophisticated activity when confronted with a child! There is a demand that you have to simply 'BE' there. Clearly one has to inwardly recognize this pure essential quality of personhood there. The words which are required to be spoken are not of the 'head'. It is some sort of heart to heart communication that is supposed to happen; and this is what is just so unnatural to me. Interesting to see the parallel way Edgar Schneider speaks of his association with children. (5)

Now it might be asked by the reader just how I got on during my own brief periods of fatherhood. Well going back to my own children, it must be understood that this was in some ways to be considered and seen as 'business'. I was designated by nature to be 'the father', and the children were my responsibility, representing a pretty solid job of work and on-going activity. Thus I had something of a pragmatic and active involvement with them. It was truly my inherent business.

I guess it would be with just an attitude of resigned acceptance now that I deal with children when I have to. I endeavour to relax down as deep as I can go, and to exchange the necessary brief words with the infants. Recent invitations to an associate's party for his child prompted me to attend for a short time only. I made a very rapid withdrawal after some half an hour.

Oh yes, it has been said that I could do better, and maybe would mingle more happily if I were a 'drinker', and could duly consume one of the proferred alcoholic beverages along with the rest of the guests. As it is I must admit that adult parties or gatherings can be a bit easier or acceptable to me than are the children's parties. But ultimately the same problems apply.

References.

(1) Schneider, Edgar.   Discovering my Autism.   Page 115.
(2) See Essay On   A Humour so Perverse'.
(3) See Essay 'On   My Own Children'
(4) See Essay 'On   Knowing another Person'.
(5) Schneider, Edgar   Discovering my Autism.   Page 83

Chapter 13   I WOULDN'T BE ANYONE ELSE.

On Being Myself

I've frequently been accused of appearing smug and pleased with myself.   But apparently I'm not alone among high functioning Aspies of seldom wishing I could be someone else.

Perhaps at times I've had a genuine little wish that I possessed just one or other of the certain useful characteristics that I've seen in the NTs about me. But this is rare. I am generally pleased to be who I am.

As a child, and coming out of an old fashioned church centred family, I really believed and felt that I belonged to an elite group that alone knew the truth about Life, God and the Universe.   I was clearly covering up a profound sense of inadequacy that was promoted by the rejection I endured from my peers.   It is most embarrassing now to look back on some of my snobbish and superior ways in those early times. In the long run, I did learn in my own way (and very often the hardest way) that blind confidence about truth was simplistic and ephemeral; and no matter what conclusions I came to in myself, there was always someone or some book or authority that could make me question my ideas.

I do value my own unique interests and skills now. But it took me a long time to get over the worst of the sense of inferiority that plagued me from my school days. This perception left me with the feeling that alone among my peers I was without the prospect of any good job.   My failures at University stressed this, and had me feeling that my ability to stand up and be counted was sadly deficient. I guess that I always had or showed the signs of talents and inclinations that should by rights have proven to be valued and prized in the world. But it must be admitted, the mere fact of being able to speak well in public (along with an elevated IQ) doesn't take you very far by itself, unless you have something important to talk about, and for that matter, the necessary vocational skills that other people will recognize and value.

Confessions of an Unashamed Asperger

My training in radio techniques and the accompanying acting skills were pleasing and gratifying; but unfortunately at the time of my schooling, radio was fast going out, and television was coming in. I was too immature at the time for the latter as I looked awfully young, and had nothing about me of the slick, uninhibited and sophisticated sort of Presenter of the kind that was necessary for the profession. I was at my best when well hidden behind a microphone with a script in my hands. So I became a Radio Announcer.

Yet it must be acknowledged that my eventual year and a half in radio was a time of non-distinction, to put it mildly. Added to that was the fact that there was some sort of a demand even in a country radio station that you be versatile and sophisticated, and very capable on a fast delivery breakfast session. One also needed particular skills in whipping disks on and off a record playing turntable.

Now this was in the early 1960s. Unfortunately too, a breakfast session commencing perhaps at 5.30am in the morning demands that one be awake, convincing and entertaining. I was dead-pan and very flat I fear, at that time of day. Looking back I can see this very lack of coordination needed for the fundamental job of switching records on a turntable and flicking switches back and forth for some two or three hours, found me clearly inadequate. Also even though behind a microphone, and without being under the visual scrutiny of the great public out there, I was still expected to be communicative and friendly or warm. No, it didn't work. You still had to like and reach people, in a way that does not come naturally to the Aspie. I was not the requisite spontaneous and earthy person who could be suitably uninhibited, as he projected a real personality.

My attempts through life at doing things with my hands were dismal failures. In a period when I was unemployed, I tried a couple of types of craft work, going through the required training with all the goodwill in the world. I soon learnt! I'm the sort of person who will set out to do a craft or handyman sort of job, and get delayed for a couple of hours just trying to get the lid off a bottle, or struggling with the preliminary job of removing a screw from an appliance. Or again, maybe even more humiliating, endeavouring to work out just how to square up a crooked piece of timber I've just been sawing. No, Trade and Craft work was simply not viable for this person.

Through my years in the public service, I did get more and more experience in the extra-curricular sorts of work and activity that appealed to me, and I progressively learned just what I could do well and pleasingly. I reverted in my fifties to the work of the Public Platform, as I put together audio-visual presentations for the public, on some of my favourite topics. I discovered that I had skills in this field and a somewhat unique sort of approach in my presentation to an audience. I returned too, to my earliest love, which was Acting. I found an Agent, and took on a few jobs as an extra in Television and Film. When I eventually retired from the workforce, I labelled myself as a professional actor, and found more and more to do in these spheres.

I can aver now that I would honestly not want to be anyone other than who I am. My particular faults and weaknesses are quite familiar to me, and I can live with them. I have always tended to fail in occupations and situations of the regular kinds. I was never any good at set and conventional areas of study or training. But my public speaking skills developed fast, as well as my understanding of the Thespian art. By the time of my retirement in 1994, I had a fine reputation in the community theatre scene in my city, with many opportunities for stage roles.

I have got to the point where I can see clearly that there is practically no one else around who does just what I do. All the things in which I've achieved success, have been in unique areas of study or practice that are not in the normal range. And my essential qualifications have come about autonomously, and not from official institutions or teaching persons. I do best when I pursue things by myself, under my own steam and at my own pace. The only success I've ever had with a formal bit of study was in the form of one little unit, in a mail operated, but legitimate University course. My choice of topic was on the subject of 19th century art. This I succeeded at very well; but it must be recalled that it did happen to be a subject with which I was already pretty well acquainted, and in which I have had experience in front of the public.

I do value greatly the particular friends I've accumulated. These are mostly unusual people, and ones who invariably have some activity or interest in common with me. I don't know of any folks of my last 20 or 30 years who became friends merely for the sake of friendship alone.

When I took on new jobs during my working days, I sometimes took up to 6 months to a year to be able to identify my various work-mates, being cursed as I am with lousy facial recognition ability. I would often confuse two or three of them, and for some peculiar reason, especially the women. It would turn out to be particularly embarrassing at times, when I would be told to take some document or file and give it to person X or person Y. More than once I recall I would hopefully and blindly pick the wrong individual, not wanting after working with them all for maybe three or four months, to have to ask "Are you person X?" Then there would be the inevitable inquisition on why did I give it to person A when I had been told to give it to person X or Y. Such a process of confusion doesn't make it practicable to make friends or to socialize easily.

Happily, I do manage though, through good fortune or divine guidance, to locate those very few who are good for me to be with. However, I think I still carry some of the wariness that I exhibited in my married relations. This meant that I was never truly confident about my ability to hang on to the friend any more than I could an intimate. At any moment the relationship might nose-dive. But nevertheless, I have found a greater confidence in these my later years, that I am capable of finding a select group of people who will like me almost as much as I like me.

I see myself first and foremost as a person, rather than a male. Though totally heterosexual, I have few particularly masculine characteristics that stand out in me. I seem to have a series of gaps in my gender makeup. For example, as I have endeavoured to describe it, I possess something of a male 'urge' rather than the male 'instinct'. Presumably it explains a lot about so much of my fumbling efforts in my life, to be a male, and to deal romantically with women.

I don't choose my friends just for the reason that they might boost my ego, or confirm my opinion of myself. My best friends are there for two major reasons. First, they don't interfere or intrude. And second, because they have essential interests in common with me. There is a real me that can go on living in my own inner private planet, at the same time as my virtual self lives on this mundane planet, and interacts with its inhabitants.

This virtual self is like a projection of myself … an acted out manifestation of me… a computerised image and something of a shadowy version of the real me. My best friends are the special folk who manage to break through occasionally and to contact that distant and real me on my own planet. The other people, who aren't my best friends, see and are aware of the virtual me only. Now, that virtual me is highly susceptible to hurt, criticism, manipulation, emotional blackmail, etc. Though they are not aware of it, the best friends are able to see through a window into that other world, and can glimpse, I believe, something of the real me. Of course they would not be aware of this fact. My marriage partners have I think, fluctuated wildly between their occasional perceptions of the real me and their common perception of the projected me, and naturally becoming very confused. Their lack of knowledge of a real me has shown itself by the fact that they were typically unable to predict just what I might be likely to do under unusual circumstances.

I think I've always had a strong and clear sense of just who I am. But the business of living in that world of other people just complicates the way my projected self organises its life and determines its path. For this reason, depending on whether people discern the real me or the projected me, I give out strange and mixed signals and identifications. I'm aware that this could sound like a Schizoid-type neurosis; but the fact remains that I do manage to run my life pretty successfully. I retain good health, hold down this select group of close friends, and maintain a pretty good relationship and reputation within the larger circle. As an actor, I am held in good respect for integrity and reliability. Above all, it must be said that my pussycats hold me in the closest love and respect. And what greater compliment can any AS individual require in life?

My eventual first viewing of the old movie Rain Man just a couple of years ago represented a wonderful experience. Wouldn't I just love to portray an autistic character on stage or screen! Though mine is a thoroughly manageable HFA with no savant abilities, I could still follow every mood or extravagant feeling that Dustin Hoffman depicted.

The major advantages I've enjoyed that must have mitigated against the potential disablement of the Asperger Syndrome, would have to include the following. A good intelligence, which it was pointed out to me, enabled me to make decisions and moment by moment adjustments in my life that provided me at least with the appearance of socialising skills. Then there was a conscientious and sympathetic nature that held some degree of concern about other people's feeling as well as a considerable patience.

My sense of humour has been invaluable at all times; and has taken on at times, I admit, a somewhat perverted course. (1) Many of us Aspies do tend to take serious things a bit more lightly than do our NT confreres; and just maybe, the opposite can apply as well, when we find ourselves taking the lighter things rather too seriously. Anyway, humour has always been healing for me, enabling me to laugh at myself, and not take myself too seriously.

A vital advantage was the fact that I grew up in a very secure loving and encouraging family, and that gave me a clear sense of my own identity, and the chance to discover my interests and my talents. Then there was inherent good health and a practical pragmatic disposition that has helped me to maintain it.

I've manifested enough commonsense and financial awareness to be able to keep my affairs in good order and to make suitable decisions in life. I have an inquiring mind, that has enjoyed the search and study into my own extensive psyche; as well as a sufficiently open mind to accept the things that I find there, regardless of the shocks and surprises involved.

It is interesting to note that I had the unwitting help of a mother who as an overly clinging and intrusive parent, enforced degrees of socialising and interaction upon me. Presumably this factor was effective in giving me the advantages of an excellent home life for an Aspie. As I claim elsewhere, I appear to have had extremely good luck (or Karma) in my choices and contacts, as well as in the opportunities that have come my way.

It goes without saying that a big advantage I have enjoyed has been the fact that my AS is high functioning. I have never been literally disabled by the Syndrome. Though many in my life have thought I was strange, no-one ever detected the need for a specific diagnosis. I value my own company and the peacefulness of my inner world. Then there are the cats that I love so much to have sharing in my life. Cats have so many wonderful features that complement my life and my meditations. I value my self-sufficiency - to be able to get on day by day without relying on another person to cook, wash, sew or house-keep. Sure, there are things that I occasionally need others to do around the house, or to deal with electronic equipment that I can't handle. I just bring people in to fix those issues. They don't usually interrupt my inner life, or disturb my essential autonomy.

Then, as any book lover will understand, I can say that my books are like close friends. They bring me real joy, never interrupt and never argue and contribute so very much to the riches of my life. There is my love of solitude, which I see as a remarkable gift. It almost seems like a religious vocation, that this life was a singular opportunity to seek out the truth or the beauty and goodness that means so much to me.

I can feel smugly grateful I don't smoke, or drink for that

matter. I don't take recreational drugs. I don't feel impelled towards taking risks in daily life. With no involvement in physical activities or sports, I retain a relative safety in life and limb. Happily I seem to appeal to sufficient persons to attract sufficient friends and colleagues into my life. It was probably my long-suffering patience more than anything that got me through my working life in the public service. So that after 29 years, I came through with a usable superannuation payout, and was able to invest in whatever fashion that I wished. I followed my nose as it were, and it seems after all these years, that I did make the most suitable decisions on how to handle the funds.

Now in regard to the business of the most suitable investment, I can say that sharing the decisions with an intimate, like a partner, would have been most painful for me with so much negotiation, research and discussion. This would have driven me round and round in circles; whereas working by myself, I was fully prepared to make mistakes, as I usually am in daily life. As it happens, my instincts led me largely in the right ways, leading often to advantages never dreamed of by my old work place associates.

Of course it must be admitted that strictly speaking, those same old colleagues would have been sharing with wives and partners; and thus would have invested the greater part of their income and ambitions into family and children, and presumable have gained something of the blessings of family, in ways I have not known. Since I found myself alone at a suitable time in life, the interference of family demands and pressures didn't take away my available earnings along with the potential for investments of the kind that I chose. I consider this a great advantage for myself. I was lucky to have been raised in a family that instilled the practical and ethical values I largely hold to this day, as well as fostering peace and quiet along with the more intellectual or artistic life. I had the benefit too, of locating and affiliating with groups, churches and fraternities that encouraged and enlarged my talents as well as my pleasures.

I was advantaged too, in being born at the time that I was, and entering the workforce in the early 50s when I went to the city to live. It's still startling to recall just how I went into a bookshop I fancied, and speaking to the Manager over the counter, asked if I could get a job there. He simply said "Yes and when will you be able to start?" Unimaginable in these more straightened times, I fear. Other jobs I took on were not as productive as this one was, as my opportunities to learn about books and to enlarge my library and knowledge were magnified here.

Fate took an interesting turn when one of my theatrical associates invited me to join in a touring show, and for a year I trotted round the country on a new learning adventure. Jobs like the radio announcing of course, did give me valuable experience; and the eventual joining of the public service, put me in a position for some 29 years that kept me safe and well fed, until retirement. Advantage after advantage, I believe. Sure, I now have almost everything I can want in life, especially the chance to study and read what I want, and to work at lectures and at acting and film making. A beautiful house too, that gives me the space that I can psychically fill out in my consciousness. Big advantages and many blessings, indeed!

On the Fantasy of being 'Cured'

It is apparently not uncommon for small children to have fantasies or nagging feelings that there are 'secrets' about their life, or maybe about their origins. Bad or deficient relations with a parent may make them wonder if they really belong in the particular family. Religious beliefs and theories may make them wonder about their own states of goodness or Godliness. Now when it comes to children with disabilities, and the natural comparison that they will make of themselves against the normality of their peers, it is pretty well to be expected that they will fantasize over the ultimate reasons for their problems.

I'm not sure that much research has ever been done into the 'being' and 'identity' fantasies that abound in the minds of young persons with Asperger Syndrome. It may well be that few will have had the right questions asked of them by their therapists, in order to determine such a matter. For that matter, many therapists, at least until recently, have appeared unable to imagine that persons on the Spectrum do indulge in fantasy lives at all.

But just what sorts of imaginings will you be going through, if you have always felt like an alien, an outcast and one who doesn't seem to fit the everyday and the normal? As we well know, the taunts and bullying that all too many children undergo from their peers will bring about innumerable troubles and maladjustments; and the inherent bewilderment about their status in the world, that is typical of the mind of the Asperger, must be pretty drastic to cope with.

In the days prior to my hearing of Aspergers Syndrome, as I've stated elsewhere, I made copious notes about myself, my quirks and my peculiarities. I was not able to determine just what it all meant. I did feel like an alien, since somehow the way other people described their social experiences and emotions seemed foreign to my thinking.

On the surface, it would seem that I had been adequately socialised by my family, thank heaven. I knew pretty well just how to get on reasonably well with my peers, my work associates, etc. But a nagging feeling kept hitting me that I was not quite as with it, as I managed to appear in my day to day living. Was there something inherently wrong with me? And if so, then what exactly was 'wrong' or out of balance? At times it seemed that I was living with the greatest of difficulty, moment by moment, while restraining my real self.

Well, some twenty odd years ago, an idea struck me. I was not someone who was naturally whole or correctly socialised. Somehow it seemed that I had been 'cured' of something. But what on earth could it possibly have been? No-one had any idea or had ever suggested that there was any discrepancy in my integrated self. Sure, I had occasionally given other people the impression that I was eccentric or odd. This was not all that surprising. The things I wanted to study or practise were marginal things, and alternative or esoteric in nature. I didn't drink, drive, swim, dance, smoke etc, and I was not drawn to mixing with my peers, and swapping small talk. I just went through the motions of normal living and feeling, and I sort of skated over the business of being part of the world at all.

The older I got, the more that word 'ALIEN' kept hitting me. There actually were big discrepancies in my psyche. I found that I was genuinely different from my associates and the people in the world about me as I came in contact with outsiders and drop-outs, as well as eccentrics. But these others who manifested peculiarities didn't seem to be as respectable as me. They seemed to be lost in pessimism, in depression and all sorts of misdoings, and not to mention their destructive addictions.

So where was I uniquely different? I had to keep some sort of restraint on myself, so that my slack, inefficient self didn't take over, and so that certain of my childlike characteristics didn't manifest too embarrassingly. It seemed not so much as though I was living a lie, as it were; but perhaps I was a bit like a person who once had or been born with an illness or an unstable mental condition, and who had learned or been trained to cope with it, and to behave in an acceptable fashion. I had been cured somehow, of something unknown and unsuspected, and there were only shadows or barely recalled memories of what had ailed me. If only we had known of Asperger's Syndrome in those early days!

Various terms and labels had been heaped onto me over my life, especially by the women who had been with me. I recall being called narcissistic, schizoid, passive-aggressive, angry young man (many years ago, that one!), having a tending to Personality Disorder, and even being Devil-possessed. Once, prior to knowledge of Aspergers Syndrome, I found an encyclopaedic reference to the common features attributed to the Psychopathic personality. I was deeply intrigued, as certain of the characteristics sounded like me. Of course, I didn't have any of the anti-social or heartless bits, but some of what might be best described as the un-human things seemed to fit. If only I had known what I know now!!!

Anyway, to follow up on the possibility, I made some inquiries, and a patronising professional good humouredly referred me for diagnostic tests, provided by an independent psychologist.

This lady made use of the TAT, or Thematic Apperception Test, and lost no time in getting me to free associate with some twenty or more black and white line drawings of people in sundry situations and relations with each other. I duly found it very stimulating, and a fun opportunity for the indulgence of my fluid imagination. The lady apparently considered it beneath her dignity to even refer in her report to my psychopathic fancy; but provided a very interesting summary of her assessment several days later. (2)

In relating the above story in my public talks, I quote what is probably one of my best jokes in the way of an Aspergers play on words. I go on to say "And just think... if I had turned out to be a Psychopath, then this presentation tonight could be described as a Hannibal Lecture!!" (Boom Boom). For some reason, this usually goes over pretty well, which is very gratifying to an old theatrical ham, like myself.

My other major piece of word play on the subject suggests that in having me come into the family in the first place, it was perhaps like my parents going into MacDonald's and ordering a meal. My father wanted a hamburger, my mother wanted a chickenburger. But of course, what they finished up being served with, was - an Asperger. Perhaps not quite so good a joke, but it's not a bad throw-away line. Of course that comparison or rhyme of Asperger with hamburger is not original with me.

An Aspie you Ain't!

It would make a fascinating exercise to tabulate the verbal reactions people make on the announcement that one has been diagnosed with Aspergers. I recall one old friend, whose daughter had become a most successful Clinical Psychologist, looked at me a bit pityingly and told me something to the effect of "Ah well, if my daughter got hold of you for a few weeks, she'd soon have you over that little fantasy."

After a few weeks of knowing me, one Psychologist that I was recommended to, simply refused to admit me to the hallowed halls of Aspergia. He declared that there was just no way that I could have the Syndrome. Presumably I looked him in the eye too directly, and appeared just too sociable.

I might compare this sort of misjudgement about Aspies with the misunderstanding of persons in the homosexual community. I suspect that in the old days, the only 'Gays' who came to the attention of the psychiatrists and counsellors, were the ones who were badly disturbed emotionally, or those who fell foul of the law. Naturally as a consequence the good professionals of those times tended to carry a limited idea of just what homosexuality really was; and they found it hard to conceive that the community might just have even a few well-balanced people among them. Now that society has cast aside many of the old prejudices about the Gay population, a more balanced idea of their being has happily become known. And so, extremes in particular traits and mannerisms that used to be regarded as typical of the class, and thus to be deplored as pathological, are now seen to be just that... as some of the extremes.

Just so, for those professionals who even today still deal with none but the more disturbed Aspies, the thesis that there might happen to be some reasonably well adjusted adults with Aspergers, would seem somewhat unlikely. If, they argue, the person being interviewed or assessed is not singularly disabled, and if he appears to be able to look after himself, or can hold down a job or get himself married, and needs no mentor -well then, ipso facto, he just can't be an Aspie.

There was one old friend, a doctor who I managed to track down after some 25 years, to talk to again. On my hearing of my diagnosis, he actually mused "Hm, I just wonder who you paid or persuaded to give you that diagnosis." For all his learning (and he's a pretty bright chap), he apparently hadn't been confronted with the most up to date findings on Aspergers Syndrome.

I think too of my brother, an admirable being at all times. He was singularly unimpressed when I told him. I suspect that it was only after I had described my successful lecture appearances, in front of audiences that combined professionals and other diagnosed Aspies that he tended to take the idea at all seriously. I still have a few misgivings about his averred acceptance. As a typical elder brother perhaps, he has always treated my special interests or eccentric pursuits with amused though indulgent disdain. But just the same, I have to give it to him he has been most kind in promoting this present interest by providing me with a couple of exceptionally brilliant books, along with some useful articles and press releases.

I have learnt not to be too concerned when friends or associates I've told of the AS diagnosis and characteristics, just laugh it off, or reckon the idea to be a typical result of my obsessive readings in popular psychology books. It is doubtless, they condescendingly assume, either symptomatic of a Psychic Hypochondria, or maybe even the manifestation of an infantile desire to be special and 'different'. Another popular comment is that the label offers one an excuse for different behaviour.

One lesson that has taken me some years to get to grips with since my diagnosis is this business of the standard preconceived notions of just what actually constitutes Asperger's Syndrome. With all the good will in the world, even some professionals, who have the experience and over-view of a wide variety of Aspies, can give the impression in their writings that there is only one single consistent pattern of thinking and behaviour that is common to all AS individuals.

Like many innocent persons on the Spectrum, when I was first diagnosed, (and for that matter, before, while I was still anticipating a diagnosis) I jumped to the happy conclusion that we would have to be all alike. I rejoiced in wonderful fantasy dreams about what a predominantly Asperger's world would be like. All of us very special people (angelic beings every one, of course!) would be capable of sharing a unique society, wherein there would automatically be justice, tolerance, and universal understanding. We would have similar ideals, needs, interests and so on; and no longer being a despised and rejected class, we would all be tolerant and progressive. We could and would create a wonderful world.

Though I've had to change my mind well and truly, especially under the influence of biographical literature by and about Aspies, as well as from meeting a number of the 'fraternity', I still find myself pulled back to this Aspie fantasy at times, and I literally do have to fight it off.

I can never forget my first attendance at a talk given by a prominent person with Autism/Aspergers. It all felt so right and familiar, and I looked forward enormously to meeting the speaker at the close of the lecture. But I got a shock when on introducing myself, the speaker seemed just to close down - to retreat back into self; and was in no way available in the fashion I had anticipated, even in the company of a fellow Aspie.

What a further surprise it was for me when I first met and talked to other Aspies in the social situation. It was I admit, a profound disillusionment and let down for me. The anticipated Utopia of Aspiedom proved to be a chimera, and I was fooling myself. I saw just as many difficulties, conflicts, misconceptions and confusions as I'd experienced with the NTs. I was disappointed to observe that I could get just as confused and lost or uncomfortable when listening to these fellow 'paragons of virtue' as I had with the NTs. In fact I learnt to value more the clarity of speech and thinking that I found among many of my NT friends. Furthermore, the experience forced me to watch the ways in which I might be coming across to them in return.

I certainly didn't go into a feeling of oneness with them individually, nor did I automatically become close friends with them. Just occasionally, an introduction over the phone suggested to me that there would be close affinities; but the subsequent meeting in person was all too often a let-down.

Now don't get me wrong... I'm not saying that I have no sense of oneness with the Aspie population. From the first time in my life, perhaps some fourteen years ago, when in excitement and fascination I listened to interviews with Autistics on the radio, I felt a genuine and unique sort of affinity with the people presenting. These have been perhaps the only occasions on which I've experienced anything that might have been described as empathy. Regardless of our different views and experience, or the severity of our AS symptoms, somehow I knew just what they were on about. I saw such films as Rain Man, Man of Flowers, and A Beautiful Mind; and the thinking behind the AS behaviour appeared crystal clear and just so familiar to me. It doesn't mean that I necessarily came to the same conclusions as the characters in these films, but I could clearly see where they were coming from.

As it happens, we vary enormously, I discovered, in everything from our daily habits and requirements, our attitudes to other people, our processes of eating and of hygiene, etc. We have among us optimists and pessimists, depressives galore, as well as quite a few who are burdened by a lot more problems than just their AS. Just a study of the varying codes of ethics that we've developed will show the variations. Look at the attitudes to religion among Aspies. In these few years, I have run across just as many spiritual (and non-spiritual) paths followed by Aspies as in the great unwashed of the NT population on the outside. I know vehement and educated Atheists, beautiful and sincere born-again Christians, as well as respectable conservative church people of all creeds. (I have to add, AND well-informed Pagans like myself). I discovered that it is not at all easy to delineate the basic essentials that are most common among us all.

Only this evening, I was taking a look through a number of the volumes on my Aspergers shelf, and got fascinated at the variations between the characters of the AS males who populate the accounts. It was a sobering experience to read these records again. Look at Patrick McCabe in 'Living and Loving with Asperger's Syndrome'. Compare with the fascinating and chaotic Danny, in Jacob's 'Loving Mr Spock'. Then shift over and read Edgar Schneider's revelation of himself in 'Discovering my Autism', and just compare again with yours truly in this present volume. We can be just poles apart in habit and temperament... we vary every bit as much as do our NT counterparts.

Sure, I might look a little enviously on Danny's charm, on Edgar's guts and mathematical skills etc. I feel inferior when I read of Patrick's drive to completion of tasks and his overall perfectionism. I am lost in admiration of the respect in which the latter two gentlemen are held. There is Danny who can excel on the sporting field. And so on. Just what truly common features do we all possess at base? Merely looking at the criteria of behaviour and outer characteristics pressed on us by the professionals, I feel, can be inadequate. (3) It is my contention that the great majority of odd behavioural diversions of the Aspie are not automatic or 'essential'. Rather they can just represent self-protective procedures or peculiar adaptative   methods of fitting in.

What is my own personal list of the most essential characteristics of AS? Well, I would stick my neck out and list the following generalisations...

*A lifelong history of being confused by the NT persons about us.

*A similar lifelong history of causing confusion to the same NTs in return.

*Some sense of being an alien... of not belonging to the rest of humanity; (or of seeing the rest of humanity as aliens).

*Having a different and eccentric rhythm that carries us along.

*Being frequently distracted by 'parts of things', or odd details that grab us; or, as is commonly put, not easily seeing the wood for the trees.

*Being engaged in a lifelong and sometimes vain search for real friends.

*A passion for collecting, and other hobbies (all too frequently of an impractical variety), described by the experts very politely as 'Special Interests'.

*A seeking for fairness in the world, with something of an inevitable desperation at its seeming absence.

*An incapacity in comprehending the accepted meanings attached to such things as Love, Intimacy, Bonding etc.

*The greatest difficulty in contacting the hearts and minds of our NT peers and loved ones.

*An extraordinary difficulty in locating or even in identifying the person behind the outer characteristics they observe in others. They simply can't KNOW another person.

*A difficulty achieving true spontaneity when with others.

*An obsessive reliance on routines and rituals as well as somewhat rigid rules in order to cope with the business of daily living.

*Discomfort in switching from the rich inner world of one's rigid isolation, in order to deal with the confusing arena of the 'commonsense' world of other people.

*A disconcerting and embarrassing naivety about day to day matters, that can manifest regardless of the subject's age, experience and intelligence.

*A difficulty in co-ordinating with other people in pairs or in teams.

I think that the foregoing allows for so many of the variations that we see. I've come to the conclusion that the outer symptoms or observable behaviours of the Aspies, as repeatedly tabulated in the literature, delighted in by the Media, as well as being relied on by the experts for diagnostic purposes, are secondary issues. As I say, they are largely brought about by our habitual and defensive responses to the pressures and demands of the family and schooling and the world that we experienced.

The business of being saddled with a 'label' apparently disturbs some of our number very badly, suggesting to them that they are 'sick' or somehow malformed. It never struck me like that. Sure, there are some strong arguments against the giving of names and labels to people; and in some particular societies or even family groups (where one would hope to get better understanding) the individual can be ostracised or singled out for bad treatment, when so defined. However for me, as I hope I have made plain, the determination of the AS label was only beneficial and progressive. It was entirely up to me as to whether or not to tell the world at large about it. For that matter as well, I was free to choose for myself if I even accepted the diagnosis in the first place. If I had found it objectionable or detrimental, or for that matter undemonstrable, I'm sure that I'd have rejected it out of hand.

As I see it, so long as it is taken the right way, with all its limitations and qualifications, the process of labelling with a term like Asperger's gives some degree of an idea to the savvy observer, of just what kind of behaviour and blank spots are likely to be found in the person. It surely must be essential for a person to admit to being correctly labelled as an Alcoholic for example, or as a Diabetic - or even as a chronic worrier. Those about him and those who have to deal with him are better prepared for the sorts of treatment or handling which are most suitable for employment. And even if it were ever proved that AS just happened to be a purely behaviouristic phenomenon, without any neurological cause, at least the sufferer could be better handled and directed towards the most progressive treatments and guidance.

However, since many other labels that get dropped onto sufferers and problem people point the way to particular treatments, and for that matter do unfortunately suggest that these folk have either abused their bodies and minds rather badly in the past, clearly this label of Asperger's is situated in a different ball park. Our native sense of alienation, of just not belonging, is to a greater extent pretty unique among human beings. Normally as far as I know, only that group of the psychopaths, drug addicts and mentally disturbed people have anything like it. No, to me the issuing of a label to those who are shown to have one of these extraordinary Syndromes appears like a most sensible move. For the great part, at any rate, our Aspies are people with a recognizable Syndrome which is definitely not to be seen as a Pathology. And as far as I'm concerned, every newly diagnosed individual should be encouraged to recognize the fact, along with the distinction involved.

It does get a little tiresome when the NTs about me suggest more or less seriously that they themselves must be AS because they share one or two traits like the ones I've detailed above. I've had to find ways of explaining the difference. When I observe how so many NTs resemble us in particular ways, it strikes me that one way of considering the difference is to picture it this way. A neurotic person in the normal NT world is still essentially part of that world. He/she belongs to it, and recognizes that fact. It represents the gravest hurt and pain to him that he tries over and over again to fit in, to be accepted and to be able to take his rightful place as a legitimate member. But sadly it doesn't work as a rule. If it does, it is unsatisfying and perhaps comes in temporary bursts. Persons like this find themselves virtually chucked out, rejected and repulsed by those who they know all too well are essentially of THEIR OWN KIND.

However for the Asperger, at least the one who has an interest in the social world, and who actually desires friends and acceptance, it is a different scenario. For us, the world is largely alien. WE ARE SIMPLY NOT AMONG OUR OWN KIND. We are just not of this planet (or so we feel). We hover about the other people of the world and of the society, looking on in wonder and curiosity. We observe the ways in which those alien inhabitants get on together and find their varied and strange sorts of satisfaction.

We are outsiders who want to get in, though admittedly on our own terms, and in our own time and rhythm. This is totally different from the former neurotic group who are already part of the group, but who can't find a home in it. So we try to move in FROM OUTSIDE.

I found an extraordinary attitude in one lady. She observed that I was making a lot of friends from Internet Asperger''s groups. I'd had useful correspondence with authorities both here in Australia and abroad. Then as well, I've been asked to speak on Asperger's for support groups etc.

This particular lady indicated a profound envy for my diagnosis, coming to the conclusion that to have AS, or at least to be diagnosed with it, had proven to be very beneficial to me, giving me access to all sorts of interesting people, as well as even appearing to offer me some mysterious sort of higher status in the community. I even got the impression that it was considered that I just didn't deserve these benefits. She seemed to think that a similar diagnosis of AS for herself might just lift her own deprived life into a state of importance and acceptance. Just because I was helped and so relieved to get the DX, she thought it must be a great thing to have. Naturally enough, with this idea in mind, she had to ignore all the difficulties and distresses, misunderstandings and losses that I've had to endure over my years, in order to get just where I am. Let me tell you, it ain't been no bed of roses, as any Aspie will tell you, no matter how 'high functioning' he may be.

"Oh, I'm like that too!" How often have I had that or similar comments delivered to me, when I've explained just what is involved in the experiencing of Asperger's Syndrome. As I've had to come to terms over the matter, and then to describe it all to others, there are certainly very few items within the repertoire of awkward and bizarre symptoms experienced by us Aspies that you won't find within the life and moment by moment experiences of certain NTs about us. Of course, very frequently the same symptoms will be described as different things, and given different reasons or causes.

The commentary given by the post-Freudian analyst Karen Horney back in the 40s/50s, of the type she describes as 'People who move away from people', is at first sight an almost perfect description of certain of us Aspies. (4) Since in those pre-AS defining days, her book is dealing with the 'normal' of the population, the NTs, - clearly she is detailing persons afflicted with neurotic or schizoid problems; but for a time you might say that she had me fooled. Then I just happened to read Edgar Schneider's valuable and as far as I've been able to discern, unique tabulation of the specific distinctions between the essential schizoid characteristics and the Asperger's ones. (5) On the surface, they do look most alike. And it is only when you examine the motivations and the pressures behind the manifestations, that you see they are not the same.

Let's face it, many NT people in the world outside, are retiring in nature. They call it shyness. Many have tricks and mannerisms of speech that they've developed. These might be called defensive mechanisms. Many perform the actions that look like the Asperger practices known as stimming. Apart from possibly having nervous ticks, or for that matter, indications of Tourettes Syndrome, it is not uncommon for NT people to tap fingers, twirl pencils, pull locks of hair, apparently beat time with their hands or feet, or appear to be mentally dancing to an indiscernible melody or rhythm. Loads of NTs collect things or develop fads, or take on peculiar hobbies. And the tricky or embarrassing proclivities of persons with obsessive/compulsive trends are well known.

It is not surprising that on being told about their friend's or relative's AS diagnosis, a lot of regular commonsense-ridden people will look at one rather pityingly, and simply say "Oh yeah? I'm like that too." Or perhaps with something of a sarcastic look, "Maybe I could get that diagnosis too." The implication is conveyed that the Aspie is doing a job of 'special pleading', and is manipulating the system for privileges and unusual exemptions.

The temptation at such times is to protest, to try to batter the sarcastic one with a whole lot of facts, figures and intimate details. It can be literally something of a heartbreaking experience. You want desperately to have this matter understood and believed. You want others to appreciate just what you've discovered after perhaps a lifetime of research, pain and puzzlement. You may possibly be desperate to give the explanation to your peers and relatives for the things in you that they've put up with all these years. So many who consider themselves to be well informed and psychologically sophisticated will even sneer, and come to the conclusion that you are fundamentally just a hypochondriac who is going through the thrill and excitement of discovering an 'Illness' that no-one has heard of before.

Then of course you have to go through the inevitable process of explaining over again that Asperger's is not a Pathology, not a mental illness, not a neurosis, - but a Syndrome. "Yeah," they say, "What the heck is that?" and you have to start all over again.

But then, and it happens to represent one of the supreme joys of the twice-born Aspie when he discovers and communicates with someone who actually 'understands' - one who has heard of it... and who perhaps has someone in his family or their circle filling the same bill. And heaven knows, you really feel that you have been sent on earth with a mission to do some good when you have the opportunity to help someone realize that their difficult younger son, or their aged father or uncle possibly, is or was of the Asperger fraternity. Some of my most gratifying moments in recent years have been when some colleague has come back to tell me that the revelation about myself has led to their own problem son or relative being suitably diagnosed with AS, and is now on the right track for appropriate help.

Yes, it is quite true that other people are often 'like that'. But I think I can say with a degree of confidence that in many cases an Aspie would be able to spot the difference between genuine Asperger's symptoms and those common neurotic features. I've often considered that experts who offer their services to diagnose AS in the population, might do well to have assistance and advice from those who hopefully know the business best... the Aspies themselves.

Just in the last few days, I've been studying certain individuals in my circle who despite knowing and acknowledging my Aspie classification have insisted on picking on the odd eccentric characteristic, and saying "But I'm like that, too. Doesn't that mean that I'm AS?" Just watching these folks over an odd hour or two is enough to give the absolute lie to such claim or suggestion. I observe their repertoire of NT emotional expression, and I can easily see the warmth of emotional expression with their every utterance. I recognize perhaps their free and empathic mixing with other people in a party or crowd situation. I feel their ability to spontaneously reach out towards myself or others in order to make them feel at home and get under their skin, as it were.

Then look at another characteristic. Some Aspies may talk an awful lot; but there is a world of difference between the monologue/lecture style of the AS individual focussing on his pet topics, and the sharing/chatting approach that characterises the friendly NT person or partner. NTs are simply not aware of these differences, unless and indeed until they specifically get frustrated or puzzled by the curious ways in which their tame Aspie converses or reveals his feelings and explanations.

On My Personal Relationship to Aspergers

Confessions of an Unashamed Asperger

There is always a debate going on over the question about whether we Aspies are 'ordinary' persons with an unfortunate overlay of Asperger's Syndrome, or if on the other hand, that Asperger's is of the very essence of our natural self, our real being; and that any 'normal' is just a veneer or overlay that sits comfortably or otherwise on the top.   Like many others of our 'fraternity', I can't conceive of myself without the experiences and perceptions of AS.   The fashion in which other (normal) people appear to live is unfathomable to me. Their much vaunted advantages too often give me the impression of characteristics that are actually negative, and that can just repulse me.   I absolutely identify myself with the Asperger's.

The NT population of the world seem to carry so many burdens that are curious and unenviable. I am disturbed by the reliance on unspoken messages that they seem to believe is a crucial part of their intercourse with others. They depend so much for their conclusions and their motivations on hints, body language, intuition, and as well, this peculiar and inexplicable capacity they claim for 'reading' their fellows. That same person who may completely reject any such faculty as a mental telepathy, or some other psychic sense, will readily exhibit and vehemently defend this extraordinary capacity for sensing something of the real personhood behind the outer shell of their fellows.

So very often I have been shocked at the sophisticated individuals in my milieu priding themselves on their insight into other folk.   And of course I see those looks of pity, focused on me, as they note that I don't share their thoughts and their judgments about others.   But, I've observed, these insightful people appear so often to be just as often deceived about others as I am, and perhaps on occasions even more so. I am grateful for the unique perceptions I have about the world, and for the gifts that I've been given.   Somehow the greater growth of sophistication in those same people seems just to make them more cynical, more suspicious, and also perhaps, even to age more.

It may be that pessimism, world-weary sophistication and lack of trust, are among the accepted means of looking after oneself; but for me they are too depressing and destructive to one's values.   I have been heavily criticized so often for my naïve optimistic approach that can appear to my intimates as being unrealistic.   But I feel terribly sad when I observe persons about me who with all their prized down to earth realism and cynicism have only succeeded in losing their ability to grasp and treasure the simplest of beautiful things about them.

We Aspies may bear the residual marks of the child about us, but I've yet to be convinced that this is just automatically a bad thing, if and when we don't allow them to interfere with the competent handling of everyday life.   Perhaps the only reason that occasional childlike characteristics may be detrimental, is because others don't share the factor, and are over-sophisticated.   Cut out the reactions from others, and probably most of these troubles just dissipate.   But maybe I'm being too hopeful and optimistic.

Perhaps another area of childlike nature is in the way we interact with our beloved animals. I watch my pussycat, and admire the wonderful way in which she greets the day, the sunshine and her comfortable padded basket. She has this enviable capacity to play, and to bound about as if she were a kitten still. Yes, there is one of my aims and objects - to be mature like this - a middle-aged creature in this time zone, and still to have the preparedness to get joy from the simplest of things. No wonder so many of us Aspies regard and treat our cats as Honorary Aspies. A compliment indeed! Or wait a second. Should it strictly be the other way round? That we Aspies might be considered as Honorary Cats??? (6) Like our cats, we Aspies can be hooked into pleasure or excitement very readily, as we get pulled into simple repetitive routines or delight in pretty things that would leave the mature and cool NT viewer completely unmoved.(7)

So, about the inevitable question of a cure. If a cure were developed for AS, would I personally be in it? Well, when I compare myself with the NTs of this world, AND since I don't really see myself as being distinctly disabled by the condition, I can say that I would definitely choose NO 'cure'. The Syndrome is not any sort of pathology. It is not a discrete something in us that can be healed. We Aspies are individuals whose brains are wired in a different set of ways. AS is not to be conceived of as a psychological affliction either; though almost inevitably that is the way the innocent onlooker will envisage it.

An AS person can of course, have other personality problems or mental health difficulties. He may well have neurotic symptoms; but in itself, AS is not a neurosis. The latter may well prove responsive to psychological intervention. Naturally, it has to be acknowledged that the unique behaviour patterns displayed by the Aspie have a psychological component. They are comforting and they offer a sense of control; they help establish a predictability in daily life or even an escape from stress. Nevertheless they have to be recognized as symptoms or outcomes of what is underneath, rather than representing the real essence of the AS condition.

Can the Aspie 'change', any more than a Siamese Cat may change its points? Of course, and innumerable testimonies have been given in recent times of genuine turn-abouts in their disturbing behaviours by long-term adult Aspies. And some of these persons have been known to exert huge efforts in order to alter their ways of relating, and to reduce their 'bad' habits. But I feel that caution must be applied by anyone who seeks for such change. It cannot be simply demanded of the person. Any motivation for change must come sincerely and wholeheartedly from within him. In the long run, it is his responsibility; and fortunately, some degree of change, correction and modification should be within the capability of any reasonably stable Asperger's person.

Intervention by a Counsellor or Psychiatrist might well help the individual in the process of identifying and modifying certain of his actions. But there is no evidence that it can in any way change the facts and nature of his underlying Asperger's being. Under harsh or deep emotional coercion perhaps an Aspie might find it pressed on him to alter certain of his inappropriate ways; but the likely outcome is that he will fall into some substitute habit that will turn out to be worse than the original one. With the depth of pain he suffers in such a turnaround, he may be left with profound resentment and frustration. Perhaps his innate capacity to trust may suffer, and the greater part of any developing intimacy will go. Any spontaneity will undoubtedly be dampened down, and the 'cured' state may turn out to be worse than the original condition. There is clearly little advantage in eliminating his bad habit, only to find that the Aspie has retreated or withdrawn from closeness.

Elsewhere, I offer my own list of the things that Aspies seems to share together. (8) These are not the simplistic and media-publicized features that always come up in conversation. Some are subjective attitudes and perceptions that may distort the understanding. But I'm sure that it is certain crucial GAPS in the workings of the inner life that distinguish one as AS, and which lead him to ineffectiveness when dealing with human interactions. These gaps represent the source of his biggest problems They manifest through the inability to recognize and to contact the person behind the mask in his partner, or in any of his fellows; and in his sheer incapability to understand just what is really meant among NT humans by words like love, intimacy, empathy and such like.

To put it all another way, the primary distinctions that make the Aspie what he is, are NOT directly observable features of his behaviour. Some of these may well be typical of many Aspies, but they only represent possible ways in which the underlying state of being might be manifesting. The real primary causes are neurological ones, but I hasten to admit that they will be better delineated by minds more informed than my own. And the immediate reasons for the 'different' or difficult behaviours will be those same gaps I just discussed. Practices that are common to many Aspies, like stimming, rigidity of habits, fixed routines, collecting things and avoiding company, are chosen and developed to enable easier living as well as self-protection (each with his own selection of them).

The behaviours, words and factors of appearance that we can observe objectively in the Aspie, and which lead him most often to the room of the psychologist, are purely the secondary symptoms of AS. These are the things that in their obsessive or bizarre appearance can lead the unthinking mind astray. Recall that a blind person is not defined or diagnosed as blind by the carrying of a white cane, or by walking with a seeing-eye dog. Neither will a blind person be cured of his blindness by giving him a cane, or by keeping obstacles out of his way, though each action can bring about a change in his behaviour, and make life more liveable for him.

Sadly, all the same, the only readily accessible aspects of Autism/Asperger's are behavioural or psychological, with the necessary and sufficient physical causes remaining unknown. There is still no reliable objective test, and diagnosis is essentially based on observation of behaviour. Effects both good and bad of any interventions can only be based on observing behavioural changes. I look forward to the day when not only may there be scanning tests that will detect the real autistic factors in the brain, but also when newer and better questionaires may be devised that can bring out the truth about the inner experience.

I am reminded of the differences between the males and the females of our human species. Our knowledge of this matter has only been identified in relatively recent years. The body shape and figure, the texture of skin, sound of voice, and fat/muscle distribution, are our normal and immediate means of telling the difference between the sexes. But they and even the genitals themselves are only the secondary signs of gender. The primary differences lie deep within the genes, hidden out of sight or reach of the regular human senses.

So as for this issue of a cure for Aspergers Syndrome. As we say in Australia, "If it ain't broke, then don't fix it!" AS is not the indication of a 'broken' individual! It is not Pathology. It is just what we are. But again I stress, it is NOT simply to be identified with that much publicized AS behaviour. The essence or origin of AS is not to be seen on the surface. I suppose that the very fact that the unusual behaviours can vary so much from person to person shows that they are not the primary things. Each individual Aspie will take on his own selection of habits, in the attempt (and often a desperate attempt!) to deal with the world, and for self comfort.

Finally. summing up with a relevant last word on it, as one of my associates put it most aptly, "Autism/Aspergers is a neurological condition most often handled on a psychological basis. That's less a reflection of scientific/medical incompetence, and much more an indictment of our profound ignorance of what autism really is". (9).

I wouldn't want to be 'cured' of my Asperger's Syndrome. Sure I'm pretty self- contained, (some might say self-satisfied?). Yes, I can be quite oblivious of the moods and feelings of my companions. I engage in a significant number of eccentric behaviours commonly associated with AS folk. But I have at the same time developed or had to develop what is for me a profound code of ethics, to arm myself for dealing competently and not too intrusively with the other persons in the world. I learnt a number of basic rules from my family, but they did not come naturally or easily. I had many things to learn the hard way, as I grew up.

One of the major characteristics of AS folk is that they need rules, in order to live and grow. They need guidance, and constantly will be falling back on the rules that were imposed on them when small. Many of the Aspies of the world show a remarkable trend towards honesty. It is hard or unpleasant for them to be anything but frank and open. Literal fact is open and honest, and they find it hard to work out why one should lie or obfuscate. For that matter, lying can be plain downright difficult for many of us, since we don't understand the inner workings of our NT colleagues enough to be able to lie convincingly. Further, if you can't mind-read, you probably can't calculate sufficiently to work out how to manipulate the consciousness of another.

I've never understood the necessary delay that NTs seem to go through, when they are getting familiar or intimate with someone. I have this quality of virtually being perhaps just about as close as I'll ever be to the other party from the first moment I chat to them. Whether this is good or bad, I leave it to the good graces of the reader to determine, though I have my own ideas of what most would say.

I certainly do make myself vulnerable by my childlike trust in others, and I have often stuck my neck out by chatting to or befriending folks that have appealed to me. Having little pride, I've not been backward at introducing myself to people that I might find useful or compatible. Sure, often it doesn't work. But the number of times it has worked and delivered me real benefits has made it a valuable exercise. It reminds me of the old story of the lupine young man who made a habit of asking every woman he met to have sex with him. "You must get an awful lot of knock-backs," he was asked. "Oh sure" he answered, "but you should see the number of wins that I get too."

I feel that if you don't suffer from too much human pride, then you do stand a good chance of finding or creating opportunities that others don't dream of. You run risks as well of course, but heavens above, what about the risks that heavy drinkers, fast drivers and energetic sportsmen take every day? At least I must be reducing the inherent risks by the way I make a point of selecting my contacts from within the most suitable social groups. Knowing that I don't have the vocabulary for small talk with my peers, I've made up for it, I would claim, by deliberately creating around me a very exciting and exclusive circle of friends that are satisfying and life affirming. And these indeed, are people that I can talk to with joy and profit.

No, I would not want to be cured of my AS. I have not got world weary. I can enjoy the fantasy life of the child. I can still be enthralled by children's books and films. I can retreat into the land of dreams without embarrassment. Though I take care to retain a degree of dignity in my public life, I have no hesitation in expressing my child self there too, as well as in private. I guess that is part of the reality as well as the privilege of the Actor in me. What an extraordinary opportunity and privilege it is to take on the job of performing, taking on or creating a part in a play, where one can express an infinite number of emotions and motivations – indeed, many of the same that normally constitute none of my everyday experiences. This is a world where I can drop the convention ridden inhibitions legitimately and safely; and no-one will despise me for childlike things that would lose me credence in the outside world.

I have little hesitation in relatively harmless areas of self indulgence. I do feed myself on a pretty healthy sort of diet, but I am quite prepared to enjoy pleasant foods that will do nothing for my nutrition. Luckily I have not shown any significant propensity for increase in weight. I get a great kick out of lying down on a bed and snoozing, maybe a sense, you might say, of returning to the womb. And none of this is enhanced by means and benefit of alcohol or dangerous drugs.

Oh, yes, I do sound smug quite frequently. I guess I am too. I only hope I'm not too much of a snob as well.

References.

(1) See Essay on   A Perverse Sense of Humour.
(2) See Appendix no.2 Test Profiles. TAT description.
(3) DSM IV... Diagnostic Characteristics of Asperger's
                Syndrome.
(4) Horney, Karen.   Our Inner Conflicts.   Moving
                        Away from People.   Page 73.
(5) Schneider, Edgar   Discovering My Autism.   Page 96.
(6) Hoopman, K   All Cats have Aspergers Syndrome.
(7) See Essay on   Peak Experiences.
(8) See Essay   An Aspie You Ain't.
(9) Loughman, W.D.   Quoted with permission from personal
                        correspondence.

APPENDIX I

LIFE HISTORY IN BRIEF.

Full Name   Ronald Ian Hedgcock..

Born.   10pm, 4th November, 1935. (Astrologically Scorpio, but more like my Gemini Rising, and Moon in Aquarius.)

Where   Dandenong, Melbourne, Victoria, Australia. Presently living in retirement in Ballarat, Victorian Regional City.

=============================

Parents.   Mother - old-fashioned, loving and gentle house-wife. Musician/Singer.
Father - Postmaster, Lay Preacher (and other offices) in Methodist Church. Organist/Choirmaster/Composer. Freemason, Active in civic life. Kindly gentle man, held in great respect in all his spheres.

Sibling.   Brother Murray. 4 years my senior. Journalist living in London. Authority on cricket, with huge library on same.

Marriages   Three marriages between 1959 and 1986. Living singly since then.

Children   Two surviving children, born 1960 and 1965.

=============================

Education   State School in Upwey and Maffra, both Victoria. High School to equivalent of Year 11 (Leaving Certificate) at Mount Gambier, in South Australia.

Higher Ed.   Two years only of part time University. No Degree achieved. With studies in Psychology and Philosophy.
Extra-Curricular training in Public Speaking and related skills.
Professional training in Radio, Television and Stage Acting.

=============================

Work.   3 Years Salesman in Bookshop, immediately after leaving School
1 Year touring with Stage Hypnotist.

1 Year Attendant in Cinema and Hotel.
2 Years Storeman in Cigarette Warehouse.
2 years as Radio Announcer in North Queensland.
29 Years in the Public Service as a Clerk.
Retired at age of 56, and shifted back to Victoria.
Now classified as Professional Actor and Lecturer.
============================

Army Service. National Service Army Training, (Artillery) and
Citizens Reserve Forces, 1954 to 1956.
No overseas or active Service.
============================

Churches. Methodist upbringing. One marriage in Anglican
Church.
Seven to eight years in non-professional Clergy
of Liberal Catholic Church, eventually ordained
as Priest.
Now, no church affiliation.   Religious Inclinations
toward Gnostic/Humanist/Pantheist/Pagan.
============================

Hobbies & Art History, Classical Music and Opera, Cats,
Pursuits.   Book collecting, Esoteric studies, Lecturing in
my various lines of study.
50 years of membership in AMORC Fraternity.
Volunteer for 15 yrs in Historical Museum Park,
where I portrayed 1850s Phrenologist.
Professional Entertaining.
Mental Magic, & Literary/Poetry readings.
In early days, a Semi-Professional Palmist, and
Practitioner of Stage Conjuring.

APPENDIX II

TEST PROFILES, and PSYCHOLOGICAL ASSESSMENTS.

I have to confess that I am a sucker for tests and assessments. I see an article in a magazine that offers to tell you where you are at, and just what sort of a person you are, and I'm hooked.   The Internet regularly comes up with items of this kind as well, and of late these have provided conclusions that appeared to me to be pretty valid. And in my library are a number of books (of varying standard) that offer the same sort of self-assessment.

My favourite work in the category is by the controversial but stimulating Hans Eysenck, along with fellow researcher Glenn Wilson. It bears the title of Know Your Own Personality. From my answers to the exhaustive questionaires that are in the book, I've selected a range that may be of interest or use to the reader of my confessions.   They are arranged in the form of one's position on a scale; and I give a rough idea of how I appeared.   The first ones detailed below are made up of a number of separate tests.

SCALE TOPIC.   MY POSITION.

-Introversion/Extraversion
    Activity...   Inactivity   Median score
    Sociability... Unsociability   Very High on Unsociability
    Risk Taking...Carefulness   Very High on Carefulness
    Impulsiveness...Control   Slight tendency to Control
    Expressiveness/ Inhibition   Moderate on Expressive
    Practicality - Reflectiveness.   Strong on Reflectiveness.
    Irresponsibility/Responsibility   Median score.

           Score   Moderate 'Introvert'.
    ===================================
-Tough minded/Tender minded.
    Assertiveness..Peacefulness. Very High on Peacefulness
    Achievement..Unambitious.   Slight tendency to
                           Achievement
    Manipulation... Empathy   Strong on Manipulation
    Sensation-seeking..Unadventurous   Very High on
                                 Unadventurous

Dogmatism......Flexibility   High on Flexibility
Masculinity......Femininity   Median

Score High 'Tender Minded'
==

-Emotional Instability/Adjustment
    Inferiority ..Self Esteem   High on Inferiority
    Depressiveness...Happiness   High on Happiness
    Anxiety..Calm   High on Calm
    Obsessiveness..Casualness.   High on Casualness
    Dependence..Autonomy   Moderate on Autonomy
    Hypochondriac.. Sense of Health.Moderate on Sense of
                              Health.
  Guilt.. Guilt Freedom   Moderate on Guilt.

Stability and Adjustment....Score Moderate..
==

 -Radical/Conservative scale...   Mildly Radical
==

-Humour   Score very high on most forms of humour
==

-Sex/Libido   Score mildly high on Libido
==

-When we come to the popular but rather controversial Myer
  Briggs Scale, I showed up essentially as INTJ.
==

-In Internet Research tests from University of Cambridge,
  the following scores were determined.
AQ 36 (described as Very High Autistic)
EQ 23 (described as Low Score for Empathising)
SQ 66 (described as Average Score for Systematising)
==

-Fun Tests from the Internet.
In a recent test which is designed to determine one's
Empathy/Systematic rating, I showed up with EQ of 25 and
SQ of 20. EQ here matches reasonably closely with the
Cambridge Score above, while I guess that the Systematising
score was determined on some different sort of scale.
==

A further set of questions were intended to detect any
tendencies to Personality Disorders. My results gave low
ratings to Paranoid, Schizoid, Anti-social, Borderline,

Histrionic, Dependent and Obsessive-Compulsive.
I showed up with high scores on Avoidant and Schizotypal, and with very high on Narcissistic.

=======================================
Also from the Internet, there was a curious quiz to determine one's kind of thinking.   My results showed me to be a fairly even balance between a Linguistic thinker and an Existential thinker.

=======================================

My standard IQ rating is somewhere in the middle 130s.

During a torrid period in the middle of one of my marriages, I was referred to a psychologist who specialized in assessment tests. She administered what is known as a TAT, or Thematic Apperception Test.

This was administered with the aid of a pack of cards, each of which had an evocative and perhaps rather ambiguous drawing of a person or persons in various life situations and relationships. The figures were clear and in no way abstract as in the classical Rorschach tests.   The client or subject was required to look at each picture and relate either a story or an interpretation, or maybe just a response to the image that is seen.

I have to admit that I enjoyed this test; and found the eventual assessment that resulted to be of great interest.   Below is the text of this document, but with just a couple of discretionary omissions.

"The first story in this protocol portrays a boy who is 'sick to death' and 'fed to the back teeth' with his task of playing the violin, which was foisted on him too early by his parents. He describes the impotence of a child, unable to fight authority.
He says his mother was a loving but neurotic disciplinarian.
His second story portrays a wife who has taken over the motherly role, and is confident she can handle her man. The violent feelings the man is experiencing represent the

rebellion within him and the aggression he has repressed.
His themes centre on coercion and the desire to escape. He
is in a state of conflict about his future, knowing he has to
face decisions he is not enthusiastic about making.

He is a man with a pressure of ideas, which lead him in all
directions. His imagination is fertile. He is very intelligent and
usually makes intellectual decisions rather than letting his
feelings dictate his actions.

His flexibility is at times astonishing. One idea leads to
another. He is fluid and inventive and creative in his thinking.
He resists boundaries and often tends not to see them, after
having escaped the restraints of childhood with such a sense
of relief.

He enjoys drama and fantasy which take care of his
instinctual frustrations and longings. Acting also expands his
experience in a way that is very therapeutic and stimulating
for him. He probably enjoys acting more than real life at
times, when life deals him frustrating blows.

His aggression is largely catered for through sublimation and
fantasy, or in intellectual pursuits, allowing him to be friendly
and independent but not deeply involved in the affairs of
others. He likes to see justice done and is therefore on the
side of the law, but he dislikes regimentation. He has
repressed his dependency conflicts – which are seen through
the themes of his stories.

He is able to conjure up the comforts and advantages of a
protective mother figure who would shelter her child or love
object from the hardships of life, yet he can also envisage
women as witch-like and destructive. He is obviously very
ambivalent about women. He can see the witch and the
mother in the same person.

He objects to violence and brute force, and does not seem
himself as the muscle bound prototype, but as a non physical
aesthete, sensitive to pain, and unwilling to be a hero or to
perform feats of endurance. He is the thinker, the dreamer
who enjoys philosophising. He has no wish to be anyone but

himself, although he likes the actor's role.   He has compensated for being of slight stature and no challenge to the macho male by excelling in other areas and developing an appreciation for less tangible things.

He is the product of a narrow Methodist upbringing, in revolt against dull morality and accepted tenets.   He has a great deal of intellectual curiosity and a desire for unusual experiences that give life extra meaning.   He likes to help educate other people.   He says he was a mentor to his wives and his daughter.

In his acting roles he loves to be a comic like Charlie Chaplin – entertaining himself   as well as others.

He can offer friendship and affection to a woman, but lacks real passion.   His mind is always busy.   He admits he is not always empathic, and is a bad judge of character.

He is psychologically self-sufficient to a degree, and is not prepared to submit to persons who attack his self-esteem.   In relationship difficulties, he protects himself by drawing further away.   With his many resources, he can live in his head if reality becomes too tough, and he would never allow anyone to own him.

He is a very interesting person."
===

APPENDIX III

Criteria for my self-Diagnosis of Asperger Syndrome, pre-2000.

I was first made aware of the Autistic Spectrum in about 1990, with descriptions of this extraordinary condition known as Asperger Syndrome; and I duly recognized the fact that I displayed features in common with it. However, it was not until some stage in the year 1996, as I read more on the subject, that I became convinced that a great number of the eccentric aspects of my personality simply had to indicate the nature of AS. From my hastily acquired library of key texts and autobiographies on the subject, I collated a comprehensive listing of all the standard characteristics and symptoms that are commonly found in AS individuals. These I divided into three categories which represented Strong, Moderate and Weak (to non-existent); and sorted all the features I could recall or detect within myself into these headings.

Extra facets of my experience and personality that were not specified in the literature, but which appeared to me to have a possible relevance to the picture of AS, I added to each category; and as it happened, more than one authority with expertise in AS allowed that my list was on the whole pretty valid, and my conclusions legitimate.

For the greater part, I believe that this early and occasionally rather naïve listing of data was demonstrably accurate; and I have on many occasions come back to it to double check the material, and to duly compare with the updated and better informed conclusions of today as are amplified in the present volume.

In this Appendix I offer the same listing that I prepared some 12-14 years ago, though with a very small number of revisions. The benefit of hindsight as well as a great deal of study into the intricacies of Aspergers has made me rethink a very few of my old ideas. I guess that I have learnt a bit more about myself over these few years, and some few of my hastily tabulated items have shown themselves to be inadequate - if not in their definition, then probably with regard to the categories in which they were originally distributed, or the degree of their influence. So here is an edited and re-organized version of my original tables. It must be noted that I am using my own terminology, without reference to DSM IV.

==
a. STRONG and PREDOMINANT FEATURES.

Difficulty in Socialising.

Little understanding of how to play with other children in groups. Largely indifferent to peer pressure. Found other children's talk and games confusing. I was always the last to know or to understand anything that was of common knowledge or gossip.
Had no instinct for self-defense. Was easily bullied. Stuck to rules and regulations.
In adulthood; -
Hard work to remember social conventions and expectation. Totally lost and floundering at parties. Always most comfortable with only one or two persons.

====================================
Lack in Empathy and Intimacy

Oblivious of other people's inner lives and motives. Had no concept of my parents' thoughts or realities.
Never experienced or had any understanding of empathy. Unable to 'read' another or to interpret their emotions or motivations. No comprehension of intimacy, which for me is like an invasion or being overwhelmed. Inability to develop and maintain normal comfortable intimate relations. I become passive in intimate situations. I experience all people as aliens, though lovers, wives, family and friends may be friendly and benevolent aliens. Can tend to exhibit an instant intimacy with just about anyone, whether stranger or casual acquaintance. Relationship with partner carries very little depth and is just about the same as with friends and associates. Can presume and fabricate or act out intimacy in casual relationships. Have no understanding of principles like bonding, loyalty or love. I substitute such intellectually

chosen concepts like duty, respect, kindness, habit and formality. Unable to interpret emotions and attitudes of others. Can't really forgive, because I don't truly love or hate.

=====================================
Tendency to Solitude and the Inner Life

As a child, I was happy to play games by myself... jigsaws etc. I avoided social contact with other children at lunchtimes and recess periods. I lived very much in an inner world of fantasy and imagination, as fuelled by my reading.
In Adulthood; -
I have limited tolerance for the company of any human, and eventually find it uncomfortable to share my house and daily routine with anyone, male or female, old or young. I come alive most when by myself. I am a loner with a very select group of friends. My real world is internal and rather secretive. I enjoy jokes and humour by myself. I intensely dislike sharing and combining in committee fashion with anyone, including a partner. Play Patience (Solitaire) for hours very regularly. Enjoy the exclusive companionship of my cats, who I talk to a lot. I have always hated being in charge of or responsible for other people.

===
Self Centredness

Instinctively self-centred. But fundamentally unselfish. I have had no real interest to know about the inner life of other people. I don't really understand how one can 'know' another person anyway. No concern or grief at the death of anyone. It is always with effort that I break out of my own inner world to take notice of another, or deal with their issues. I have to concentrate painfully in order to take in what another is talking about. Commonly I approach others for my own needs. I am rarely put off by what others do or have done, so long as it doesn't affect me. In relationships, out of sight is out of mind. I have only a mild need for reassurance from others. I always had a profoundly naïve and unsophisticated view of everything. I want and need a modicum only of rescue and reassurance from other people. I don't seem to need people, and find it hard to determine anything specific I might want from marriage.

======================================
Idiosyncrasies in Communication and Literal Mind

I have to be careful to restrain my facetious and intended funny comments. I enjoy the use of repetitive jokes and routine comedy routines in daily life. I have a lack of appreciation of social cues. I turn conversations round to my special interests. I have a marked lack in non-verbal communication. I don't comprehend the principle of giving and receiving messages with the eyes. I am detached from feelings or intentions of others unless spelt out literally. I have a strong tendency to take any comments and statements as automatically true. I have no inclination to scepticism. I have an unthinking trust in people. I frequently fail to ask or seek clarification from a person, so can fail to understand. I tend to take things for granted. I can report my feelings accurately and in a detached way, but am usually incapable of expressing them spontaneously.
I can give embarrassing and inappropriate responses and comments that will disturb or shock others. I can be over-anxious to speak well and clearly, and thus can sound unnatural or pedantic, especially if engaged in intimate talk. I can talk too much in bursts, and have to watch carefully to make sure I'm not over-doing my talk. I can occasionally exhibit gauche or clumsy body language. I'm inconsistent in the way I might share confidences or experiences with others.

======================================
Physical and Sensory issues

I couldn't play team or body contact sports. I am averse to putting myself at any physical risk. I have relatively poor motor coordination, sometimes surprising clumsiness, and lack of bodily rhythm. I was slow or late in riding a bike, tying shoelaces, whistling, blowing my nose, balance, poor to moderate in catching and throwing or clapping. I could never skip (jump rope), no rhythm in piano playing, typing or shorthand. Dancing is something of an impossibility, the attempt can make me feel physically sick. I am hopeless at crafts and very weak in handyman jobs. I am rather weak in muscularity, though I have good long term stamina. As a child I enjoyed simplified kiddie construction games and toys. I find difficulty in understanding instruction leaflets or guides to appliances. I could often do best in boring repetitive work. I find sharing jobs with others rather painful. I rarely seem to go through anything like shock after an accident or emergency. I am disturbed by unexpected touches, jabs or tickles to my body or neck.

Having a real body/mind split, I identify myself with my mind and eyes. I am often oblivious to body issues, though I am normally quite sensitive to genuine pain. I can experience considerable distress in crowds amid the loud hum or buzz of talk that goes on.

==
Collecting and Special Interests

I am an inveterate hoarder, and a keen book collector. I find it hard to throw away printed matter that interests me. I was a hobbyist from early childhood. I was always attracted by the unusual and esoteric ...the unorthodox. I have a tendency to become an expert and impromptu lecturer on my pet topics of expertise. I gravitate to clubs and groups as well as to friends who have direct interests in common. In hobbies, I have tended to be theorist, with intellectual knowledge of the relevant topics, and little or no practical skills or training. I compulsively enjoy studying patterns, such as tracing patterns visually on ceiling timbers and wardrobe doors, etc. I tend to keep elaborate lists and tabulations. Over the years I have made extensive notes on my own life and psychology, this latter practice now being largely confined to the study of my Aspergers tendencies.

Reading and studying are crucial for me, though not within Academia. I greatly enjoy discussion and debate on my favourite topics and special interests. I enjoy arranging items in my collections into order and special systems. I love entertaining audiences, giving lectures, performing monologues, comedy routines, telling jokes, reading poetry and acting roles. As an actor I find the scripts in the theatre far more real than the features of everyday life. I enjoy being encyclopaedic in my interests and my knowledge.

==
Other relevant criteria

I was very fussy in eating food as a child. I have very clear memories of images in my early childhood, from possibly 1 or 2 years old. In particular I can clearly recall my thinking and way of seeing the world. But it was never people centred. I was always self centred or 'things' centred. I never developed an instinctive moral sense. I could only learn rules and conventions of respectability. My therapist indicated to me that in the consultation situation I never seemed to go through classical Transference. I have many times disturbed the professionals that I've consulted with my detached intellectual style of talk. I like to either lead or follow. But I find equal sharing very difficult. I am most afraid of being captive of another person, or of being dominated. Other people's emotions worry me, whether their anger or their distress. I'm easily bluffed or manipulated. I am deeply disturbed by chaos (of that which doesn't make sense or of that which is out of control). I'm not afraid of death or dying. I have a fascination with parts of objects and things in the world. I can miss the coherent facts, as I often see details or parts, only. Thus too I may observe a woman or any person as a collection of particular pieces of data or information. I never seem to see the total person or to recognize the real being underneath.

==
Sexuality

I experienced slow and late sexual maturity and awareness, despite normal heterosexuality. I greatly enjoy the company of the opposite sex, and tend to be attracted to women in a casual undiscriminating fashion, regardless of the absence of physical contact with them. I have no understanding or experience of sexual chemistry or body language signals. Perhaps I had some degree of a retarded adolescence in the sexual nature. I have no sense ever of what could be called passion or lust towards women. I tend towards a head-centred sexuality. Love talk tended to be formal and contrived. My body was not automatically rhythmical in the sex act. I found to my shock and surprise that I didn't enjoy the routine sharing of my bed with partners.

==

b.   MODERATE and OCCASIONAL CHARACTERISTICS.

I generally have a tendency to want to avoid other people, but force myself to contact them routinely.   I have a liking or preference to adhere to well established routines and repetition.   I have a tendency to experience a free flow between conscious and unconscious minds.   I can be disturbed or put out by any interruption to my routines and my thoughts.

==
========================

c.   WEAK RARE OR ABSENT CHARACTERISTICS.

Routines and rituals…All that I engage in are for pleasure, comfort or self-defense.
I have no unpleasant or destructive compulsions.
Clumsyness.   Not commonly to be observed in my daily life. I'm aware of the tendency however.
Strangeness of Gait.   No peculiar tendencies here in running or walking.
Flapping or Rocking.   No tendencies here.
Facial Grimaces or Ticks.   Nothing I've ever been aware of.
Rote without meaning.   Nothing like this.
Limited Face expression or gesture.   Can present a blank face. Gestures can be restricted, despite expressiveness in acting or in platform work.
Stiff Gaze.   Yes, some slight tendencies here.
Lack of Hand gesture.   No sign of this.
Style of gesture.   No large or clumsy gestures.
Reading of non-fiction. Do prefer for the most part, but also like some fiction.
Lack of Cohesion in conversation… For the most part very coherent talking.
Lack of Precision describing emotion. No lack of precision here.
Literal interpretation of metaphor etc.   No problem with handling metaphor or figures of speech. Use of language is my strength.
Inability to repair conversations.   No, can usually do this.

Confessions of an Unashamed Asperger

Physical objects and input upsetting.   Not for the most part.
    But hate loud talk or dazzling bright lights.

Coming too close to others.   No I don't do this.

Lack of interest in making friends.   No, I set out to make a
    few select friends.

Expect others to mind read.   No, I don't expect others
    to know what I'm thinking feeling or experiencing.

Inability for pretend play as child.   No, I had good capacity
    for this.

Unlikely to engage in lying.   Not true for me. With my
    natural secretive tendency, have learnt to lie for
    privacy and self-protection.

Difficulty holding down job.   No, I was in the work place
    for some 40 years. With last employer for some 29
    years, albeit without any high office or advancement,
    and finished with reasonable financial security.

Signs of Syndromic restriction.   No, few would have
    imagined I could have AS.   Frequently dismissed as
    eccentric or odd. But that's all.

Scared of appearing in Public.   No, I very naturally and
    happily turned to the Public Platform or stage during
    my maturity with success and good reputation. Greatly
    enjoy being in front of the public. Can be awkward
    when in social converse.

==

APPENDIX IV (Humour)

ALL CATS ARE AUTISTIC. (Preface)

The text of this important document is published here, by kind permission of the author Alice Loftin.   It is intended to complement the Essay in the body of this work, entitled 'Cats and the Aspie'; and should be considered carefully, clause by clause.

I must express my sincerest thanks to Ms Loftin who graciously gave her consent for such reproduction with no reserve. (1) As a most vital exercise in research, it may bring enlightenment and comfort to many Aspies as they seek for fellow aliens among the other animal species of the world.   I would also thank my own furry little collaborators Tamino and Felecia for their valued advice on this and certain other matters dealt with in this book.   Their expertIse was invaluable.

References. Loftin, Alice.   All Cats are Autistic. Private
                              Communication   2006.

==

ALL CATS ARE AUTISTIC (V1.3)
(based on the DSM-IV Criteria)

A.   A total of six (or more) items from (1), (2) and (3), with at least two from (1), and one each from (2) and (3).

(1)   Qualitative impairment in social interaction, as manifested by at least two of the following:

(a)   Marked impairment in the use of multiple nonverbal behaviours, such as eye to eye gaze, facial expression, body postures and gestures to regulate social interaction.

Except when agitated, interpretive behaviour is limited.   Cats show very little change in facial exression, and posture is usually relaxed.   Eye-to-eye contact is difficult, as cats are seemingly unable to bear looking into the eyes for a period of time.

(b)   Failure to develop peer relationships appropriate to developmental level.

There is a marked deficiency in friendly social interaction with other cats. Cats must have been in consistent contact with each other for an extended period of time (delayed achievement of "comfort zone") before interacting in any social manner; and the relationship is tenuous even then. This often applies to interaction with humans as well.

(c)   A lack of spontaneous seeking to share enjoyment, interests or achievements with other people (e.g. by a lack of showing, bringing, or pointing out objects of interest)

Cats do not point out or retrieve objects for others. Cats are not concerned about whether or not their interests are similar to those of other entities. Cats find your interests irrelevant.

(d)   Lack of social or emotional reciprocity.

Cats are concerned with their own interests only. They will not lick your fur for the sole purpose of bringing you enjoyment.   If they do so at all, it's either because you taste good, or you are dirty and need cleaning.

(2)   Qualitative impairments in communication, as manifested by at least one of the following:

(a)   Delay in or total lack of, the development of spoken language (not accompanied by an attempt to compensate through alternative modes of communication such as gesture or mime).

Many cats do not speak, or do so only occasionally. Nor are they able to gesture their needs beyond the very basic, such as leading you to the empty food dish.

(b)   In individuals with adequate speech, marked impairment in the ability to initiate or sustain a conversation with others.

Cats do not converse well. Even in situations where it appears they are carrying on a dialogue with a person, mutual misunderstanding of each other's meaning is inevitable.

(c)   Stereotyped and repetitive use of language or idiosyncratic language.

All cats with speech perseverate on the word "Meow" and its variations.

(d)   Lack of varied, spontaneous make-believe play or social imitative play appropriate to developmental level.

        Often older cats will engage in play which on a developmental level is more appropriate to kittens. Their pretend and imitative abilities are limited as well.

(3)   Restricted, repetitive, and stereotyped patterns of behaviour, interests and activities as manifested by at least one of the following:

(a)   Encompassing preoccupation with one or more stereotyped and restricted patterns of interest that is abnormal either in intensity or focus.

Cats are generally fascinated and often obsessed with Entomology, (Insects), Ornithology (Birds), Ichthyology (Fishes). Sometimes obsessive interests also include string-like and ball-shaped objects.

(b)   Apparently inflexible adherence to specific, non-functional routines or rituals.

Cats have little tolerance for changes in routine, including the routines of the individuals they live with. They find it distressing and will often attempt to remedy the situation with control measures (waking you up at 5am on a weekend.) Cats also ritually bathe.

(c)   Stereotyped and repetitive motor mannerisms (eg. Hand or finger flapping or twisting or complex whole-body movements).

Cat's tail. "Nuff said!

(d) Persistent preoccupation with parts of objects.

Strings. Dangling bits of objects. Flying objects. Crawling objects. Single bits of kibble. Shadows. Laser Pointer lights.

B. Delays or abnormal functioning in at least one of the following areas, with onset prior to age 3 (Cat) years: (1) social interaction, (2) language as used in social communication, or (3) symbolic or imaginative play.

Not enough study done in relation to normal society.

C. The disturbance is not better accounted for by Rett's disorder or childhood disintegrative disorder.

Other Symptoms common to Autism.

Sensory Issues.

Sounds

Cats are easily distracted and disturbed by a wide variety of noises. Sudden noises are particularly distressful, although very quiet noises are distracting also.

On the other hand, cats are prone not to hear or understand specific words, such as their Name or "Come", causing them to appear as though they are ignoring the speaker, particularly when hyper-focused on another subject (usually nothing).

Smell/Taste.

Cats typically have hypersensitive smell and taste in comparison to humans. As a result, they tend to be extremely finicky. Few cats will eat vegetables.

Touch.

Cats are often hypersensitive to touch. They may shrink away when an attempt to touch them is made. However, rubbing/scratching certain areas of their persons can be quite pleasurable to them. These places include, but are not limited to: behind the ears, cheeks, under the chin, and the shoulders.

Self-Stimulation, or Stimming.

Purring is an activity cats engage in which increases their calm and receptivity. Stretching and scratching are also prevalent stimming activities.
Some cats have been known to make kneading motions on soft blankets and on people.

Alice Loftin.

==

APPENDIX V.

BIBLIOGRAPHY

Books Dealing Specifically with Aspergers and Autism.

Aston, Maxine   The Other Half of Asperger Syndrome. 2001
                 (National Autistic Soc.)
Frith, Uta (ed)   Autism and Asperger Syndrome.   1991
                 (Cambridge).
Grandin, T & Scariano M. Emergence.Labelled Autistic. 1985
                 (Warner Books)
Grandin, T & Johnson, C. Animals in Translation.   2005
                 (Bloomsbury.)
Jacobs, Barbara   Loving Mr Spock.   2003
                 (Penguin Books).
O'Connell, Sanjida.   Mindreading.   1997
                 (Heinemann)
Ratey J. MD & Johnson,C. Shadow Syndromes.   1997
                 (Bantom books).
Sacks, Oliver   An Anthropologist on Mars,   1995
                 (Picador.)
Shore, Stephen   Beyond the Wall   2003
                 (AAPC).
Williams, D   (Sundry) incl. Somebody Somewhere,   1994
                 (Doubleday.)
 DSM IV. The Diagnostic and Statistical Manual of   1994
of Mental Disorders. (American Psychiatric Association)

(Following Titles are Published by Jessica Kingsley, London)
Aston, Maxine   Aspergers in love.   2003
Attwood, Prof Tony   Aspergers Syndrome.   1998
Henault, Dr I. Asperger's Syndrome and Sexuality.   2006
Hoopman, Kathy All Cats have Asperger's Syndrome.   2007
McCabe, P. & J. Living and loving with Asp. Syndrome.   2003
O'Neill, Jasmine Lee Through the Eyes of Aliens.   1999
Schneider, Edgar   Discovering My Autism.   1999
                           Living the good life With Autism 2003
Slater-Walker, G & C. An Asperger Marriage.   2002
Stanford, Ashley   Aspergers Syndrome and Long   2003
                           Term Relationships.
Willey, Liane Holliday   Pretending to be Normal.   1999

====================================

Various other Books consulted or quoted

Brandon, N & E.Devers Romantic Love Q and A Book. 1982
                (Tarcher Inc.)
Carnegie, Dale.   How to Stop Worrying.   1957
                (Worlds Work.)
Coward, Noel   Fumed Oak (One act play)   1935
                (Windmill Press).
DeBono, Edward   The Happiness Purpose.   1979
                (Pelican Books.)
Eysenck H. & Wilson, G. Know your own Personality.   1975
                (MacMillan.)
Horney, Karen, MD   Our Inner Conflicts.   1966
                (Norton Books.)
Howell and Ford,   True History of the Elephant Man. 1980
                (Penguin Books)
Keirsey, D & Bates M   Please Understand Me.   1984
                (Prometheus Nemesis Book Co).
Lee, John Alan   Love Styles   1976
                (Abacus Books.)
Scott Peck, M. MD   The Road Less Travelled.   1991
                (Arrow Books)

==

www.ingramcontent.com/pod-product-compliance
Lightning Source LLC
Chambersburg PA
CBHW022351280326
41935CB00007B/150